CLASSICAL MYTHOLOGY
IN THE
PLAYS, MASQUES, AND POEMS
OF
BEN JONSON

❧

PUBLISHED WITH THE AID OF
THE CHARLES PHELPS TAFT MEMORIAL FUND

LONDON: HUMPHREY MILFORD
OXFORD UNIVERSITY PRESS

CLASSICAL MYTHOLOGY

IN THE

PLAYS, MASQUES, AND POEMS

OF

BEN JONSON

BY

CHARLES FRANCIS WHEELER, Ph.D.

Assistant Professor of English
Xavier University

PRINCETON
PRINCETON UNIVERSITY PRESS
FOR THE UNIVERSITY OF CINCINNATI
1938

FOREWORD

THE text of Jonson's works which I have used is that edited by W. Gifford and revised by F. Cunningham, published in London, 1875. Lines are not numbered in this edition. Hence it should be understood that, throughout, the Arabic numerals used in references to Jonson's plays, masques, and poems are *page* numbers, though these are not preceded by "p." or "pp." In addition in references to the plays I have, wherever possible, given act and scene numbers respectively in large and small Roman numerals. References to works other than Jonson's are to be understood as references to the editions listed in my Bibliography.

Upon the completion of this study, I feel sincerely grateful to those who have in various ways assisted me.

My debt to my guide and friend, Professor Robert Shafer of the University of Cincinnati, must be the first to be acknowledged. All who have been associated with Dr. Shafer have experienced the inspiration of his learning and his ideals, and at the same time have been struck by the fact that learning and ideals have not robbed him of common sense. Steady judgment based on common sense, it seems to me, is that which distinguishes scholarship from pedantry. I owe thanks also to Professor Frank W. Chandler, head of the Department of English in the University of Cincinnati. His genial personality and his unflagging devotion to literary studies have long exerted an infectious influence upon a very large number of students.

Several of my colleagues at Xavier University have encouraged and helped me. Dean Edward Carrigan, S.J., heartened me on more than one occasion. Professor Robert Manning, S.J., Mr. Raymond Fellinger, and Mr. Vincent Eckstein gave me help with translations. Mr. Fellinger's assistance when I was getting my manuscript into its final form also was invaluable.

Lastly I wish to speak of the daily cooperation of my beloved father, who passed from earth last Easter Sunday, and of my cherished mother. To them, James F. and Mary E. Sweeney Wheeler, I dedicate this book.

C. F. W.

March 1, 1938

CONTENTS

INTRODUCTION: THE PLAYS

FROM *Cynthia's Revels,* his only attempt at dramatic fantasy, Ben Jonson experimentally learned that myth lacks the vitality essential for even the shallowest of plots. This comedy, the fourth of his sixteen completed plays, satirizes the trait that modern psychologists politely and professionally term Narcissism; it also attempts poetically to justify the action of Queen Elizabeth in permitting the execution of her erstwhile favourite, the Earl of Essex. But no matter how clever the dramatist's inspiration may be, his merging of the story of Echo and Narcissus with the allegory of Cynthia and Actaeon and with the byplay of Cupid and Mercury makes honest human interest and a unified plot quite impossible. The play fails emotionally and structurally; yet its abundance of fable, its satirical moments, its lyric loveliness, and its judicious moralizations munificently compensate every reader. Its myths will be more fully evaluated later.

After *Cynthia's Revels* Jonson resumed his practice of introducing only learned allusions to mythology into his dramas; that is, like the poets of the Alexandrian age, he offered his audiences no more than a fleeting suggestion of a fabulous situation. He realized, possibly, that if his plays were to satisfy his humanistic ideal of presenting truth adorned with beauty, he would need to embellish them somewhat artificially. The virtuous and sensible conduct of a few men and women—perhaps like himself?—who were immune from the humours and were guiltless of the crimes that he proposed to castigate would not suffice. Even Marlowe, although poetry is inherent in the unbounded aspirations of Faustus and Tamburlaine and the Jew of Malta, had endowed his tragedies with the imaginative but artificial richness of myth.

To Jonson, then, as he portrayed the petty and commonplace annoyances of daily life with which a realist must deal,

myth was far more necessary. He understood, however, that
he could not delay the action of a realistic drama with the
lengthy myth-digressions of a *Faerie Queene* or a *Paradise
Lost*. His alternative was to use the ornamental loveliness of
Greek and Roman legend only when he wished to brighten
or perhaps to soften his satire and his tragedy. In dedicating
Volpone to the English universities he seems to utter his
aim:

> If my muses be true to me, I shall raise the despised
> head of poetry again, and stripping her out of those
> rotten and base rags wherewith the times have adulter-
> ated her form, restore her to her primitive habit, fea-
> ture, and majesty, and render her worthy to be em-
> braced and kist of all the great and master-spirits of
> our world.
> *Volpone,* Dedication, p. 160.

And Asper—Jonson, himself—renders this prose declaration
of purpose into verse and myth:

> Gracious and kind spectators, you are welcome;
> Apollo and the Muses feast your eyes
> With graceful objects, and may our Minerva
> Answer your hopes, unto their largest strain!
> *Every Man out of His Humour,* The Stage, p. 14.

Jonson, who wrote to satisfy himself as well as to please
his audience, did not feel completely frustrated if the un-
learned public did not recognize his "blue-ey'd maid"[1] whose
weapon is her spear as the huntress, Diana. And if they did
not know that his "mad Thespian girls"[2] associated with
Apollo are the Muses, or that his "many-mouthed vulgar
dog"[3] is Cerberus, he could hope that these mysterious allusions would at least awe them into tolerance. Thus his humanistic craving to present his wisdom, for the sake of
beauty, against a background relieved by fancy would be

---

[1] *Sejanus,* IV, v, 102.
[2] *Every Man in His Humour,* III, i, 61.
[3] *Every Man out of His Humour,* I, i, 44.

appeased. The learned and the aristocrats, moreover, would be won by the charm of his presentation as much as by his censures of the immoral and the ridiculous. These were the eager, imaginative, and beauty-cherishing Englishmen whose glory lasted from the springlike flowering of the Renaissance to the autumnal frost of the Puritan régime.

Scholars and aristocrats attending a performance of *Volpone* three centuries ago must have caught the poetry of Mosca's speech upon the power of gold:

> Why, your gold
> Is such another med'cine, it dries up
> All those offensive savours: it transforms
> The most deformed, and restores them lovely,
> As 'twere the strange poetical girdle. Jove
> Could not invent t'himself a shroud more subtle
> To pass Acrisius' guards.   *Volpone,* V, i, 289, 290.

Perhaps, hearing these lines, some recalled Venus' loosening "from her bosom the broidered zone, curiously-wrought, wherein are fashioned all manner of allurements; therein is love, therein desire, therein dalliance—beguilement that steals the wits even of the wise."[4] They may also have thought of Jove's consorting in the guise of a golden shower with the imprisoned Danaë, whose son, it had been foretold, would overpower his grandfather Acrisius; they may even have known Sophocles' choral strophe:

> Like to thee that maiden bright,
>   Danaë, in her brass-bound tower,
> Once exchanged the glad sunlight
>   For a cell, her bridal bower.
> And yet she sprang of royal line,
>   My child, like thine,
>   And nursed the seed
>   By her conceived
> Of Zeus descending in a golden shower.
>   *Antigone,* 944-952.

[4] *Iliad,* 14. 214-217.

Likewise, some spectators at *Sejanus* may have understood Caius Silius' allusion as he anticipates the conviction that his enemies hope will carry with it the sentence of death :

> This boast of law, and law, is but a form,
> A net of Vulcan's filing, a mere ingine,
> To take that life by a pretext of justice,
> Which you pursue in malice !
>
> *Sejanus,* III, i, 70.

To appreciate the metaphor in these lines the hearers needed only to know of the "bonds which might not be broken or loosed . . . fine as spiders' webs, so that no one even of the blessed gods could see them, so exceedingly craftily were they fashioned."[5] Vulcan made these bonds to entrap his unsuspecting wife, Venus, in her clandestine union with fierce Mars.

And even though the colour and richness of these mythological touches were not always obvious to the Elizabethan and Jacobean spectators of Jonson's dramas, there was still the possibility that the fullness of his acquaintance with the literature of fable would impress them. They may have realized that for practically any idea—serious or comic—Jonson could find a somewhat relevant parallel in classic story; to be so prodigal of his store, and ordinarily so apt, he had to possess an abundance of ancient learning. Very often by referring to two or more tales or deities in a single passage, he confirms one's opinion that his resources were almost inexhaustible. Thus he utilizes a double allusion with humorous intent to allow Ned Clerimont to gull Captain Otter; the latter desires to win the consent of his wife to his keeping a bull and a bear, and Ned advises him to offer her the cogency of this pseudo-reasoning: "Did not Pasiphaë, who was a queen, love a bull? and was not Calisto, the mother of Arcas, turn'd into a bear, and made a star . . .?"[6]

[5] *Odyssey,* 8. 272-281.
[6] *Epicoene,* III, i, 390.

Frequently, also, Jonson enumerates not two but several fabulous situations. In such a passage the unholy Sir Epicure Mammon, growing enthusiastic over the possibilities of transforming metals of little value into the glistering gold he so much covets, likens alchemy in its effects to Jason's golden fleece, to "Pandora's tub" (the box in which the ills of mankind were confined until the inquisitive Pandora lifted the lid to peek, whereupon they escaped to plague succeeding generations), and to "Medea's charms." Among the riddles of his newly discovered art, Mammon includes

> the Hesperian garden, Cadmus' story,
> Jove's shower, the boon of Midas, Argus' eyes.
>
> *Alchemist,* II, i, 48, 49.

The most impressive of these passages cumulative in nature is Jonson's parody upon the stressing of physical beauty and upon the extravagant conceits of the Cavaliers' Platonic poems. Jonson's characters, Pennyboy junior and his "jeerers" or wits, laud Pennyboy's mistress Pecunia, who so lifelessly personifies wealth:

> Her smiles they are love's fetters!
> Her breasts his apples! her teats strawberries!
> Where Cupid, were he present now, would cry,
> Farewell my mother's milk, here's sweeter nectar!
> Help me to praise Pecunia, gentlemen;
> . . .
> *Fit.* A lady
> The Graces taught to move!
> *Alm.* The Hours did nurse!
> . . .
> *Fit.* A voice, as if that harmony still spake!
> *Alm.* And polish'd skin, whiter than Venus' foot!
> *Fit.* Young Hebe's neck, or Juno's arms!
> . . .
> Leda might yield unto her for a face!
> *Alm.* Hermione for breasts!
> *Fit.* Flora for cheeks!
> *Alm.* And Helen for a mouth!
>
> *The Staple of News,* IV, i, 253, 254.

Had his scholarly taste not prevented him, how Jonson could have outdone the Cavaliers' effusive "Platonic" trivialities!

Another avenue to an appreciation of the mythology in Jonson's dramas lies in a study of the relation of it to characterization. Here is revealed an illuminating consistency. In the comedies of contemporary London and Venice the myth content is proportionally slight; in the comedies and tragedies of Rome and Fesulae and Gargaphie, as one expects, it increases ponderously. Without being too statistical one may observe that of the twenty-two characters named in the *dramatis personae* of *The Case Is Altered*,[7] but six express themselves in its nineteen mythological passages; the latter concern only Cupid, Vesta, Venus (Cypris), the Destinies, Fortune, the Lars, Elysium, Plutus, "the infernal gods," Nature, Rhadamanthus, and Melpomene. Of the twenty-five characters in *The Poetaster* approximately eighteen employ the lines which amount to a Jonsonian Pantheon. In the later comedies these passages range from five in *The Devil Is an Ass* to almost forty in *The Staple of News*. After 1604, of course, Jonson's masques evidence his learning in fable.

Direct characterization occurs rarely in the theatre, but Jonson describes Carlo Buffone—who is said to be a prototype of Jonson's rival dramatist, Marston—as "a public, scurrilous, and profane jester, that more swift than Circe, with absurd similes, will transform any person into a deformity."[8] (Circe is the Homeric enchantress by whose magic power Ulysses' men are changed into swine.)

Indirect characterization has two aspects: It is contained in remarks to or about someone, and it is demonstrated by the speech of the one characterized. The first type is utilized when Macilente, disgusted with Carlo Buffone's two-faced con-

[7] Professors Herford and Simpson assign this play to 1597-8.
[8] *Every Man out of His Humour*, p. 6. *Cf. Odyssey*, 10. 135-11. 22.

duct and hypocritical greeting ("I am glad to see you so well return'd, signior"), replies tartly, "You are! gramercy, good Janus."[9] *Sejanus* particularly abounds in this form of characterization, two forceful instances of it being spoken by Arruntius. He, when Caesar feigns to offer his resignation to the senate, comments that the ambitious Sejanus answers "more nimbly than Vertumnus."[10] (Disguised alternately as a reaper, a gardener, a soldier, a fisherman, and an old woman, Vertumnus wooed Pomona.) Arruntius, too, declares that rather than trust an employee of the Roman state he would "sooner trust Greek Sinon,"[11] the captive who by treachery brought about the destruction of Troy after he had won the confidence of his captors. And at the moment of the arrest of Sejanus, the provost exclaims, "Come down, Typhoeus."[12] (The latter, monster-child of Earth and Tartarus, warred on Jove.)

If any skeptic questions Jonson's skill in his adaptations of myth for his dramas, let him analyze the fitness of these and other mythological invectives. An excellent instance of this characterization of a person from the comment of others occurs in Arete's delineation of Crites: He deserves well, she says, because he causes his "potential merit" to become actual; he is "one whom the Muses and Minerva love" and "whom Phoebus, though not Fortune, holdeth dear." These facts appear "even through the ungentle injuries of Fate."[13] Because it is spoken of a mortal, this is the highest kind of praise, and Cynthia in her reply stamps Stoicism of this order as acceptable to her divinity.

The second type of indirect characterization—allusions by the one characterized—results accidentally from all the foregoing passages. One realizes, for example, that Arruntius'

---

[9] *Every Man out of His Humour*, I, i, 37, 38.
[10] *Sejanus*, III, i, 66.
[11] *Ibid.*, IV, v, 103.
[12] *Ibid.*, V, x, 142.
[13] *Cynthia's Revels*, V, iii, 341, 342.

love of justice is sincere, and that the provost, in arresting Sejanus, feels no pity for him. In *The Poetaster* the vacuous nature and gross manner of Tucca are similarly exposed. His swashbuckling and his flattery are satirically but poetically bared when he says to Albius, "Give me thy hand, Agamemnon; we hear abroad thou art the Hector of citizens: . . . are we welcome to thee, noble Neoptolemus?" Reassured by a hearty response, he asks, "Which of these is thy wedlock, Menelaus? thy Helen, thy Lucrece?" She being indicated, he rhapsodizes, "She is a Venus, a Vesta, a Melpomene: come hither, Penelope; what's thy name, Iris?" Then he swears by Jove that the gods were goslings to accomplish the union of "so sweet a breath" with Albius: "Thou hadst ill fortune, Thisbe; the Fates were infatuate."[14] Subsequently, during the burlesque banquet of the gods, Tucca blusters as "enraged" Mars at Ganymede, the beauteous cupbearer.[15]

The improvident Jonson's concern over the Renaissance tendency towards the accumulation of wealth has evoked this comment: "Even the love of wealth for its own sake has aspects less ignoble than those which belong to the pursuit of it for the sake of a luxurious way of living unknown to earlier generations or less affluent neighbours."[16] This truth is demonstrated when several of Jonson's characters use fable to reveal their natures. Jaques, the beggar, bemoans the loss of his hoard of ill-gotten gold, but in his soul there is a bit of poetry: Gold is his "dear Lar," the deity of his household; when he discovers a trail of the missing coins, he is in the "odorous and enflower'd fields" of Elysium, where "blessed ghosts do walk."[17] His delight in wealth, then, is

---

[14] *The Poetaster*, IV, i, 445, 446.
[15] *Ibid.*, IV, iii, 452 ff.
[16] A. W. Ward in *Cambridge History of English Literature*, V, 396.
[17] *The Case is Altered*, V, i, 378, 379.

entirely sensuous and miserly. He does not enjoy it for its legitimate or illegitimate uses; rather he glories in possessing it secretly in his poverty.

Sensuous enjoyment of his gold also is a characteristic of Volpone, who in a definitely Hesiodic manner salutes his treasure at daybreak:

> O thou son of Sol,
> But brighter than thy father, let me kiss,
> With adoration, thee, and every relick
> Of sacred treasure in this blessed room.
> Well did wise poets, by thy glorious name,
> Title that age which they would have the best;
> Thou being the best of things, and far transcending
> All style of joy, in children, parents, friends,
> Or any other waking dream on earth:
> Thy looks when they to Venus did ascribe,
> They should have given her twenty thousand Cupids;
> Such are thy beauties and our loves!
>
> *Volpone,* I, i, 166, 167.

(Hesiod recounts that the gods first "made a golden race of mortal men. . . . And they lived like gods without sorrow of heart, remote and free from toil and grief: miserable age rested not on them. . . . When they died, it was as though they were overcome with sleep. . . . They dwelt in ease and peace upon their lands."[18] The same poet mentions "golden Aphrodite."[19] Nowhere, either in Hesiod or in the other writers, is the number of her *Erotes* specified.)

But Volpone uses, as well as possesses, his wealth when he finds fiendish amusement in the machinations of the would-be inheritors of his fortune. One of these even has commanded his wife to submit to Volpone's pleasure. When she

[18] *Works and Days,* 109-120.
[19] *Ibid.,* 65.

proves intractable, the leech himself woos her with the
story of his infatuation. For her, he says, he

> would have contended
> With the blue Proteus, or the horned flood.[20]
>
> *Volpone,* III, vi, 246.

After addressing to her the appealing lyric, "Come, my
Celia," he catalogues many exceptional entertainments he
will provide for her: precious gems, rare dishes, perfumed
baths, potent drink, and vile performances,

> Whilst we, in changed shapes, act Ovid's tales,
> Thou, like Europa now, and I like Jove,
> Then I like Mars, and thou like Erycine:
> So, of the rest, till we have quite run through,
> And wearied all the fables of the gods.
>
> *Volpone,* III, vi, 251.

Of the same sensual ilk is Sir Epicure Mammon, who,
even before he has acquired wealth through his alchemical
endeavours, plans to gratify his unchaste desire by wooing
Dol Common. He avows that he will

> talk to her all in gold;
> Rain her as many showers as Jove did drops
> Unto his Danäe; shew the god a miser.
>
> *The Alchemist,* IV, i, 113.

Jaques, Volpone, Mammon—and there is one more. Jonson
shows that cupidity is not confined to man alone, and that
financial gain motivates the woman who grants her favours
even as it is offered as an inducement by the man who seeks
them. Fulvia—a Roman courtesan—grimly states the terms
of her bargains:

> They shall all give and pay well, that come here,
> If they will have it; and that, jewels, pearl,
> Plate, or round sums to buy these. I'm not taken

[20] These and following allusions will be discussed in succeeding paragraphs.

With a cob-swan, or a high-mounting bull,
As foolish Leda and Europa were;
But the bright gold, with Danaë. For such price
I would endure a rough, harsh Jupiter.

Catiline, II, i, 223.

Thus with mythology Jonson mitigates the ugliness and foulness of Mammon, Volpone, and Fulvia; otherwise their covetous and lustful natures would be almost too repulsive for dramatic presentation. But fully to comprehend Jonson's achievement, one must be mindful of the classic versions of the myths to which allusion is made. Sophocles' account of Danaë has previously been quoted. Proteus, with whom Volpone says he would have fought, is the immortal prophet of the sea, who, when in strife with Agamemnon, "turned into a bearded lion, and then into a serpent, and a leopard, and a huge boar; then he turned into flowing water, and into a tree."[21] So also does he transform himself when in battle with Aristaeus.[22] "The horned flood," which Volpone would have dared, is Achelous, a river-god who struggled, in the guise of a horned bull, with Hercules unsuccessfully for the love of Deianira.[23] Like the promises of most seducers, these of Volpone are flagrantly insincere.

His anticipation of re-enacting the Jove-Europa myth, contained as it is in a line, hardly intimates the charming development of the Ovidian story: Jove "took upon him the form of a bull. In this form he mingled with the cattle, lowed like the rest. . . . His colour was white as the untrodden snow. . . . His horns were small, but perfect in shape as if carved by an artist's hand, cleaner and more clear than pearls. His brow and eyes would inspire no fear, and his whole expression was peaceful. . . . Presently she drew near, and held out flowers to his snow-white lips. The disguised lover

[21] *Odyssey,* 4. 456-458.
[22] *Georgics,* 4. 405-410; 440-442.
[23] See article on Achelous.

rejoiced and . . . kissed her hands. . . . He jumps sportively about on the grass, now lays his snowy body down on the yellow sands. . . . He yields his breast for her maiden hands to pat and his horns to entwine with garlands of fresh flowers. The princess even dares to sit upon his back . . . and soon [he] is in full flight with his prize on the open ocean. . . . And her fluttering garments stream behind her in the wind."[24]

One aspect of the illicit love of Mars and Erycine (Venus) —the bonds forged by the wronged Vulcan—has already been quoted. From the Homeric tale, too, one learns of the watchfulness of Mars for Vulcan's departure from his home; of Mars' eager invitation to Venus; of Vulcan's terrible anger; of the "unquenchable laughter" of the gods when "they saw [that] the craft of wise Hephaestus" had the lovers in toils; of Mercury's wanton envy of the cause of Mars' shame and chagrin; and of Poseidon's guaranteeing Vulcan that Mars would pay him "the fine of the adulterer" to recompense him for the dowry he had given to wed Poseidon's daughter, Venus.[25] Leda's experience, which Fulvia mentions, is related by Euripides; the speaker is Leda's daughter, Helen of Troy:

> The tale
> Telleth that to my mother Leda flew
> Zeus, who had stoln the likeness of a swan,
> And, fleeing the chasing eagle, wrought
> By guile his pleasure.
>
> *Helen,* 17-21.

It is illuminating, after having read one or more versions of a myth in the classic authors, to re-read Jonson's reference to it. One feels then a renewed admiration for him who could so deftly fit it to so many and such diverse characters and situations.

---

[24] *Metamorphoses,* 2. 850-875.
[25] *Odyssey,* 8. 266-359.

Besides employing myth for ornamentation and for character portrayal, Jonson finds it also of value for the expression of his criticism of life. At times this is of a nature which may be termed philosophical; more often it remains on a different level, and is to be discovered merely in his way of phrasing, by a kind of metonymy, the problems of contemporary life. Philosophy, for example, is evident in the words of the dour Macilente, the envious scholar who is grieved not only by the meagreness of his own exchequer but also by the financial abundance possessed by Deliro, his benefactor. In his opinion, to be thus undiscriminating, Fortune must be "blind"[26] and "the strumpet";[27] Chance he once describes as "the old lady,"[28] but later he complains that "that dog call'd Chance" has no reason to "fawn upon" Deliro more than on him.[29] He explains that his words, "One of those that fortune favours," mean "that you are one that lives not by your wits."[30] And acknowledging Deliro's kindness, he says aside,

> And yet the muffled Fates, had it pleased them,
> Might have supplied me from their own full store,
> Without this word *I thank you* to a fool.
> *Every Man out of His Humour,* II, ii, 73.

Macilente, his opening speech reveals, is no Stoic; he is "no such pill'd Cynick" that he will agree "that beggary is the only happiness," or "of these patient fools" who "sing: *My mind to me a kingdom is.*"[31]

Boldly in contrast with Macilente's covetousness is the resignation and fortitude of the aged Count Ferneze, whose

---

[26] *Every Man out of His Humour,* I, i, 36; II, ii, 77.
[27] *Ibid.,* I, i, 39.
[28] *Ibid.*
[29] *Ibid.,* II, ii, 73.
[30] *Ibid.,* I, i, 37.
[31] *Ibid.,* I, i, 27, 28.

son has been captured in battle. The Count stoically says to
a noble hostage, whom he holds prisoner,

> But since it is the pleasure of our fates,
> That we should thus be rack'd on fortune's wheel,
> Let us prepare with steeled patience
> To tread on torment, and with minds confirm'd,
> Welcome the worst of envy.
>
> *The Case Is Altered,* III, iii, 354.

In *Sejanus,* a minute before Caius Silius stabs himself
rather than submit to the persecution of his political enemies,
he remembers "his guards . . . against fortune's spite."[32]
Sejanus' philosophy includes scornful defiance of all deities
except Fortuna. Dauntlessly daring to acquire unrestricted
control of the Roman state, he refuses Terentius' suggestion that he offer sacrifice. Religion, he says, makes men
"excellent fools."[33] The gods are powerless to "change the
certain course of fate," and even if they had such power,
they would scarcely use it in return for the offering of "a
beeve's fat, or less."

Sejanus is not averse, however, to adoring the "grateful
image" of Fortune with a "grain of incense." During his
sacrifice, when the goddess turns her head from him, he
angrily exclaims,

> I, the slave
> And mock of fools, scorn on my worthy head!
> That have been titled and adored a god,
> Yea sacrificed unto, myself, in Rome,
> No less than Jove: and I be brought to do
> A peevish giglot, rites! perhaps the thought
> And shame of that, made Fortune turn her face,
> Knowing herself the lesser deity,
> And but my servant.   *Sejanus,* V, iv, 120.

So reckless an attitude toward the gods, of course, notably
increases the horror aroused by the catastrophe of the trag-

[32] *Sejanus,* III, i, 73.
[33] *Ibid.,* V, i, 113.

edy, for it seems as if that aspect of chance celebrated under the title of Fortuna deals most unkindly and mercilessly with arrogant fatalists.

Among the numerous examples of Jonson's strengthening his observations on contemporary life by applying mythological parallels to them are his satirical tirades on his rivals in the field of literature. Few of these are more effective than his complaint that "every servile imitating spirit" who is

> Plagued with an itching leprosy of wit,
> In a mere halting fury, strives to fling
> His ulcerous body in the Thespian spring,
> And straight leaps forth a poet! but as lame
> As Vulcan.
>
> *Every Man out of His Humour,* The Stage, p. 15.

Another mythological parallel was inspired by Queen Elizabeth's happiness at receiving the title of Cynthia, the chaste huntress associated with the moon; her pleasure seems to have suggested to Jonson, when he penned the dedication of *Cynthia's Revels* some time after the accession of James I, the thought of terming him Phoebus, the sun-god and twin of Cynthia.

In addition to Elizabeth's pleasure in her complimentary title, the similarity of the Diana-Actaeon myth to her harsh treatment of Essex inspired Jonson's obvious reference to Cynthia's unremitting justice. Actaeon had seen Diana bathing; Essex, entering the Queen's apartment inopportunely, saw her in négligé. Ovid comments upon Diana's heartlessness and upon the public judgement passed upon her:

> *Rumor in ambiguo est; aliis violentior aequo*
> *visa dea est, alii laudant dignamque severa*
> *virginitate vocant.*[34]
>
> *Metamorphoses,* 3. 253-255.

---

[34] "Common talk wavered this way and that: to some the goddess seemed more cruel than was just; others called her act worthy of her austere virginity."

Jonson wisely offers no direct explanation of the cause of his Queen's wrath; his Cynthia merely says,

> For so Actæon, by presuming far,
> Did, to our grief, incur a fatal doom.
> *Cynthia's Revels,* V, iii, 352.

To have said more might have been to say too much; there is some question about the propriety with which a playwright —who had only a short time before claimed benefit of clergy after a duel in which he had slain his opponent—may appear uninvited as the champion of a mighty Queen.

Jonson's handling the Essex affair in this mythological manner is as timely as is his paralleling the humour of egoism with the legend of Narcissus. Cynthia's declaration, too, that her chastity scorns, not love, "but giddy Cupid, Venus' frantic son,"[35] is her queenly condemnation of flirtation and infatuation. And Crites' remark that to provide a masque at Cynthia's request is "a labour more for Hercules" not only describes the effort required to create such an entertainment but also possibly foreshadows Jonson's own reactions later when Queen Anne bestowed like commissions upon him.

If the remark really proved prophetic, did Jonson, like Crites, have a wise, reassuring Arete (Virtue) to sustain him? When he thought that the vapid courtier-actors would "confusion prove," perhaps his Arete likewise reminded him that the Queen's sceptre would check their "eccentric property,"

> as Hermes' wand
> Charms the disorders of tumultuous ghosts;
> And as the strife of Chaos then did cease,
> When better light than Nature's did arrive.
> *Cynthia's Revels,* V, ii, 336, 337.

Crites, undertaking his masque, invoked the god of the Muses and the god of wit—"Apollo and Cyllenian Mercury." Some-

---

[35] *Cynthia's Revels,* V, iii, 340.

what similarly, Jonson turned to the deities in Graeco-Roman mythology and found in their stories the material which made him the preferred masque-poet at the court of James I.

THE MASQUES AND POEMS

The enthusiasm which Jonson had for his vocation as dramatist and poet rested as much upon his humanistic scorn for imperfection as upon his desire to entertain; he takes his stand with Horace in attempting to bring about intellectual and spiritual improvement, as he writes in *Epicoene*.[36] Relieving this ethical motive were two innate characteristics of genuine importance: Jonson's appreciation of delicate beauty and his fondness for robust humour. Had he aimed merely to elevate mankind, he might, like Bacon, have devoted himself to the essay, and even to the cause of science; but Jonson possessed both comprehensive knowledge and a vigorous imagination—and he became a satirist and poet. What he knew of mythology—and probably none of his contemporaries knew more than he—became the vehicle by which he was not only to embellish but actually to animate his masques. As a result, even his *pièces d'occasion* gain artistic significance by classical association.

One of the earliest of these is the pageant and speeches which he prepared as part of the civic welcome and coronation exercises for James I; and Jonson's talent for joining contemporary events to classical fable, which has been noticed in the discussion of his plays, particularly asserts itself during the exercises conducted at Temple Bar.[37] There a temple had been erected in honour of *Janus Quadrifrons* because, according to Jonson, Janus "fills all parts of the

[36] The ends of all, who for the scene do write,
Are, or should be, to profit and delight.
Epicoene, Prologue, p. 332.
[37] The following summary has been made from *Part of King James's Entertainment,* 416-426. For information about the subjects introduced, see the articles under Sources.

world with his majesty," or "by reason of the four elements, which brake out of him, being Chaos," or because "the year . . . , under his sway, is divided into four seasons." Janus, too, "had four faces, yet he thought them not enough, to behold the greatness and glory of that day." Lastly, under his titles of Patulcius and Clusius, the doors of his temple remained open or closed to signify that a nation was engaged in warfare or was enjoying the blessings of peace, respectively; at James' advent, consequently, they were closed.

Inside this temple various personifications appropriately symbolized the condition of the times in England: Irene (Peace), Plutus (Wealth), Enyalius ("Mars, groveling"), Eleutheria (Liberty), the Genius Urbis, and others. "The noise, and present tumult" of the royal reception had awakened a Flamen Martialis, who recalled that

> The Ides of March were enter'd, and I bound
> With these, to celebrate the genial feast
> Of Anna styled Parenna, Mars's guest.

The Genius admitted that this was the fifteenth day of March, but explained that Mars' statues had long ceased to be, and that the Anne being honoured was one far superior to Anna Parenna.

By this happy unification of the Janus myth with that of Anna and of the Genius and with the ancient celebration of the Ides of March in tribute to the god of war, Jonson succeeds in raising a political and social event to the dignity of a literary performance. The piece is graceful enough, and highly complimentary to the King and Queen; yet it is tinged with that incongruity—the error and confusion of the rudely awakened Flamen after the slumber of some fifteen centuries—that generally marks intellectual comedy, as Meredith has defined it. Playfulness and myth similarly mingle in Jonsonian poetry, as witness his rueful "Execration upon

Vulcan,"[38] wherein he attributes to the lame smithy the destructive fire which ruined his library and his manuscripts, including his own translation of Horace's *Ars Poetica* and his commentary upon it from Aristotle. The "Execration" taunts Vulcan with allusions to all the embarrassments, misfortunes, and misdeeds that the god endured or committed, and demands the reason for his animus towards a certain better-deserving author!

Another kind of appreciation of Jonson's masques is derived from a knowledge of their genesis in classic sources. To give the genesis of all the masques or of the more lengthy ones would require many weeks of Herculean labour, but fortunately *The Masque of Lethe,* one of Jonson's shorter creations—being little more than six pages in the Gifford-Cunningham edition of 1875—can be presented as typical of the growth of most of the other creations of this genre, and probably will not prove too tedious.

In *Lethe* the personifications of Humanity, Cheerfulness, and Readiness in the "FRONT *before the* SCENE" have no mythological value. The scene is of "CHARON *putting off from the shore, having landed certain imagined ghosts, whom* MERCURY *there receives, and encourageth to come on towards the river* LETHE, *who appears lying in the person of an old man. The* Fates *sitting by him on his bank* . . . MERCURY, *perceiving them to faint, calls them on, and shews them his golden rod.*" The god exhorts the shades not to fail "so near the fields of rest," where "no more Furies, no more torments dwell," for one "who hath been once in love, hath proved his hell," and Lethe will afford them the relief of forgetting the past. To Lethe's inquiry about the newly arrived ghosts Mercury answers:

> They are the gentle forms
> Of lovers, tost upon those frantic seas,
> Whence Venus sprung.

[38] *Underwoods,* LXI.

They have died, Mercury, laughing at their sentimental complaints, continues, because they were drowned by Love. One of them insists, however, that *"he is not dead"*—and the Fates substantiate his claim. Their rock, their spindle, and their shears, they say, prove that not only he but the others still live. Mercury, disconcerted, exclaims,

> I 'gin to doubt, that Love with charms hath put
> This phant'sie in them; and they only think
> That they are ghosts.

The Fates advise these unfortunate lovers to drink of Lethe to obliterate their sorrow and trouble, and the water proves efficacious; the ghosts become men. Thereupon Jonson philosophizes:

> *2 Fate.*   Love at the name of Lethe flies.
> *Lethe.*   For, in oblivion drown'd, he dies.
> *3 Fate.*   He must not hope, though other states
>   He oft subdue, he can the Fates.

The first dance of the masque follows.

Jonson developed Charon, the ferryman of the Styx, either from Vergil[39] or, more probably, from Lucian,[40] who also presents a scene similar to that in *Lethe*. Elsewhere Lucian[41] associates Charon with Mercury. The latter's "golden rod" is the caduceus described as golden by Homer[42] and by Apollodorus.[43] Homer[44] and Pindar[45] mention the "fields of rest" (Elysium), and Homer,[46] Euripides,[47] and Vergil[48] charac-

[39] *Aeneid*, 6. 295-330.
[40] *Of Mourning*, 10 (for Charon) and 5 (for the scene).
[41] *Dialogues of the Dead*, 4; *Charon*, 1.
[42] *Odyssey*, 5. 87.
[43] 3. 10. 2.
[44] *Odyssey*, 24. 13, 14.
[45] *Olympian*, 2. 68-74.
[46] *Iliad*, 19. 259, 260.
[47] *Orestes*, 28-38; 255-265.
[48] *Aeneid*, 6. 566-574.

terize the Furies as torturers. That Venus was born from the waves is related by Hesiod.[49]

The discussion of the effect of love may well have been suggested by Lucian's *Voyage to the Lower World*,[50] in which among those being transported by Charon were "seven who killed themselves for love. Also Theagenes, the philosopher, for love of the Megarian courtesan." Some on this voyage "turn about, and must ever be looking back at what they have left behind them, far off though it be,—like men that are sick for love." Another resemblance to Lucian's *Charon*[51] exists in the satire upon the various lamentations of the love-sick ghosts, for Lucian writes that Charon, being conducted by Mercury around the upper world to see the sights, asks about men: "But what are all these misty shapes that beset them on every side?" His guide replies: "Hopes, Fears, Follies, Pleasures, Greeds, Hates, Grudges, and such like. . . . Look closely, and you will make out the Fates up aloft, spinning each man his spindle-full; from that spindle a man hangs by a narrow thread." Allusion to the Fates' rock, spindle, and shears is usually derived from the *Latin Anthology*.[52] Lucian,[53] as well as Vergil[54] and Tibullus,[55] implies that love is subject to the domination of the Fates, while the introduction of Lethe as the river which induces oblivion is traceable to Lucian,[56] Plato,[57] Vergil,[58] and Claudian.[59]

After the first dance the masque resumes with an unimportant dialogue between Cupid and Mercury; the latter's

[49] *Theogony*, 188-200.
[50] 6 and 14.
[51] 15, 16.
[52] 1. 792.
[53] *Charon*, 16, 15, and *Voyage*, 3-5.
[54] *Aeneid*, 6. 440-466.
[55] 1. 1. 69.
[56] 50. 5.
[57] *Republic*, 10. 621A.
[58] *Aeneid*, 6. 713-715.
[59] *Rape of Proserpine*, 1. 282, 283.

reference to his "snaky rod" recalls the appearance of his caduceus in pictures and in Martial's *Epigrams.*[60] Following the main dance and the revels (Cupid meanwhile has been encouraging uninfatuated romance), Love offers the masquers his paraphernalia—quiver, bow, and torches, so that they who love may have him "naked and entire." This passage, ending with Mercury's warning "that Love disarm'd" is no "less a fire," conforms to the characterization of Eros in Moschus' *Idyls.*[61] Cupid's remark about Mercury's wit accords with the latter's rôle in an *Homeric Hymn.*[62] The reconciliation of the deities, with which *Lethe* concludes, is not inconsistent with their earlier rivalry, which has been teasing and friendly, rather than vicious.

Thus from a thought that seems to have been suggested by a chance sentence in Lucian—the seven shades who had killed themselves because all was not well with their love affairs—Jonson built *Lethe,* adorning it with ideas gleaned from his reading of some dozen other sources, himself contributing only the pacifying of the gods, which is symbolical of the acquiescence of wit and love to each other. This optimistic note struck at the end of the masque would scarcely have suited Lucian's cynical view of the gossamer aspirations of men. The investigation of the genesis of *Lethe* indicates that one's enjoyment of Jonson's mythological masques and poems will be keen in proportion to one's background in the humanities. Otherwise the caustic treatment of sentimentality in *Lethe,* of alchemy in *Mercury Vindicated,* and of voluptuousness in *Epigrams* XXV will be obscured or defeated. So much for the satirical element in Jonson's masques and non-dramatic works.

There remains a note of comedy, however, even amid the lovely beauty of some of the more delicate creations, of

[60] 7. 74.
[61] 1. See the following discussion of *The Hue and Cry after Cupid.*
[62] 4. 496-512; 574-576.

which mythology so frequently is the woof and warp. Such skilful weaving has made *The Hue and Cry after Cupid* one of the most interesting tapestries, from the literary point of view. The inspiration of this masque, as Whalley says in his edition of it, is Moschus' *Idyls,* I :

> Cypris one day made hue and cry after her son Love and said : Whosoever hath seen one Love loitering at the street-corners, know that he is my runaway, and any that shall bring me word of him shall have a reward ; and the reward shall be the kiss of Cypris ; and if he bring her runaway with him, the kiss shall not be all. He is a notable lad ; he shall be known among twenty : complexion not white but rather like to fire ; eyes keen and beamy ; . . . makes cruel play. . . . All naked his body. . . . He's winged like a bird and flies from one to another. . . . He hath a . . . little golden quiver, but in it lie the keen shafts with which he ofttimes woundeth e'en me. . . . Let any that shall take him bind and bring him and never pity. If he see him weeping, let him have a care lest he be deceived ; if laughing, let him still hale him along ; but if making to kiss him, let him flee him, for his kiss is an ill kiss and his lips poison. . . .

In Jonson's *Hue* Venus summons the Graces to cry her son ; they describe him with practically no additions to Moschus' poem :

> Beauties, have you seen this toy,
> Called Love, a little boy,
> Almost naked, wanton, blind ;
> Cruel now, and then as kind ?
>
> . . .
>
> She that will but now discover
> Where the winged wag doth hover,
> Shall to-night receive a kiss,
> How, or where herself would wish :
> But, who brings him to his mother,
> Shall have that kiss, and another.

He hath marks about him plenty:
You shall know him among twenty.
All his body is a fire.

.   .   .

Wings he hath, which though ye clip,
He will leap from lip to lip.

.   .   .

He doth bear a golden bow,
And a quiver, hanging low,
Full of arrows. . . .
                              If he have
Any head more sharp than other,
With that first he strikes his mother.

.   .   .

Not a kiss but poison bears;
And most treason in his tears.

Upon Cupid's sudden appearance, Venus, curious because he seems so blithely joyful, inquires if he has shot Minerva or the Muses (Minerva and they are immune to the boy-god's arrows, according to Lucian); or has caused Rhea again to love Atys; or has occasioned again the Moon's (Selene's) stopping over Endymion; or has brought Hercules again to spin for love of Omphale; or has led Jove again to assume a disguise and to leave his thunder. All of these exploits of Cupid are related in Lucian's *Dialogues of the Gods*;[63] but the question that Venus puts to Cupid was inspired by a very like passage in an epithalamium of Claudian's:

> *"quid tantum gavisus?" ait; "quae proelia sudas*
> *improbe? quis iacuit telis? iterumne Tonantem*
> *inter Sidonias cogis mugire iuvencas?*

[63] Jonson cites 12 and 19; the Hercules myth, however, without mention of Cupid, is from 13.

an Titana domas? an pastoralia Lunam
rursus in antra vocas? durum magnumque videris
debellasse deum."[64]   *Epithalamium*, (X), 111-116.

Though these do not show exhaustively the sources of
Hue, they suffice to demonstrate not only the indebtedness
which Jonson's invention owes to his source material, but also
the delicate merging of comedy and beauty which gives to
his masques and verses their lilting gracefulness. In this
respect, when he is at his best, he has no superior in English
literature. Still, without the criticism of life—trivial as it
sometimes is—which these compositions invariably possess,
they would prove insipid. They derive zest from their presentation of some kind of thought; *Hue*, for instance, would
be inane were it not for the exposition of the emotion of
love which is metaphorically expressed in the Graces' description of the missing Eros.

By means of a negative example this can perhaps be made
clearer: Near the conclusion of *Hue* Vulcan enters upon a
comparatively lengthy disquisition of the marriage state:
The sphere which he has displayed in honour of this occasion—a court wedding—is "formed round and even," and,
like the heavens, possesses "the perfect'st form" and reveals
"the heaven of marriage." In the zodiac of this nuptial
heaven Vulcan has placed the "twelve sacred powers" of
"nuptial hours." Gemini, for example, signifies the power
"that twins their hearts, and doth of two make one." Aries
symbolizes their pride in youth and beauty, and suggests
the bride's graces. Lofty and ingenious as this device upon
matrimony is, it does not possess the appealing fancifulness

[64] " 'Whence comes thy joy?' she asks; 'cruel child, what battles hast
thou fought? What victim has thine arrow pierced? Hast thou once more
compelled the Thunderer to low among the heifers of Sidon? Hast thou
overcome Apollo, or again summoned Diana to a shepherd's care?
Methinks thou hast triumphed over some fierce and potent god.' "

of the characterization of Love in *Hue,* where the presence
of non-emotional comedy has already been discussed.

Other instances of this trait of Jonson—his presenting
humorous mythological material in his masques—are not
scarce. A pretty scene in *The Masque of Beauty* presents
"in the back-part of the isle, a grove of grown trees laden
with golden fruit, which other little Cupids plucked, and
threw at each other, whilst on the ground leverets picked
up the bruised apples, and left them half eaten." This, it
may be mentioned incidentally, Jonson must have gathered
from Philostratus' *Imagines,*[65] chiefly through a process of
astute selection.

And the name of this author brings to mind another occasion when Jonson uses his work:[66] *Pleasure Reconciled to
Virtue.* This opens with a merry chorus in honour of Comus,
"the god of cheer, or the Belly," followed by the bowl bearer's monologue-discussion of Hercules' bowl, which he carries. After an anti-masque, Hercules appears in dreadful
anger to compare these celebrators to earth-nourished monsters like Antaeus. (Hercules killed Antaeus in a wrestling
contest by lifting him away from the ground, his source of
invincible strength.) Later, when Hercules lies down to sleep
at the foot of Mount Atlas, there is another anti-masque,
this consisting of pygmies, who utter dire threats against
the slayer of their "brother" Antaeus. These enemies in-
stantly disappear when Hercules awakens and receives from

[65] I. 6: "Cupids are gathering apples. . . . Here run straight rows of
trees with space left free between them to walk in. . . . On the ends of
the branches apples golden and red and yellow invite the whole swarm
of Cupids to harvest them. . . . Two of them are throwing an apple back
and forth. . . . I will describe the wrestling also. . . . In pain the Cupid
whose finger is being bent back bites the ear of his opponent. The Cupids
who are spectators are angry with him for this as unfair and contrary
to the rules of wrestling, and pelt him with apples. And let not the hare
yonder escape us. . . . The creature was sitting under the trees and feed-
ing on the apples that fell to the ground but leaving many half-eaten."
[66] *Ibid.,* 2. 21; 22.

the hands of Mercury a crown of poplar in reward for his being the "active friend of Virtue."

The philosophic opinions which Jonson implies in this masque include moderation in eating and drinking—perhaps because of his own derelictions in both respects—and in general the preferring of virtue rather than pleasure. Yet were the masque devoid of the comic element in the anti-masque, it would deserve small praise, for small effectiveness would it have. Even the most excellent moralizations, like those in the masques of Jonson's contemporary, Daniel, require the poetic gifts of a Milton or the learned comedy of a Jonson to escape dullness.

The allusions to nature in Jonson's masques and poems also occasionally possess that kind of gaiety that results from the incongruous, although more often the blending of mythology with the seasons and the winds and the heavens and the seas and the skies is accomplished by thoughtful and luxurious personification. In the lighter vein Jonson creates a satyr somewhat like Puck[67] to mingle with the fairies and Queen Mab of English folklore in *The Satyr*, and this hybrid satyr observes that the Prince has "Cyparissus' face," and that his mother, Queen Anne, has "Syrinx' grace!"

Again, when the King and the Queen were entertained with *The Penates*, May 1, 1604, at Highgate, Jonson, thinking probably of James' interest in learned presentations, arranged for Mercury to greet the guests in the garden, which he describes as the bower on "the Arcadian hill Cyllene" where Maia bore him. Welcoming the visitors this May Day are Maia, "the blushing Aurora," the "gentle wind Favonius," Flora, some mountain nymphs, and "the Dryads of the valley." After a song, Maia congratulates the royal guests, and in mythological language speaks about na-

[67] Herford and Simpson, II, 261.

ture. Mercury relates the erotic fable of his love for Penelope, upon whom he begot Pan. The latter, summoned from leading the sylvan dances of the wood nymphs about "the fount of laughter, or Bacchus' spring," approaches the group, and insists, in ribald speech, that they all partake of his liquor to insure their merriment.

The descriptive part of this entertainment—Mercury's welcome to the royal guests—should probably be designated as the magical treatment of nature according to Arnold's classification, for here indeed "the eye is on the object, but charm and magic are added."[68] Consider, for example, this brief excerpt from Mercury's ecstatic salutation:

> Behold my mother Maia . . . gladding the air with her breath, and cheering the spring with her smiles. At her feet, the blushing Aurora, who, with her rosy hand, casteth her honeydews on those sweeter herbs, accompanied with that gentle wind Favonius, whose subtile spirit, in the breathing forth, Flora makes into flowers, and sticks them in the grass, as if she contended to have the embroidery of the earth richer than the cope of the sky. Here, for her month, the yearly delicate May keeps state. . . . But see! upon your approach . . . the birds are hush'd, Zephyr is still, the morn forbears her office, Flora is dumb, and herself amazed.

But a few moments later, with the introduction of Pan to the merry assembly, Jonson's most capricious mood asserts itself, and a jovial spirit pervades the concluding part of the entertainment, demonstrating once again the author's faculty for providing a charming and learned background for a comparatively trivial and passing social occasion.

In *The Vision of Delight*[69] another lofty description of spring causes Wonder, at the sight of Peace (Eirene, one of the Hours) in the bower of Zephyr, to exclaim:

[68] Arnold, *On the Study of Celtic Literature and on Translating Homer,* London, 1903, p. 136.
[69] Pp. 290, 291.

Grows

The wealth of nature here, or art? it shows
As if Favonius, father of the spring,
Who in the verdant meads doth reign sole king,
Hath roused him here, and shook his feathers, wet
With purple swelling nectar; and had let
The sweet and fruitful dew fall on the ground
To force out all the flowers that might be found:
Or a Minerva with her needle had
The enamour'd earth with all her riches clad,
And made the downy Zephyr as he flew
Still to be followed with the Spring's best hue.
The gaudy peacock boasts not in his train
So many lights and shadows, nor the rain-
Resolving Iris, when the Sun doth court her.

As Gifford has noticed, Jonson is indebted to Claudian[70] for this description. It must be added, however, that the rendering of the passage is Jonson's own work and proves his independence of a rigid adherence to his source. Apparently, too, Jonson had Claudian's passage in mind several years

[70] *The Rape of Proserpine,* 2. 71-100 [Henna addresses Zephyrus]: " 'Gracious father of the spring, thou who ever rulest over my meads with errant breeze and bringest rain upon the summer lands with thine unceasing breath, behold. . . . Grant that now all the trees be thick with newly-grown fruit, that fertile Hybla may be jealous and admit her paradise surpassed. All the sweet airs of Panchaea's incense-bearing woods, all the honied odours of Hydaspes' distant stream, all the spices which from furthest fields the long-lived Phoenix gathers, seeking new birth from wished for death— . . . with generous breath refresh my country. . . .'
"So spake she, and Zephyrus shook his wings adrip with fresh nectar and drenches the ground with their life-giving dew. Wheresoe'er he flies spring's brilliance follows. . . . He paints the bright roses red, the hyacinths blue and the sweet violets purple. What girdles of Babylon, meet cincture of a royal breast, are adorned with such varied jewels? What fleece so dyed in the rich juice of the murex where stand the brazen towers of Tyre? Not the wings of Juno's own bird display such colouring. Not thus do the many changing hues of the rainbow span young winter's sky when in curved arch its rainy path glows green amid the parting clouds."

later when he composed *Pan's Anniversary*,[71] in which a
shepherd invokes three nymphs to shower some thirty kinds
of flowers in Pan's honour,

> That when the altar, as it ought, is drest,
> More odour come not from the phoenix' nest;
> The breath thereof Panchaia may envý,
> The colours China, and the light the sky.

The last two lines particularly suggest Claudian's *"ramos
Panchaia, vellera Seres."*[72]

Less poetic but certainly not less elevated is the treatment
of nature in the last part of *King James's Entertainment*.
When the paraders upon this occasion reached the Strand,
they beheld two pyramids seventy feet in height supporting
"a rainbow, the moon, sun, and those seven stars, . . . the
Pleiades." Because Electra, one of the Pleiades, "is rarely
or not at all to be seen," Jonson devised the scheme of having "her hanging in the air, in figure of a comet," from
which position she spoke:

> The long laments I spent for ruin'd Troy,
> Are dried; and now mine eyes run tears of joy.
> No more shall men suppose Electra dead,
> Though from the consort of her sisters fled
> Unto the arctic circle, here to grace,
> And gild this day with her serenest face:
> And see, my daughter Iris hastes to throw
> Her roseate wings, in compass of a bow,
> About our state, as sign of my approach:
> Attracting to her seat from Mithra's coach,
> A thousand different and particular hues,
> Which she throughout her body doth diffuse.
> The sun, as loth to part from this half sphere,
> Stands still; and Phoebe labours to appear
> In all as bright, if not as rich, as he:

[71] 42.

[72] *Panegyric on the Third Consulship of Honorius*, 211: "Panchaia per-
fumes, and China silk."

> And, for a note of more serenity,
> My six fair sisters hither shift their lights,
> To do this hour the utmost of her rites.[73]

The sun, the rainbow, the moon, and the Pleiades can now all be seen simultaneously, Electra continues, because

> great king, this day is thine,
> And doth admit no night.

She hopes that, since James has closed the gates of Janus' temple, Justice is entering upon another Golden Age, this an English one.

The trouble to which Jonson went to evolve this entertainment is evidenced in the dozen footnotes and quotations with which he documents it. But his patience, his ingenuity, and his whimsical playfulness here and later during the spring in *The Penates* were rewarded. He was commissioned to create the Twelfth Night masque for the following year and thereafter for some twenty years. His appointment is the more remarkable because, after his expulsion for disorderliness at Daniel's *Vision of the Twelve Goddesses,* he must have been for a time in something like disgrace at court. He immediately established his place in the King's esteem, however; probably his inspiration and his effectiveness lie equally in his Rabelaisian comedy and in his happy ability to poeticize nature and myth.

When he speaks of the sea, he pictures Oceanus "in a human form, the colour of his flesh blue; and shadowed with a robe of sea-green; his head gray, and horned, as he is described by the ancients: his beard of the like mixed colour: . . . and in his hand a trident."[74] Or he makes his scene an island, Delos, whither Latona took refuge from Juno's jealous wrath to bring forth her twins, Apollo and Diana; and the sea-deities, Proteus, Portunus, and Saron, praise Nep-

[73] Pp. 429, 430.
[74] *The Masque of Blackness,* p. 7.

tune while Galatea, Doris, and the Sirens play their parts.[75] When he uses a mountain setting, he presents Atlas, *"an old man, his head and beard all hoary, and frost, as if his shoulders were covered with snow; the rest wood and rock. A grove of ivy at his feet."*[76]

Thinking of the air, he accepts the Greek interpretation that Juno is "the air itself," and the high clouds, opening, reveal *"Juno, sitting in a throne, supported by two beautiful peacocks; her attire rich, and like a queen, a white diadem on her head, from whence descended a veil, and that bound with a fascia of several colour'd silks, set with all sorts of jewels, and raised in the top with lilies and roses: in her right hand she held a sceptre, in the other a timbrel, at her golden feet the hide of a lion was placed: round about her sat the spirits of the air in several colours, making music: above her the region of fire, with a continual motion, was seen to whirl circularly, and Jupiter standing in the top (figuring the heaven) brandishing his thunder: beneath her the rainbow, Iris,"* and eight ladies who symbolize Juno's powers as guardian of marriage.[77]

To celebrate the coming of spring in an entertainment for Shrovetide, he devises a scene marked with flowers, leafage, picturesque clouds, a child Zephyrus, and a personification of spring as "a beautiful maid, her upper garment green, under it a white robe wrought with flowers." But this order is disturbed by Spring's relating to her *Naides* that Love has defied the gods and his own mother, and gone to hell to create a fury. The anti-masque presents the upheaval caused by Cupid's action; there are storms, winds, lightning, thunder, rain, and snow personified appropriately, until Juno, the queen of the air, intervenes. The scene then changes to the colourful and fragrant bower of Chloris, god-

[75] *Neptune's Triumph.*
[76] *Pleasure Reconciled to Virtue*, p. 299.
[77] *Hymenaei*, pp. 55, 56.

dess of flowers, surmounted with Iris' rainbow, and Cupid begs pardon for his unseeming action.[78]

Expecting these and a myriad other pleasures, the epicure who today comes to Jonson to appease his craving for learning, comedy, natural loveliness, or realistic satire repeats the comment made by the Elizabethans and the Jacobeans : The sparkling vintages of classic mythology, usually mellow but sometimes sour, perfect these feasts. From the first of Jonson's entertainments (*The Satyr,* 1603) to the last (*Love's Welcome at Bolsover,* 1634), his resources of Greek and Roman fable were ever available and helpful to his Muse.

APPRECIATION

That which Fortune denied Jonson—wealth, title, position —he wrested from the Muses. They, with drapery like that woven by Pallas and Arachne, decently and becomingly adorned his stark, acrimonious contempt for men's follies. Both Melpomene of tragedy and Thalia of comedy distinguished his plays from the lustreless ones produced by many of his contemporaries. The Muses' voices softened his cynical and embittered comment as he characterized Mammon, Volpone, Fulvia, Sejanus, and Catiline. Their loveliness enhanced the virtue of Crites, Arete, and Celia. Eventually Fama Bona bestowed her highest honours upon Jonson's efforts.

The theatre, however, restricts the Muses' liberty. Their entrances, no matter how timely or lyric, must not retard dramatic action. A play is not an epic, a spectator is not a reader. The drama, therefore, allowed the Muses only partly to fulfil their possibilities as Jonson's inspiration.

Opportunely the summons came for him to compose entertainments and masques. In these his virile and occasionally vulgar nature could not have done without Euterpe, Terpsichore, and Urania in music, the dance, and the scene. With

[78] *Chloridia,* pp. 96 ff.

lyrics of mirth and of love Thalia and Erato, too, graced his work. Greatly through their literature Jonson created masques that reached a new peak of poetic, tuneful, graceful, and spectacular entertainment. While he laboured year after year for the court-festivals, the Muses could range with complete freedom through classic story. At last Jonson had accomplished his early ambition:

> In this alone, his Muse her sweetness hath,
> She scorns the print of any beaten path;
> And proves new ways to come to learned ears;
> Pied ignorance she neither loves nor fears.
> Nor hunts she after popular applause,
> Or foamy praise, that drops from common jaws:
> The garland that she wears, their hands must twine,
> Who can both censure, understand, define
> What merit is.
>
> *Cynthia's Revels,* Prologue, p. 215.

THE SOURCES

ABBREVIATIONS

Al.	*The Alchemist*
Au.	*The Masque of Augurs*
Ba.	*The Barriers,* following *Hymenaei*
Be.	*The Masque of Beauty*
B.F.	*Bartholomew's Fair*
Bl.	*The Masque of Blackness*
Ca.	*Catiline*
Canaan	*The New English Canaan*
Case	*The Case Is Altered*
Chl.	*Chloridia*
Christmas	*The Masque of Christmas*
C.R.	*Cynthia's Revels*
D.A.	*The Devil Is an Ass*
E.M.I.	*Every Man in His Humour*
E.M.O.	*Every Man out of His Humour*
Ent. of Two Kings	*The Entertainment of the Two Kings of Great Britain and Denmark* . . .
Epi.	*Epigrams*
Epic.	*Epicoene,* or *The Silent Woman*
Expostulation	*An Expostulation with Inigo Jones*
F.I.	*The Fortunate Isles, and Their Union*
F.M.	*The Fall of Mortimer*
For.	*The Forest*
G.A.R.	*The Golden Age Restored*
G.M.	*The Gypsies Metamorphosed*
Henry's Ba.	*Prince Henry's Barriers*
Hue	*The Hue and Cry after Cupid*
Hy.	*Hymenaei*
K.J.E.	*The Entertainment for King James* . . .
Lethe	*The Masque of Lethe*
L.F.	*Love Freed from Ignorance and Folly*
L.R.	*Love Restored*

L.T.	*Love's Triumph through Callipolis*
L.W.Bol.	*Love's Welcome; the King and Queen's Entertainment at Bolsover*
L.W.Wel.	*Love's Welcome; the King's Entertainment at Welbeck* . . .
M.L.	*The Magnetic Lady;* or *Humours Reconciled*
M.O.	*The Masque of Owls*
M.P.	*Miscellaneous Pieces*
M.V.	*Mercury Vindicated from the Alchemists*
N.I.	*The New Inn;* or *The Light Heart*
N.N.W.	*News from the New World* . . .
N.T.	*Neptune's Triumph for the Return of Albion*
Ob.	*The Masque of Oberon*
Ode	*Ode Allegorike* in Miscellaneous Pieces
P.A.	*Pan's Anniversary;* or *The Shepherd's Holiday*
Panegyre	*A Panegyre on the Happy Entrance of James* . . .
Pen.	*The Penates*
Po.	*The Poetaster*
P.R.	*Pleasure Reconciled to Virtue*
Qu.	*The Masque of Queens*
Sat.	*The Satyr*
Se.	*Sejanus*
S.N.	*The Staple of News*
Tilt	*A Challenge at Tilt*
T.T.	*A Tale of a Tub*
T.V.	*Time Vindicated to Himself and to his Honours*
Und.	*Underwoods*
V.D.	*The Vision of Delight*
Verses	*Verses Placed over the Door at the Entrance into the Apollo*
Volp.	*Volpone;* or *The Fox*
Wales	*For the Honour of Wales*

ARTICLES

ACHATES. *Po.,* V, i, 484.

"Fidus Achates," companion of Aeneas, is named ten times in *Aen.,* 1, and frequently in the other books.

ACHELOUS. *Volp.,* III, vi, 246.

When Volpone boasts that he would have contended with the "horned flood" for the love of Celia, he alludes to the myth of the river god Achelous, who, in the form of a horned bull, fought with Hercules for the love of Deianira. Ovid (*Met.,* 9. 80-88) relates the story most fully; *cf.* also Strabo, 10. 2. 19; Apollodorus, 2. 7. 5; Diodorus Siculus, 4. 35; and Hyginus' *L.F.,* 31.

ACHERON. *Epi.,* 233; 237.

Speaking of the Stygian river, Acheron, J. follows classical tradition (*e.g., Geor.,* 2. 490-493; *Aen.,* 6. 295-297; 7. 569, 570; Lucian's *Of Mourning,* 3), but exaggerates for humorous purposes.

ACHILLES. *E.M.O.,* IV, iv, 145; *N.I.,* I, i, 325; IV, iii, 390; *M.L.,* III, iii, 58; *Qu.,* 132 footnote; 139, 140 setting; *For.,* 268.

Like Homer (*Il.,* 1. 131 *et passim*), J. characterizes Achilles as great, valorous, and furious. Root notes that Chapman's *Il.,* 7, p. 98, contains the phrase "great Thetis' son"; this is found in *E.M.O.* where the quarrel between him and Agamemnon is the subject (*Il.,* 1. 53-356). The *Qu.* footnote tells of the slaying of Penthesilea (*cf.* MARS), queen of the Amazons, by Achilles at Troy, and of his remorse when he discovered her beauty; J. cites Justin's *History,* (2. 4. 31, 32)[1]; Diodorus, 2. (46); and Propertius'

---

[1] Whenever J. cites or quotes his sources, they are credited to him, but in such cases any additional information (*i.e.,* corrections, specific section, etc.) is included in parentheses.

Elegies, 3.10 (but this should be 3. 11. 13-16). J.'s description of Achilles as not the first

> that lock'd in brass
> Gave killing strokes,

suggests the armour of the hero at *Il.,* 19. 367-399.

ACONITE. *Qu.,* 126 and footnote.

Conforming to "all the magic masters," J. sees a resemblance between the liquor furnished to witches by the devil and aconite, mentioned in *Met., 7.* (406-419), and Pliny's *N.H.,* 27. 3. (8). See CERBERUS.

ACRISIUS. *Volp.* V, i, 289, 290. *Cf.* DANAË.

The tale of Acrisius' concealing Danaë in a brazen chamber so that she might not bear a male child—an oracle had told him that a grandson would kill him—and the subsequent visit of Jove in the guise of a golden shower, resulting in the birth of Perseus, is in many sources (*e.g.,* Apollodorus, 2. 4. 1; Pherecydes' *Fragments, 26*; Lucian's *Sea-Gods, 12*; Zenobius' *Centuria,* 1. 41; Sophocles' *Antigone,* 944-952). Here, however, the use of the myth to illustrate the power of gold parallels Horace's *Odes,* 3. 16. 1-11.

ACTAEON. *C.R.,* I, i, 219; 223; V, iii, 351, 352; *Sat.,* 449.

For J.'s justification of Elizabeth's severity to Essex see Introduction. Gargaphie (*Met.,* 3. 156) is the place where Actaeon was torn to pieces by his own hounds (*Met.,* 3. 193-251). Root calls attention to Golding's translation of *Met.,* in which an English dog name, "Ringwood," is substituted for the last hound named by Ovid; this accounts for J.'s,

> The dog of Sparta breed, and good,
> As can RING within a WOOD (*Sat.*)

Gifford specifies Ovid's *"Spartana gente Melampus"* (*Met.,* 3. 208) as the suggestion for "Sparta breed."

ADONIS. *E.M.O.*, IV, vi, 153; *C.R.*, V, iii, 351; *P.A.*, 42.

The first two passages mention Adonis' garden as do Theocritus (15. 112-118) and Pliny (*N.H.*, 19. 4. 19); "Adonis' flower" in the third is from *Met.*, 10. 728-739, where Cytherea creates it to be an annual memorial of her love for Adonis.

AEACUS. *Epi.*, 239; *Canaan*, 348, 349.

There is considerable divergence of opinion about the duties of Aeacus, Minos, and Rhadamanthus in the infernal regions. Aeacus is said to be a judge by Plato (*Apology*, 41 A; *Gorgias*, 524 A); to hold the keys of Hades by Apollodorus, 3. 12. 6; to be a gate-keeper by Lucian (*Dead*, 20; *Cataplus*, 4; *Menippus*, 8) and by Claudian (*Against Rufinus*, 2. 466, 467); to be a toll-collector by Lucian (*Charon*, 2); and to be an assessor along with Pluto and Proserpine by Isocrates (*Evagoras*, 15). Minos is said to be a judge in *Od.*, 11. 568-571; Apollodorus, 3. 1. 2; *Apology, l.c.; Dead*, 12; 30; *Menippus*, 11-13; *Against Rufinus*, 2. 476-527; and Vergil's *Culex*, 372-380. Rhadamanthus is sometimes a judge (*Apology, l.c.;* Apollodorus, *l.c.;* Pindar's *Ol.*, 2. 75, 76; Lucian's *Voyage to the Lower World*, 23-29), and at other times a torturer (*Against Rufinus*, 2. 478-480). Apollodorus, 3. 12. 6, praises Aeacus for his piety, and many (*e.g.*, Apollodorus, 3. 12. 7; Pausanias, 2. 29. 6-10) praise his justice— as J. seems to do in *Canaan*: "And Eacus . . . is as sure as text." J. has Claudian most in mind when in *Canaan* he writes "grim Minos" and "stern Radamantus," for the former epithet is in *Against Rufinus*, 2. 459: *"nigrique . . . judicis"*; and the latter is in *ibid.*, 2. 479: *"rigidi . . . fratris."*

AENEAS. *N.I.*, I, i, 325; *Hue*, 94 and footnote, 95; *Qu.*, 133 footnote; 140 setting; *Epi.*, 228; 232.

The account of Aeneas' saving his father and his son during the burning of Troy is from *Aen.*, 2. 705-743. *"Pius Aeneas"* (*e.g.*, *Aen.*, 1. 220; 305; 4. 393) explains "pious," "loved," and "good" as applied to Aeneas. Many times Vergil demonstrates the love of Venus for her son, Aeneas; *cf. e.g., Aen.,* 1. 227-258; 314-401; 2. 558-562. In the *Hue* footnote J. says, "Aeneas, the son of Venus, Virgil makes throughout, the most exquisite pattern of piety, justice, prudence, and all other princely virtues. . . ." Similar virtues J. sought to confer upon his sovereign by the comparison. J. supports "swift-foot Camilla," the "queen of the Volscians," with a quotation about her part in the strife between Aeneas and Turnus over Lavinia in *Aen.,* 7. (803-811). Chaucer's *House of Fame* may have suggested the placing of the name of Aeneas among those of the heroes decorating the House of Fame. Speaking in his sonnet to Roe of Aeneas' passing through fire, J. probably has in mind *Aen.,* 2. 705-743; through seas, 1. 124-145; and through storms and tempests, 1. 81-123. Aeneas' visit to Hades is recounted in *Aen.,* 6. 268-636; see also AVERNUS.

AEOLUS. *K.J.E.,* 407.

J. confirms this passage by quoting Vergil (*Aen.,* 1. 82, 83, "where Aeolus, at the command of Juno, lets forth the wind").

AESCULAPIUS. *Po.,* V, i, 497; 501; *Se.,* I, ii, 30; *Vo.,* II, i, 208; *Al.,* IV, i, 117; *M.L.,* V, v, 102; *Epi.,* 151. See also EPIDAURIAN SERPENT.

The physician Aesculapius is found in *Il.,* 4. 194, but in linking him and Apollo, J. probably had in mind *Il.,* 1. 473; 22. 391; or *Met.,* 15. 638, 639. Paeans are sung in honour of Apollo's curative powers in *Il.,* and Paean (Aesculapius) is the physician of the gods (*Il.,* 5. 401; 899, 900). The destruction of Aesculapius by Jove's lightning, because Aesculapius had restored even the dead, occurs frequently in literature (*e.g.,* Pindar's *Py.,* 3. 47-54; Diodorus Siculus, 4. 71; Apollodorus, 3. 10. 4; *Aen.,* 7. 770-773; Servius on *Aen.,* 7. 761; Hyginus' *L.F.,* 49). With Aesculapius' golden beard *cf. "longae ... barbae"* (*Met.,* 15. 656) and *"aureus ... deus"* (669, 670). Machaon and Podalirius, sons of Aesculapius, are named as skilled physicians at *Il.,* 2. 731, 732; 11. 833-836; *Aen.,* 2. 263. The humorous quatrain based on the offering of a cock to Aesculapius in gratitude for his benefits is inspired by ancient practice (Plato's *Phaedo,* 118). *Cf.* also LYNCEUS.

AESON. *Volp.,* I, i, 189.

For the rejuvenation of Aeson by the magic of Medea, see MEDEA.

AETHALIDES. *Volp.,* I, i, 171.

Apollonius (*Argo.,* 1. 51-55) names Mercury as the father of Aethalides, whose soul "had the gift to remember all that ever was done." From Aethalides it passed to Euphorbus, who was slain by Menelaus (*Il.,* 17. 59, 60). Pausanias (2. 17. 3) relates that the victor hung the shield of Aethalides in the temple of Here at Mycenae. Horace (*Odes,* 1. 28. 9-13), Hyginus (*L.F.,* 112), and Lucian (*Dead,* 20; *The Vision of the Cock,* 4-20) all assert that Pythagoras claimed that he possessed Euphorbus' soul. Lucian's *Vision* is J.'s source, for it names many of the possessors of this soul from Apollo to the animals specified.

AETNA. *Und.,* 372; 408.

See CYCLOPES.

AGAMEMNON. *E.M.O.,* IV, iv, 145; *Po.,* IV, i, 445; *N.I.,* I, i, 325.

See ACHILLES. In *N.I.* Agamemnon is classed with the great exemplars of heroism and manhood; *cf. Il.,* 1. 130; 170; etc.

AGLAIA. *C.R.,* V, iii, 342.

See GRACES.

AJAX. *For.*, 269.

J. speaks of the exceptional bravery of Ajax; so Homer (*Il.*, 2. 768, 769; 17. 279, 280) and Apollodorus, 4. 2, have characterized him.

ALBION. *Bl.*, 13 footnote; 17; *Be.*, 24; 25; 28; *N.T.*, 27; 34; 36; 38; *F.I.*, 81.

As J. explains in the footnote, it is customary "to style princes after the name of their princedoms: so he is still Albion, and Neptune's son that governs. As also his being dear to Neptune, in being so embraced by him." In *N.I.*, however, Albion is the prince and shares his father Neptune's responsibility. Oceanus protects Albion.

ALCIDES. *Po.*, III, i, 418; *Epi.*, 234.
See HERCULES.

ALCYONE. *K.J.E.*, 428-431.
See ELECTRA.

ALECTO. *Qu.*, 114 footnote.
See FURIES.

ALPHEUS. *Bl.*, 10 footnote.
See OCEANUS.

AMAZONS. *Epic.*, III, ii, 396; 477; *Qu.*, 132 footnote.

J. apparently follows no specific source in using the Amazon tradition; *cf. Il.*, 3. 189; 6. 186; *Aen.*, 1. 490 ff.; 11. 659-663.

AMBROSIA AND NECTAR. *E.M.O.*, IV, vi, 153; *C.R.*, I, i, 225; *Po.*, IV, iii, 453-458; *Se.*, I, i, 25; *Ca.*, I, i, 194; *S.N.*, IV, i, 253; *N.I.*, II, ii, 346; III, ii, 367; *Hy.*, 46; *K.J.E.*, 414; *N.T.*, 34; 37; *F.I.*, 80; *For.*, 258, 259; *Und.*, 375; 383; *M.P.*, 330.

Having absorbed classical tradition, J. handles the ideas of ambrosia and nectar very properly, but, as far as sources go, very loosely. A few that he must have known are *Theogony*, 639-643; *Od.*, 5. 199; 9. 359; *Il.*, 4. 1-4; 19. 37-39. Phrases like "ambrosial kiss," "ambrosial hands," "ambrosiac odour," and "ambrosial muse" should be considered with Homer's "ambrosial locks" (*Il.*, 1. 529), "ambrosial raiment" (5. 338), and "anointed her with oil, ambrosial, soft, and of rich fragrance" (14. 170-172); Vergil also uses *"ambrosiaque comae"* (*Aen.*, 1. 403).

When Amorphus perceives the fount of self-love, he exclaims, "Liberal and divine fount. . . . Here is most ambrosiac water." Here J. may have in mind the description of the fountains in the Hesperian gardens (*Hippolytus*, 748), which Euripides calls ambrosial. In *Po.* nectar is the drink of the pseudo gods and goddesses at their sacrilegious banquet; *cf. Od.*, 5. 92-94; *Il.*, 1. 598; etc. Their cupbearer is Ganymede (*Il.*, 20. 232-235). There is no precedent for introducing nectar as an agency for breaking the bonds of love (*Po.*) or as an intoxicant (*N.T.*); in both cases nectar has the effect of wine. Cupid's preferring the nectar of sensuousness to his mother's milk (*S.N.*) seemingly lacks a classical explanation. Possibly the notion of vengeance as "nectar unto my famished spirits" (*Se.*) reflects the curative power of nectar for physical ills; *cf. Il.*, 19. 38, 39; 357-359; *Aen.*, 12. 419.

AMPHION. *F.I.*, 78; *Epi.*, 229.

Homer (*Od.*, 11. 260-265) without alluding to music says Amphion and Zethus "established the seat of seven-gated Thebe, and fenced it in with walls." Ovid (*Met.*, 15. 427) and Horace (*A.P.*, 394-396) speak of Amphion's music as building citadels; *cf.* J.'s "building towns." Other sources (*e.g.*, *Met.*, 6. 178, 179; Apollodorus, 3. 5. 5; Propertius, 1. 9. 10; Claudian, 22. 170, 171; Pausanias, 9. 5. 6-8; Hyginus' *L.F.*, 9) indicate that he built only the walls.

AMPHITRITE. *L.T.*, 88 setting; 89.

J. makes Amphitrite the wife of Oceanus, contrary to classical sources which make Tethys his wife (see OCEANUS), and make Amphitrite his granddaughter and spouse of Poseidon (*e.g., Theogony,* 933; Apollodorus, 1. 4. 5; Diodorus Siculus, 4. 69). Young, beautiful, royal, and not unlike Venus according to the classics, here Amphitrite encourages the courtiers to reveal their love to the ladies. Her traditional characteristics are to be found in *Theogony,* 243; 254; 930-933; Pindar's *Ol.,* 6. 103-105; *Ciris,* 73; 481-486.

ANDROMEDA. *C.R.*, IV, i, 275.

The mere allusion to Andromeda follows the sources (*e.g.,* Apollodorus, 2. 4. 3; Hyginus' *L.F.*, 64; *De A.*, 2. 11; and *Met.*, 4. 665-739). Cf. CASSIOPEIA.

ANNA PARENNA. *K.J.E.*, 420-426.

The coronation of James I, March 15, 1604, was marked by a lavish procession which included the performing of *K.J.E.* When he was commissioned to write entertainments for the occasion, J., thinking of the date and of the Roman observance of the Ides of March, recalled that "Mars' guest" on the Ides was also an Anna—Anna Parenna—an Italian goddess of very uncertain attributes.

Ovid's *Fasti,* 3. (523-696), is the source upon which J. depends in speaking of the Ides as the feast of Parenna, in associating her as a goddess with Mars, in discussing the various explanations of her identity, and in assuming finally that she is the moon by considering the etymology of her name: *"quia mensibus impleat annum"* at *Fasti,* 3. (657). Her relationship with the moon is also partly confirmed by the Roman supplication: *"ut Annare, et Penannare commode liceret"* (Macrobius' *Saturnaliorum Conviviorum,* 1. 12. (6). "She fills the year" suggests the early practice of honouring Mars as a god of nature responsible for the fertility of the fields and the flocks, but there is no evidence in antiquity that

Parenna was so invoked; apparently J. would have her partake of Mars' attributes. He interprets the line that Parenna
"knits the oblique scarf that girts the sphere" as "the meet-
ing of the zodiac in March, the month wherein she is celebrated" (*K.J.E.,* 424).

In the masque the rites in tribute to Parenna are conducted
in the temple dedicated to Janus although Ovid at *Fasti,* 3.
(523-532) says that they were held in the fields, *"non procul
a ripis, . . . Thybri, tuis."* J. may have preferred the temple
of Janus because it was noted "to be both the house of war
and peace," and in comparing Anna Parenna, "guest" of
bellicose Mars (*Fasti,* 3. 678) with Queen Anne, the model
of peace-loving womanhood—if one may trust J.'s estimate
of her—a scene common to both natures was quite de-
sirable. James I, moreover, was beginning his reign during
the spring, and Janus was the god of beginnings and of the
springtime (*cf.* "his vernal look," *K.J.E.,* 424). Lastly, field
rites would scarcely have been an appropriate greeting to the
queen, and would necessarily have been staged indoors.

ANTAEUS. *P.R.,* 302-305.

The giant Antaeus, whose sin was inhumanity to strangers,
was slain by Hercules when the latter was *en route* to obtain
the golden apples of the Hesperides. So relate Lucan, 4. 589-
653; Philostratus' *Imagines,* 2. 21; Apollodorus, 2. 5. 11;
Pindar's *Isth.,* 4. 52-55; and many others. The killing of
Antaeus aroused the pygmies to contend with Hercules
(Philostratus, 2. 22), as Gifford says, but in *P.R.* they simply
scatter at the sight of him. The pygmies' calling Antaeus "our
brother" is from Philostratus, *l.c.* See also EARTH.

ANTEROS. *Tilt,* 220; *L.W.Wel.,* 136-138.
    See CUPID.

APOLLO.

Apollo, one of "th' interpreters twixt gods and men"
(*Und.,* 335), is acknowledged by Jove as the god of arts

(*Au.,* 427) ; thus is indicated Apollo's traditional leadership in poetry, music, and divination.

As the god of poetry (*Od.,* 8. 487, 488), he is associated with the Muses (*e.g.,* Horace's *Odes,* 4.6.25;Ovid's *Amores,* 3. 12. 17, 18; Vergil's *Eclogues,* 6. 1-12; *Culex,* 11-19). As guardians of wit, he and the Muses are found in Ovid's *Tristia,* 2. 13, and Vergil's *Catalepton,* 9. 1. 2. The joining of Apollo with the Muses and the Graces (*S.N.,* III, i, 239, 240; *G.M.,* 375; *M.O.,* 53; and *For.,* 208) accords with the *H.H. to Artemis,* 27. 13-15; *to the Muses and Apollo* 25. 1-7; Pindar's *Ol.,* 14. 10; Horace's *Carmen Saeculare,* 62; Ovid's *Met.,* 5. 255. Other passages referring to Apollo and the Muses are *Po.,* I, i, 377; III, i, 430; *L.F.,* 196; *Au.,* 420; *N.T.,* 33; *Epi.,* 188; *For.,* 250; 260, 261; *Und.,* 312; 319; 335; 368; 378; 419; *Verses,* 73; and *Ode,* 354.

Apollo celebrates in music the victory (*Ob.,* 170 and footnote) of Jove over Saturn, for which J. quotes Tibullus' *Elegia,* 2. (5. 7-10). By his song Apollo can "rear towns" (*Au.,* 420; 422; J. quotes imperfectly from *"Ovidii Epistol. Epist. Parid.,"* i.e., *Heroides,* 16. (181, 182) ; see also *Met.,* 8. 15; 12. 586-593), and by his instrumental music he can raise a college "of tuneful augurs" (*Au.,* 422; cf. J.'s sources: Livy, I. (6. 4-7. 3) and Tull. I. (this source is not satisfactory; Cicero's *De N.D.,* 3. 2. 5, is closest to the sense wanted)). For *Au.,* 421 and footnotes, where the children of Apollo are named, see LINUS, ORPHEUS, BRANCHUS, IDMON, and PHEMONOE. These children assist Apollo in interpreting the auguries.

Apollo's harp (*Ob.,* 170 and footnote; *For.,* 250; 368; *Und.,* 378; see also CLAROS) and the Muses' singing to his accompaniment recall *Theogony,* 93-96; *Shield,* 201-206; *Il.,* 1. 603, 604; *H.H. to Py. Apollo,* 3. 182-203; *to Hermes,* 4. 450-455; 500-503, and other sources. The singing of Crites (*C.R.,* V, i, 338), "fit for a theatre of gods to hear," may have been suggested by Apollo's and the Muses' entertaining

the gods at *Il.*, 1. 601-604; and the "elaborate paeans" of
Crites (*ibid.*) are reminiscent of "the beautiful paean" of *Il.*,
1. 473, and *H.H. to Py. Apollo*, 3. 516-520. For the
Arcadians' assertion that Pan knows more airs than Phoebus
(*P.A.*, 46), the inspiration may have been the contest be-
tween the two at *Met.*, 11. 151-173, and *Eclog.*, 4. 58, 59.
Passages similar to the above are *Po.*, IV, iii, 457, 458; *N.T.*,
33; *F.I.*, 77, 78; and *G.A.R.*, 250, 251.

Apollo possesses, too, the power of divination. At the oracle
of Delphi he succeeded Themis, *q.v.* for *Tilt*, 219. He is the
herald of Jupiter at *Po.*, IV, iii, 453, and *Au.*, 420. Claiming
to have taught "men the tuneful art of augury" (*ibid.*), he
comes to establish a college of augurs; in connection with this
J. cites *Aen.*, 4. (either lines 56-64 or 376-378, but neither
passage is really satisfactory) and quotes Horace's *Odes*, 1.
2. (31, 32) and *Carmen Saeculare*, (61-64). Apollo interprets prophetic trances according to the practices of antiquity,
makes it clear that the Fates do not give all knowledge (see
FATES), and admits that all his predictions are subject to
the will of Jove (*Au.*, 427). For the last J. cites Orpheus'
"hym. de omnip. Jovis" (14). The same hymn probably is
the source for the introduction of the tripod as the symbol of
Apollo, the prophet, at *Verses*, 73, but *cf.* also *H.H. to
Py. Apollo*, 3. 287-293; Euripides' *Ion*, 91-93; *Met.*, 15.
635; *Aen.*, 3. 92; etc. Naturally Apollo's reputation for
revealing truth (*Se.*, V, x, 135; *Verses*, 73) grows from this
concept of his oracular ability. For historical reasons (Dio,
57) many scenes in *Se.*, V, are in or near the temple of
Apollo.

Jove is the father of Apollo (*Au.*, 427; *Met.*, 1. 517),
Latona, *q.v.*, is his mother (*N.T.*, 28, 29), Cynthia is "sister
of Phoebus" (*C.R.*, V, i, 346; *cf. Met.*, 2. 454), and she and
Apollo are also paired at *C.R.*, Dedication, 203; V, ii, 311;
338. See DELOS. In this Dedication, Phoebus symbolizes
the king as Cynthia does the late Queen Elizabeth; see

CYNTHIA. J. distinguishes between the sun-god and day (*Ca.*, I, i, 193; *L.F.*, 187; *For.*, 261; *cf.* for classic examples *Theogony*, 14; 19; 371; *Met.*, 2. 112-115).

In *L.F.*, 187, Phoebus is said to retire to his palace (*Met.*, 2. 1-18) in the west,

> to feast in every night
> With the Ocean, where he rested
> Safe, and in all state invested.

The classics (*cf. Il.*, 8. 485; *Met.*, 4. 633, 634) declare that the sun sinks into the ocean, but there is no mention of his feasting. Osgood comments upon Milton's similar "sups with Ocean" (*P.L.*, 5. 423). Phoebus' palace in the East (*L.F.*, 187) is but a graceful comparison of Phoebus and J.'s sovereign. There seems to be no precedent for the proposed marriage of Phoebus with the queen of the Orient, the eldest of the eleven daughters of the morn (*L.F.*, 187). "Apollo's goldy-locks" (*C.R.*, V, ii, 334) may have been inspired by *"flavus Apollo"* of Ovid's *Amores*, 1. 15. 35, or by *"ille caput flavum"* of *Met.*, 11. 165, or by *"crinem . . . implicat auro"* of *Aen.*, 4. 148.

The chariot of Phoebus (*L.F.*, 187; *For.*, 260, 261; *Und.*, 369) is especially found at *Met.*, 2. 47, 48; 107-110; his "fiery horses" (*Ob.*, 181) and "his frighted horse" (*Ca.*, V, vi, 332, 333) and his "hot team" (*For.*, 261) have precedent in Euripides' *Ion*, 1148, and *Met.*, 2. 119; 153-155. For *Und.* 369, see PROMETHEUS: for *Canaan*, 349, see PHAETON and CYCNUS. Niger declares (*Bl.*, 11) that his Aethiopian daughters are black because the sun loved them; with this Elizabethanism *cf.* PHAETON. At *Hue*, 90, J. cites Lucian's *Gods* (12) for his statement that at the sight of Cupid, "the sun hath turn'd," for there Cupid is blamed for Helius' delaying with Clymene. For the opposition of the sun and nature to Vulcan's alchemy (*M.V.*, 240), see NATURE.

For other allusions to the sun and nature (*M.V.*, 233; 240; 241; *Und.*, 392) see NATURE. For the sun's courting "rain-resolving Iris" (*V.D.*, 291), see IRIS; and for Hesperus' coursing "even with the sun" (*G.M.*, 367), see HESPERUS. References to Sol or to the sun—without mythological value—are *Po.*, IV, i, 448; V, i, 472; *Se.*, V, x, 150; *Volp.*, I, i, 166, 167; *Al.*, I, i, 39; *S.N.*, IV, i, 263; *Bl.*, 12-15; *Be.*, 24; *L.F.*, 188; 193; *M.V.*, 237; *Au.*, 420; *Und.*, 369; 441; *Canaan*, 348.

Allusions to Apollo's slaying the Python occur at *Po.*, III, i, 418, and at *Ba.*, 154; *cf. e.g.*, Apollodorus, 1. 4. 1; *H.H. to Py. Apollo*, 3. 355-369; *Met.*, 1. 438-446. Related to this are *Po.*, V, i, 448, and *Au.*, 420, the latter containing the epithet "far-shooting Phoebus," a common description (*e.g.*, *Theogony*, 94; *Od.*, 8, 323; *Il.*, 1. 14; *Met.*, 1. 441; *Aen.*, 6. 75). Apollo is at once the god who sends plagues to men (*Po.*, III, i, 413; *Au.*, 420; *cf. Il.*, 1. 9, 10; 44-54) and the god who succors mankind in times of physical distress (*Po.*, III, i, 420; V, i, 501; *Au.*, 420; *Und.*, 419; *cf.* Pausanias, 4. 34. 7; *Met.*, 1. 521-524; 15. 628-640; see AESCULAPIUS).

Apollo, being likewise the moulder of men (*C.R.*, V, i, 305; V, iii, 345; *cf. Theogony*, 347; Callimachus' *Hymn to Apollo*, 2. 12-16; Theophrastus' *Characters*, 21. 1-4), is opposed to Fortune's sway of men (*C.R.*, V, iii, 341, 342; *Po.*, V, i, 472), his resentment being in harmony with his ethical nature. At *C.R.*, IV, i, 282, and *L.F.*, 193, Apollo is honoured as a god helpful to love, the precedent being his own loves. In discussing the love of Apollo for Daphne (*P.A.*, 42; *Epi.*, 153; 226), J. follows Hyginus' *L.F.*, 203; *Anacreontea*, 60 A, 11-24; and *Met.*, 1. 452-566, by referring to the story and the subsequent transformation of Daphne into a laurel tree, thereafter one of the symbols of the god (*Epi.*, 216; *Und.*, 378; *cf. Met.*, 1. 557-565). Along with the laurel and the tripod, the bow and the hawk are also his symbols.

Cupid accuses Mercury of stealing the bow (*C.R.*, I, i, 215), and Mercury similarly charges Cupid (*Hue*, 90 footnote). The latter seems the more traditional (see CUPID: Trophies) though both Cupid and Mercury are notorious for their tricky playfulness. The bow is also mentioned at *Se.,* IV, v, 102. The hawk "sacred to Apollo" (*Epi.,* 188, 189) is one of the birds employed by the augurs (*cf.* Theophrastus' "De Signis," 17). J. sees the hawk as the preserving instructress of mankind,

> That they to knowledge should so tower upright
> And never stoop, but to strike ignorance.

For *Vo.,* II, i, 214, see HELEN; for *Vo.,* I, i, 171, see AETHALIDES; and for *Au.,* 427, see GODS. Other passages relating to Apollo and various deities in the classic tradition but without specific sources or parallels are *Po.,* III, i, 411; *Se.,* I, i, 26; *N.T.,* 33; and *For.,* 250.

ARACHNE. *C.R.,* III, ii, 267; *N.T.,* 36; *F.I.,* 80.

J.'s passing notices of Arachne and Pallas as weavers imply only *Met.,* 6. 1-145, where they contest in their craftsmanship, and where Pallas, because her opponent is so good, turns her into a spider.

ARCADIA. *Pen.,* 464-467; *P.A.,* 41; 43; 46; 48.

Mercury acknowledges Cyllene in Arcadia as his birthplace (*H.H. to Hermes,* 4. 2), and Pan, whom the Arcadians worship, as his son (see PAN). The Arcadians' yearly rites to Pan seem to have been suggested to J. by *Fasti,* 2. 267-281; 290-304, in some detail. *Fasti, l.c., Met.,* 11. 151-173, and Livy, 1. 5, present the background for J.'s interpretation of the Arcadian character in *P.A.,* especially in noticing Pan as a musician who challenged Phoebus (see APOLLO). *Cf.* PAN.

ARCAS. *Epic.,* III, i, 390; *P.A.,* 43.

Arcas, who ruled the Arcadians, was the son of Callisto, *q.v.*

ARETE. *C.R., passim.*

Arete, the embodiment of womanly character, is derived from the personification of virtue in the allegory of Heracles (Xenophon's *Memorabilia,* 2. 1. 21-34). J.'s development of Arete accords only with his own concepts, and whereas the Greeks ultimately united her with Athene, he associates her with Cynthia.

ARETHESA. *Bl.,* 10 footnote.
 See OCEANUS.

ARGIVE QUEEN. *For.,* 268.
 The Argive queen is, of course, Helen of Troy, *q.v.*

ARGO. *Po.,* I, i, 377; *For.,* 269.
 See JASON.

ARGUS. *Al.,* II, i, 49; *S.N.,* III, ii, 243; *K.J.E.,* 408.

The *Al.* passage, dwelling upon the luxuriousness of Argus' eyes, suggests *Met.,* 1. 722, 723; 2. 531-535; the second, wherein jealous Saturnia places Argus with his hundred eyes to watch Io, follows *Met.,* 1. 622-628; the last, Agrypnia's motto, is from Ovid's description of Argus' occupation, *Met.,* 1. 666, 667. *Cf.* Aeschylus' *Supplicants,* 303-305; and Hyginus' *L.F.,* 145.

ARIADNE. *For.,* 269.

J. would have Ariadne's crown set among the stars neither by Zeus nor by Dionysius, but by "only poets, rapt with rage divine." The legend of her crown is from Apollonius Rhodius' *Argo.,* 3. 1001-1004; Hyginus' *D.A.,* 2. 5; *Fasti,* 3. 507-516; and *Met.,* 8. 177-182.

ARION. *Po.,* IV, i, 477; *S.N.,* III, i, 241; *N.T.,* 29; 37; *F.I.,* 78.

The story of Arion, who saved his life when he was attacked by sailors by playing his lyre and thus charming a dolphin which carried him to shore, is in Hyginus' *L.F.,* 194; Herodotus, 1. 24; *Fasti,* 2. 79-118; Lucian's *Sea-Gods,* 8.

ASTERIE.
  See IDMON.

ASTEROPE. *K.J.E.*, 428-431.
  See ELECTRA.

ASTRAEA. *G.A.R.*, 247; 250-254; *For.*, 267.
  See GOLDEN AGE.

ATE. *Ca.*, IV, ii, 278; *Qu.*, 112-115 and footnotes.
  The Dame of the witches in *Qu.* is modeled upon Ate. For
her cruelty to men, her strength, and her sure-footedness, the
correct source is *Il.*, 9. 505-507, although J. suggests *Il.*, 1;
and for her walking upon the heads of men, 19. (92-94).
The other sources J. mentions in his footnote are not of
mythological consequence. The *Ca.* passage linking Ate with
the Furies in guilt finds considerable support in the *Qu.*, 114
footnote, where J. quotes Claudian's *Against Rufinus*, 3.
(27-34).

ATLAS. *Se.*, III, i, 66; V, i, 113; *Ca.*, I, i, 193; IV, ii, 288;
Hy., 72, 73; *P.R.*, 299; 305-310; *Wa.*, 317-322.
  Atlas is powerful enough to hold up the heavens and the
"Olympian throng"; *cf. Theogony*, 517-520; 746-749;
Aeschylus' *Prometheus*, 349-352; *Od.*, 1. 52-55; *Aen.*, 4. 481,
482; *Met.*, 2. 296, 297; 6. 174, 175; and others. There is a
strong resemblance between the representation of Atlas as a
mountain in *P.R.* and in *Aen.*, 4. 246-251, and *Met.*, 4. 657-
662. *Wa.* locates the mountain in Libya as do many Greek
sources (*e.g.*, Diodorus, 3. 53; Herodotus, 4. 184; Pliny's
N.H. 6. 31).
  Atlas is the father of the Hesperides (*P.R.*), who guard
the golden apples or the golden sheep, and when Hercules
slew the dragon or the "rude pirate" molesting Atlas' daughters, their father sent him

  the best sheep that in his fold were found,
Or golden fruit in the Hesperian ground.

From Atlas, Hercules received "all the learning of the sphere" and instructions about how to bear up the skies. All this material agrees closely with Diodorus, 4. 26; 27.

Again, because Hercules had slain Antaeus, *q.v.*, Atlas sends him a crown (Philostratus' *Imagines*, 2. 21). In conveying the message Mercury speaks of "my grandsire Atlas"; Mercury's mother, Maia, is, indeed, the daughter of Atlas (*e.g.*, Lucian's *Gods*, 24; *Met.*, 1. 682; Horace's *Odes*, 1. 10. 1). The clue to J.'s terming Atlas' head the "hill of knowledge" (*P.R.*, 306) is in Diodorus, 4. 27.

ATREUS. *Ca.*, I, i, 202.

"*Qui dicerent Catilinam . . . . humani coporis sanguinem vino permixtum in pateris circumtulisse*" (Sallust's *Bellum Catalinae*, 22) is the groundwork of this allusion, the effectiveness of which J. heightens by comparing the darkness of the day to that "at Atreus' feast." Atreus killed the sons of Thyestes and served them to the unsuspecting father at a banquet (Aeschylus' *Agamemnon*, especially 1217-1245; 1583-1602).

ATROPOS. *J. and A.*, 477-481.

See FATES.

ATYS. *Hue*, 93.

J. cites Lucian's *Gods*, 12, for his statement that Rhea (Ops) fell "franticly in love by Cupid's means, with Atys." The story, also found in Pausanias, 7. 17. 10-12 and *Fasti*, 4. 223-226, continues that because Atys violated his promise to her, Rhea brought about his madness, but relenting after his death, she protected his body from corruption. See RHEA and CYBELE.

AUGURS.

See APOLLO.

AURORA. *Po.*, 369; *Pen.*, 460-462; *Ob.*, 181; *L.F.*, 187; 194; *V.D.*, 294, 295.

Light's "golden splendour" (*Po.*) and the "blushing Aurora" (*Pen.*) seem remarkably close to *"lutea . . . Aurora"* and *"roseo spectabilis ore"* of *Met.*, 7. 703, and 705, respectively, and to *"in roseis lutea mater equis"* of *Fasti*, 4. 714. *Cf.* also the "golden-throned Dawn" of *Od.*, 15. 250, and *"iamque rubescebat . . . Aurora"* of *Aen.*, 3. 521. "Rose hand" (*Pen.* and *Ob.*) is equivalent to "rosy-fingered," a description frequently met in the classics (*e.g., Works*, 610; *Il.*, 1. 477; and *Od.*, 2. 1). "Morn with roses strews the way" (*V.D.*) recalls *"roseis Aurora quadrigis"* in *Aen.*, 6. 535. The dew and Aurora are united at *Met.*, 13. 621, 622, and *Fasti*, 3. 403. "The morn forbears her office" is illuminated by Ovid's *"quod teneat lucis, teneat confina noctis"* (*Met.*, 7. 706). Similarly the elaborate description of the dawn at *Ob.*, 180, reflects the pleasing actions of *Met.*, 2. 112-115 very minutely.

In *Pen.*, performed on May Day, Aurora sits at the feet of Maia with Zephyr, Aurora's son (*Theogony*, 378, 379), and with Flora, his wife (*Fasti*, 5. 193-206), but see CHLORIS. Aurora's love for Tithonus is often related (*H.H. to Aphrodite*, 5. 218-238; *Theogony*, 984, 985; *Il.*, 11. 1; *Od.*, 5. 1; Apollodorus, 3. 12. 4. Here her remark reflects especially *Aen.*, 4. 584, 585, and *Geor.*, 1. 447). "Frozen," applied to Tithonus by Aurora, is appropriate because of his age but is unusual. Aurora introduces the notion of Hemera (Day) as at *Theogony*, 124, when she says,

> But I am urged by the Day,
> Against my will, to bid you come away (*V.D.*).

The references to Aurora's eleven daughters and to her streams are seemingly without precedent.

Avernus. *Epi.,* 234.

J. clearly parodies Vergil by combining Avernus, a lake entering Hades, with the following lines:

> Sans help of Sibyl, or a golden bough,
> Or magic sacrifice, they past along!

Aeneas consulted the Sibyl (*Aen.,* 6. 42-155), who told him that entrance to the lower regions was reserved for those who had discovered the *"auricomos . . . fetus"* (141) and had offered sacrifice (243-254).

Bacchus.

J. associates Bacchus with Comus and Priapus (*Po.,* III, i, 425), the former being a god of mirth sometimes identified with Bacchus but individualized in latter times (see COMUS), and the latter being symbolic of agricultural productiveness and of human fertility (see PRIAPUS). Twice, also, is Bacchus united with Ceres, another deity of the harvest (*Po.,* IV, iii, 443; 457; *cf. e.g., Eclog.,* 5. 79, 80; *Geor.,* 2. 227-230; *Ciris,* 229, 230).

"Serve in Apollo, but take heed of Bacchus" (*S.N.,* III, ii, 243), although obviously a direction not to imbibe excessively in the Apollo room of the Devil Tavern, reminds one that the tomb of Dionysus was honoured in the temple of Apollo at Delphi (Philochorus, I. 22, 23). As the giver of wine Bacchus is acknowledged at *Pen.,* 464-468; *Ob.,* 171; and *For.,* 261; *cf.* Hesiod's *Works,* 611-614; *Shield,* 400; Plato's *Cratylus,* 406 C; *Laws,* 2. 672 A; Pindar's *Paean,* 4. 25; etc. With *Und.,* 419, where he is termed "the father of wines," *cf. Od.,* 9. 198 scholium, Diodorus, 3. 63; 4. 1, 2.

"Lyaeus," an epithet signifying the wine-god's "freeing men's minds from cares" (*Und.,* 419; *Ob.,* 171 and footnote; *Po.,* III, i, 407), is found at *Met.,* 4. 11; 8. 274; *Fasti,* I. 395; etc. "Plump Lyaeus" (*Po.*) resembles "Lyaeus fatt" of Spenser's *F.Q.,* 3. 1. 51, of which Lotspeich says: "Spenser is apparently thinking of Silenus whom he does not distinguish as a separate person." J., who makes Silenus the tutor of Bacchus (*Ob.*, 167 footnote; see next paragraph), is more probably thinking of Comus when he uses "plump Lyaeus," for in *P.R.*, 300, the chorus salutes Comus with "Hail, hail, plump paunch!" and J. describes him on the preceding page as "the god of cheer [*cf.* Lyaeus], or the Belly." In *Po.*, IV, iii, 458, moreover, there are these words addressed to Bacchus: "Your belly weighs down your head."

J.'s assertion at *Ob.*, 169-172, that the satyrs are the "collusores, or playfellows" of Bacchus is supported by his three general references: Diodorus Siculus, (4. 4); Synesius, (*Letters*, 154); and Julian's *Caesares*, (308 C); *cf.* Julian's *Orations*, 7. 220 C. These sources also support J.'s statement that Silenus is the tutor of Bacchus. To "the stripes of the taber" these satyrs carry "Bacchus up, his pomp to vary"; for this J. cites Athenaeus (5. 198 C), and also recalls Casaubon's *De Satyrica Poesi*, (1. 2), containing a description of Rascasius Bagarrius' sculpture of the Bacchic train.

For the companionship of Bacchus and Pan (*Pen.*, 464-468; *For.*, 244) the source may be Pausanias, 2. 24. 6. In *Pen.*, praising the liquor pouring from the fount of Bacchus, Pan serves it; in *For.* the two feast together under a beech. "The green circle of thy ivy twine" (*For.*, 261) agrees with the story of the vine which wrapped itself about Dionysus shortly after his birth, as related by Euripides in *Phoenissae*, 650-656.

The comparison which J. makes of the waters of Bacchus and of Hippocrene (*Und.*, 419) may have been suggested by Boccaccio's *De Genealogia*, 5. 25 ff.: poets "are sacred to Bacchus." J.'s hope that Venus, the Graces, and Cupid will be friendly to Bacchus (*Und.*, 420) was possibly inspired by Athenaeus, 2. 36 D, or by *Anacreontea*, 5. 1-15. Certainly his desire that Bacchus' wine would become as medicinal as

Apollo's ministrations parallels Athenaeus, 1. 22 E, and Pindar's *Paean*, 4. 25.

Only one hint of the forbears of Bacchus is given. *Hy.*, 55 and footnote, states that Juno is the stepmother of Bacchus after her representation as a lion attacking Bacchus and Hercules at Argos. Plato (*Laws*, 2. 672 B) terms Juno "stepmother," and many hint at her jealousy of the wine-god (Euripides' *Bacchae*, 1-42; 278-297; 333-335; 468; Apollodorus, 3. 4. 3; *Met.*, 3. 259 ff.; etc.). J. comments (*Hy.*, 52) that the Greek ὄργια was originally equivalent to the Latin *"ceremonia,"* but "abusively" has "been made particular to Bacchus"; he specifies Servius' scholium to *Aen.*, 6; but one finds the quotation that he offers at *Aen.* 4. 301, 302.

The advanced age of Bacchus is implied at *Ob.*, 169, and *Und.*, 419; in the classics he is usually described as youthful (*cf.* Callistratus, 8. 5; *Met.*, 4. 17, 18), but *Anacreontea*, 42, 1-4, terms him "old Bacchus." Epithets applied to him (*Ob.*, 170 and footnote) are Greek ανθιος (unaccented) and Latin *"floridus."* The first should probably be referred to ἄνθος at *Orphica*, 50. 6, and the second to *"florens . . . Iacchus"* at Catullus, 64. 251.

BELLEROPHON. *N.I.*, III, ii, 372; *Qu.* 131 footnote.

Bellerophon's "brave and masculine virtue" is praised in *Il.*, 6. 155-197; *Theogony*, 325; Pindar's *Ol.*, 13. 60-92; Apollodorus, 2. 3. 1; and Hyginus' *L.F.*, 57, and *De A.*, 2. 18.

BERENICE. *Qu.*, 134, 135 and footnote; *For.*, 269.

After sacrificing her hair to Venus in thanksgiving for the safe return of her husband from an expedition, Berenice was dismayed to find that her locks had disappeared from the temple; her anguish was relieved, however, when Conon, an astronomer, declared that the hair had become *Coma Bere-*

nices in the tail of the lion. See Catullus' *Odes,* 66, and
Hyginus' *De A.,* 2. 24.

BOREAS. *Be.,* 23-26; *Ob.,* 173.

J.'s personification of Boreas (*Be.*) agrees for the most
part with Ovid's description in *Met.,* 6. 682-711: his blus-
tering and "rude voice" (685, 686); his mantle, although J.
deviates from *"pulvereamque"* (705); his icy coldness as the
North-wind (682; 686; 711); his wings (702-707); and
his "bitter and too piercing breath" striking "horrors
through the air" over land and sea (690-692). Boreas' feet
"ending in serpents' tails," J. acknowledges, is from
Pausanias, (5. 19. 1). For Boreas and Orithya, see
ORITHYA.

There seems to be no precedent for J.'s adorning Boreas
"in a robe of russet and white . . . ; his hair and beard
rough and horrid; . . . and in his hand a leafless branch,
laden with icicles"; the appropriateness and beauty of this
personified imagery of winter probably explain J.'s introducing it. It does not seem classical, either, to present Boreas as
a messenger, but J. considered him "fittest" under the circum-
stances. The *Ob.* citation is playfully in accord with what has
been said of Boreas' severity when the North-wind rages.

BRANCHUS. *Au.,* 421 *et passim.*

Branchus, J. says in a footnote, is *"Apollinis et Jances
filius,"* and he cites Strabo, 4, and Statius' *Thebais,* 3. The
former, 14. 1. 5, mentions the love of Branchus and Apollo;
the latter, 8. 198, speaks of Branchus' shrine. Lactantius on
Thebais, l.c., offers a more comprehensive explanation.
Herodotus, 1. 157; 2. 159, states that an oracle of Apollo
was located at Branchidae in Miletus.

BRIAREUS. *Epi.,* 235.

Briareus, "who hath a hundred hands," is described in *Il.,*
1. 401-404, as "him of the hundred hands, whom the gods

call Briareus, but all men Aegaeon," and he is also found in Lucian's *Gods,* 21.

BRONTES. *Und.,* 372.
See CYCLOPES.

CADMUS. *Al.,* II, i, 48, 49.
The mere reference to "Cadmus' story" as an extraordinary happening can be associated with any version of the myth (*e.g., Met.,* 3. 1-136; 4. 563-603).

CADUCEUS. *K.J.E.,* 421; *J. and A.,* 478. See MERCURY.
The caduceus is significant only in *K.J.E.* There Eudaimonia holds "in her right hand a Caduceus, the note of peaceful wisdom"; this corresponds with the manner in which the later mythologists introduce the caduceus (*e.g.,* Hyginus' *De A.,* 2. 7). The *J. and A.* passage is typical of the citations concerning Mercury's caduceus, and agrees broadly with *Od.,* 5. 47, and *Aen.,* 4. 242-244. See MERCURY.

CALLISTO. *Epic.,* III, i, 390.
Callisto, the mother of Arcas, was transformed into a bear by either Here or Artemis and then removed to become a star by Zeus (Apollodorus, 3. 8. 2; Hyginus' *L.F.,* 177, and *De A.,* 2. 1; and *Met.,* 2. 401-530). J. seems to have thought of Ovid's myth, for he names him as a story-teller in a subsequent speech.

CALYPSO. *Ca.,* IV, v, 298.
When Cethegus terms Sempronia "good Calypso," there is reflected the adventure of Odysseus "in the halls of the nymph Calypso, who keeps him perforce" (*Od.,* 4. 555-560; 5. 5-224).

CAMILLA. *Qu.,* 133.
See AENEAS.

CAPANEUS. *Ca.,* IV, v, 299.

Capaneus, one of the Seven against Thebes, was slain, as he stood on the walls, by a bolt of lightning hurled by Zeus. J., lauding the valor of Capaneus, writes:

> If they were like Capaneus at Thebes,
> They should hang dead upon the highest spires,
> And ask the second bolt to be thrown down.

This is remarkably close to Statius' *Thebais:*

> *paulum ei tardius artus*
> *cessissent, potuit fulmen sperare secundum.*

(10. 938, 939.)

Cf. Aeschylus' *Seven against Thebes,* 423-446, Euripides' *Phoenissae,* 1172-1180, and *Suppliants,* 496-501, Diodorus, 4. 65, and Hyginus' *L.F.,* 71.

CASSANDRA. *Und.,* 375.

Cassandra "all the fate of Troy foretold" (*e.g.,* Aeschylus' *Agamemnon,* 1210; *Cypria,* p. 491 (Loeb); *Aen.,* 3. 182-187; etc.).

CASSIOPEIA. *For.,* 269.

The enthusiasm of Cassiopeia for her own beauty or for that of her daughter, Andromeda, led to her placing it above that of the Nereids. This impertinence resulted in Andromeda's being chained to the rock (see ANDROMEDA) and in Cassiopeia's being transformed to a star (Hyginus' *De A.,* 2. 10).

CASTOR. *Po.,* 508 (Apologetical Dialogue); *Se.,* I, ii, 38; IV, v, 106; *Ca.,* II, i, 219; 224; 228; *T.V.,* 19; *N.T.,* 37; *Epi.,* 235; *Und.,* 426.

See DIOSCURI.

CATALOGUE OF SHIPS. *Und.,* 328.

The ships of the Greek forces are enumerated by Homer in *Il.,* 2. 484-877.

CAUCASUS. *Ca.,* III, i, 242.
　See PROMETHEUS.

CELAENO. *K.J.E.,* 428-431.
　See ELECTRA.

CENTAUR. *C.R.,* I, i, 225; *Po.,* IV, iii, 462; *Epic.,* IV, ii,
433; *Ca.,* II, i, 223; *N.I.,* I, i, 313; IV, ii, 397; IV, iii, 380;
Ob., 170; *Epi.,* 235; *Und.,* 428.

The Centaurs, a ferocious race of creatures, half-man and
half-horse, are first described by Pindar (*Py.,* 2. 21-48),
whom Apollodorus, 1. 20, Diodorus, 4. 69, Hyginus (*L.F.,*
62), and others follow. For their origin, see IXION. The
most notorious of their misdeeds is their conduct at the wedding feast of Pirithous and Hippodamia, for there, intoxicated, the Centaurs attempted to do violence to the bride. A
battle between them and the Lapithae, the groom's tribe, en-
sued (Diodorus, 4. 70; Plutarch's "Theseus," 30. 3; Pausanias, 5. 10. 8; Apollodorus, 1. 21; Hyginus' *L.F.,* 33; and
Met., 12. 210-535). *Epic., Ca.,* and *N.I.* refer to this myth.

Homer, who neither describes the Centaurs as semi-
ferine nor offers the same explanation of their strife with
the Lapithae (*Od.,* 21. 295-304), emphasizes "the feud . . .
between the centaurs and mankind" (303). With this *cf.*
J.'s Centaurs "that war with human peace and poison men"
(*Po.*). In his *Ob.* footnote J. also calls attention to Homer's
φήρ (wild creature) designating a Centaur (*Il.,* 1. 268; 2.
743) and paralleling J.'s "wild males" of *Epic. In* this play,
too, is Centaure, "a she one," a concept reflecting Ovid's
female Centaurs at *Met.,* 12. 404-406. By "the Centaur's
skill" (*N.I.*) J. suggests the fame of this race as horsemen;
in this ability they are the equals of the Thracians with
whom they are usually mentioned (*N.I.* and *Und.*). The
epithet "ugly centaurs" (*Epi.*) is justified by the usual portrayal of the tribe. See HARPY.

CEPHALUS. *T.V.*, 18.

Like Diana, who here summons him and Hippolytus to wait upon her, Cephalus pursued the hunt. After his marriage to Procris, Aurora became enamoured of him and carried him off, but he remained constant to his wife. Indignant, Aurora sent him away. She aroused in him, however, a suspicion of Procris' fidelity. By assuming the shape of a stranger and by offering Procris an extraordinary inducement, Cephalus discovered that she hesitated. When he revealed his identity, *"genus omne perosa virorum,"* she fled to become a devotee of Diana, who gave her an unfailing hunting dog and a spear certain to reach the mark at which one aimed it. These gifts of Diana, Procris gave to Cephalus when they were later reconciled. Then, because of a report that Cephalus frequently cried what seemed the name of a woman when he was hunting, Procris went to investigate. Supposing that a beast was nearby, Cephalus threw his spear and killed her. The myth is found in Hyginus' *L.F.*, 189, and Ovid's *Met.*, 7. 670-862.

CERBERUS. *E.M.O.*, The Stage, 25; I, i, 44; *Qu.*, 126 footnote; *Epi.*, 233; 238; *Canaan*, 349.

J. merely conceives Cerberus as the three-headed dog baying at the gates of Hades (*Aen.*, 6. 417-423; *Met.*, 4. 450, 451). From Cerberus' foam, spilled during his strife with Hercules, springs aconite (*Met.*, 7. 406-419).

CERCOPES. *Ob.*, 169; *Canaan*, 348.

The Cercopes, ape-like creatures, had once been human, but had suffered deformity for their impiety and impishness. They are spoken of by Diodorus, 4. 31; Apollodorus, 2. 6. 3; Herodotus, 7. 216; and Ovid (*Met.*, 14. 91-100). None of these, however, includes any explanation of the phrase "with Cercops' charm" in *Canaan*.

CERES. *Po.,* IV, i, 443; IV, iii, 457; *B.F.,* II, i, 396; *Epi.,* 208.

The rape of Proserpina, her daughter, caused Ceres, the Roman goddess of agriculture, to wander about the world in search of her until Jove promised that Proserpina should spend half of her time in heaven (*Met.,* 5. 385-571; *Fasti,* 4. 420-620; Claudian's *R.P.,* 3. 67-448, is unfinished). The germ of Ceres' "wheaten hat" is contained in *"Imposuitque suae spicea serta comae"* (*Fasti,* 4. 616). For *Po.* see BACCHUS.

CHANCE.
See FORTUNE.

CHAOS. *C.R.,* V, ii, 336, 337; *Se.,* V, x, 150; *Ca.,* III, i, 241; *K.J.E.,* 416; *Be.,* 33; *Qu.,* 126, 127; *Tilt,* 218; *L.T.,* 90.

> The strife of Chaos then did cease,
> When better light than Nature's did arrive.

These lines from *C.R.* closely parallel Ovid's description:

> *unus erat toto naturae vultus in orbe,*
> *quem dixere chaos.*
>   . . .
>
> *obstabatque aliis aliud, quia corpore in uno*
> *frigida pugnabant calidis, umentia siccis,*
> *mollia cum duris, sine pondere, habentia pondus.*
> *Hanc deus et melior litem natura diremit.*
>   *Met.,* 1. 6, 7; 18-21.

This same strife of Chaos and Nature is referred to in *Ca.* and *Qu.*

In his attempt to explain the significance of Janus' title "Quadrifrons" (*K.J.E.*) J. cites *Fasti,* 1 (the lines are 103, 104) where Janus asserts that he was originally Chaos, and that the four elements came from him. The notion that Chaos may rise again is contained in *Met.,* 2. 298, 299, very much as in *Se., Ca.,* and *Qu.* With "old deformed Chaos"

(*Se.*) and "old shrunk-up Chaos" (*Qu.*) *cf.* "*in chaos antiquum*" of *Met., 2. 299.*

J. also states that Love emerged first from Chaos (*Be.* and *L.T.*; the thought is reflected, too, at *Tilt*), and he appends a footnote to *Be.* to inform his reader that Orpheus makes known that Love was "first of all the gods; awakened by Clotho; and is therefore called Phanes, both by him, and Lactantius." See Orpheus' *Argo., 12-16,* and Lactantius' *Divinarum Institutionum, 1. 5. Cf. Theogony,* 116-121, because the concept of Love as a formative power as well as a sensual force is definitely Hesiod's. J.'s remarks about the axle that holds earth from Chaos indicate that he compares the revolution of the earth to that of a wheel, which requires an axle.

CHARIS. *Und., 293-302.*

This group of poems, among the loveliest of J.'s love lyrics, was written to one of his friends at court whose identity has not been learned. The name he bestows upon her he could have known from *Il.,* 18. 382, 383, where Charis is the wife of Hephaestus, in spite of *Od.,* 8. 266-366, which makes Aphrodite his spouse. Lucian (*Gods,* 15) explains that Aphrodite is Vulcan's wife in heaven, Charis in Lemnos. Love, therefore, sings,

> This, here sung, can be no other,
> By description, but my mother!
> So hath Homer praised her hair;
> So Anacreon drawn the air
> Of her face, and made to rise
> Just above her sparkling eyes,
> Both her brows bent like my bow (*Und., 297*).

Cf. Homer's "Charis of the gleaming veil" (*Il., l.c.*). Anacreon does not name Charis, but possibly J. had some notion of *Anacreontea,* 16. 13-21; the resemblance, however, is slight.

CHARON. *C.R.*, I, i, 217; *Ca.*, I, i, 199; *Epi.*, 233; 236; *Lethe*, 273, 274; *Canaan*, 349.

J.'s use of Charon as the ferryman of the Styx is entirely conventional, according, *e.g.*, with *Aen.*, 6. 295-330. In *C.R.* and *Lethe*, however, there seems to be a suggestion of the cooperation of Charon and Mercury, as recorded in Lucian's *Dead*, 4, and *Charon*, 1. The scene and the characterization of Charon in *Lethe* particularly resemble Lucian's *Of Mourning*, 5 and 10, respectively. With "rugged Charon" (*Ca.*) cf. *Aen.*, 6. 304: *"sed cruda deo viridisque senectus."* The notion of Charon's boat in the classics always includes sails; cf. J.'s "Their wherry had no sail too; ours had ne'er one," of *Epi.*, 233.

CHARYBDIS. *Ca.*, III, iii, 261; *S.N.*, IV, i, 253.

Charybdis dwelt opposite Scylla, and thrice daily sucked in and subsequently belched forth the water of the sea, imperiling the lives of any mariners happening by (*Od.*, 12. 101-110; 234-259; 424-444; and *Aen.*, 4. 420-424). The notion that Charybdis draws in ships that come too close to "the shelf of love" somewhat reflects Horace's *Odes*, 1. 27. 13-20.

CHIMAERA. *Po.*, I, i, 385; *Volp.*, V, viii, 316; *Epi.*, 235; *Und.*, 402.

The chimaera, in J.'s works, symbolizes that which is monstrous. He nowhere describes it, but his references imply *Theogony*, 319-324, or *Il.*, 6. 178-182.

CHLORIS. *Chl.*, 93-105. See also FLORA.

J. presents Chloris or Flora, the goddess of flowers, as does Ovid in *Fasti*, 5. 183-228, especially 195-198 and J.'s quotation, *"Arbitrium tu Dea floris habe,"* (212). Ovid recounts the assault of Zephyr upon Chloris and their subsequent marriage, but in *Chl.* J. fails to notice either, possibly through a sense of delicacy as the queen herself was perform-

ing the part of Chloris. In *Pen.* Favonius is the wooer of
Flora, perhaps implying a more intimate association. The
praise of Flora's beauty can be accounted for by Ovid's

> *quae fuerit mihi forma, grave est narrare modestae;*
> *sed generum matri repperit illa deum.*
>
> *Fasti,* 5. 198, 199.

Lactantius (*Divinarum Institutionum,* 1. 20) alludes to
Ovid's account of Zephyr and Flora.

CHRONOMASTIX. *T.V.,* 5-8.

Although there seems to be no mythological source for his
name, the impertinence of Chronomastix possibly entitles him
to the classification of a satyr, for satyrs are always characterized by their impudence and wantonness.

CHRONOS. *T.V.,* 4.

See SATURN.

CIPUS (CIPI). *Ca.,* II, i, 233.

Among the great servants and citizens of the Roman state
was Cipus, upon whose head horns suddenly grew. The
augurs declared that this portended that he was destined
to become king. To prevent this, believing that it would not
be for the betterment of the citizens, Cipus went voluntarily
into exile. Whalley has correctly pointed to this legend in
Valerius Maximus, 5. 6. (3), and *Met.,* 15. (565-621).

CIRCE. *E.M.O.,* p. 6 (characters); *Qu.,* 111 footnote; 122
footnote.

The power of Circe to transform ordinary men is related
in *Od.,* 10. 229-243; *Met.,* 14. 42-69; 277-287; and *Aen.,*
7. 10-20. In *E.M.O.* J. had no particular source in mind,
but in *Qu.* he mentions *Od., l.c.* and 10. 516-520, and *Met.,*
l.c.

CLAROS (CLARIUS). *Und.*, 368.

"Clarus" is a surname of Apollo, derived from the name of a town where Apollo was worshipped. It occurs at *Met.*, 1. 516; 11. 413; and *Aen.*, 3. 360.

CLOTHO. *K.J.E.*, 412; *J. and A.*, 479; *Be.*, 33 footnote.

Of the Fates, "Clotho is said to be the eldest, signifying in Latin *Evocatio.*" With this assertion of J., *cf.* Boccaccio's *De Genealogia*, 1. 5: "Clotho interpretari *evocationem.*" Justifying his introduction of Clotho's book, J. quotes *Met.*, 15. (809-814), and cites Martianus Capella (1. 65). Days productive of happiness were marked white, J. states, citing Pliny's *N.H.*, 7. 40; *Epistles*, 6. 11; Horace's *Odes*, 1. 36. (10); Martial's *Epigrams*, 8. 45; 9. 53; 10. 38; 11. 37 (actually 36); Statius' *Silvae*, 4. 6. (18, 19); Persius' *Satires*, 2. (1); and Catullus, 69 (actually 68 A, 3, 4; 111, 112).

COBALUS. *Und.*, 329.

This seems to be a mythological citation because it is enumerated along with other definitely mythological allusions to monsters that "Afric knew, or the full Grecian store," but no source for it has been located.

COCYTUS. *Epi.*, 233; 236.

J. stresses the murkiness and stench of Cocytus. His concept seems to reflect vaguely *Geor.*, 4. 478-480; *Aen.*, 6. 132; especially 296, 297: *"atque omnem Cocyto eructat harenam"*; and Horace's *Odes*, 2. 14. 17, 18.

COMUS. *Po.*, III, i, 425; *P.R.*, 299-303; 305; *Wa.*, 324; *For.*, 250.

Comus, whose name is from the Greek word for revel, is a god of later antiquity. He is described by Philostratus in *Imagines*, 1. 2, as youthful and intoxicated. From this description, no doubt, is derived the tendency to associate or confuse Comus with Bacchus. See BACCHUS. And from this association, possibly, comes the inspiration which J. had to portray Comus as "the voluptuous Comus, god of cheer." It has been suggested in BACCHUS that the Lyaeus aspect of Bacchus is particularly like J.'s notion of Comus.

There is also a marked resemblance between J.'s Comus and the Dionysus of Euripides' *Bacchanals*. In the latter, Dionysus is frequently referred to as Bromius, the Clamour-king (84; 116; etc.), an implied characteristic of Comus in *P.R.* Dionysus goes "to Cithaeron's glens" in *Bacchanals,* 62; *cf.* "the grove of ivy at his feet; out of which . . . is brought forth Comus, the god of cheer," in *P.R.* Again, J. writes: "They that wait upon him crown'd with ivy, their javelins done about with it," which parallels Euripides' "wreathed with ivy sprays" (80) and "the ivied thyrsus-spear" (25).

In general, the characteristics of Comus as set down by Philostratus have not been copied by others. J. seems to follow him only in adorning Comus' head "with roses and other flowers" and in the "wild music of cymbals, flutes, and tabors" produced by the revellers. Another source which J. seems to have used is Puteanus' *Comus,* wherein besides the rose crown, Comus possesses curly hair, as he also does in *P.R.* (Puteanus has not been accessible. See Dole's *Milton,* p. 422.)

The inspiration to call Comus the god of the belly and to make him of enormous proportions seems original with J. For the cup of Hercules which Comus has, see HERCULES.

CONCORD. *Ca.,* V, ii and iv (setting); V, vi, 331.

These instances are historical rather than mythological, for much of the action of the Catilinian conspiracy took place in the temple of Concord (Sallust's *Bellum Catilinae,* 46. 5; 49. 4).

CORNUCOPIAE. *E.M.I.,* III, iii, 90; *K.J.E.,* 421; *J. and A.,* 477.

Eudaimonia (Felicity) holds "a Cornucopiae filled only with flowers, as a sign of flourishing blessedness" (*K.J.E.*). On the other hand, the cornucopiae of Dyspragia (Unhappiness) is "turned downward, with all the flowers fallen out and scattered," and the Genius in *J. and A.* possesses a cornucopiae "ready to fall out of his hand." Hyginus (*L.F.,* 31; *De A.,* 2. 13), Ovid (*Fasti,* 5. 115-128), and Zenobius (*Centuria,* 2. 48) assert that the cornucopiae was one of the horns of the goat which suckled Zeus, who gave it to the nymph-owners of the animal with the promise that it should produce whatever they wished.

CORYDON. *E.M.I.,* I, iv, 38.

In alluding to the brother of Wellbred as "the Corydon," Bobadill seems to suggest "a certain mixture of rusticity and folly" in his character, according to Gifford. The name is found in Theocritus, 4, and Vergil's *Eclog.,* 2. 1; 56-59, and 7. *passim.*

CUPID.

In the many instances of J.'s alluding to Cupid, or Eros, or Love, there is much confusion, for while at times he presents definitely mythological notions, at other times he seems to be meditating philosophically upon a subject which fascinated him. This observation is particularly true when he uses the word "Love" as synonymous with Cupid, as the following illustration—an address of Cynthia to Arete—demonstrates:

> Such is our chastity, which safely scorns,
> Not love, for who more fervently doth love
> Immortal honour, and divine renown?
> But giddy Cupid, Venus' frantic son (*C.R.,* V, iii, 340).

Several times J. recalls the account of the creation of Eros as Hesiod relates it (*Theogony,* 116-120); such passages are

Be., 33, 34; *L.F.*, 186; *Tilt*, 218; and *L.T.*, 90. In contrast with Hesiod and with Plato's *Symposium*, 178 A-C (where Eros is said to be the eldest of the gods), are *Symposium*, 195 A-E (where he is the youngest), and the later concept of Cupid as a child. These together probably account for J.'s remark to Venus about "the old boy, your son" (*For.* 261) and for his characterization of Love as "the eldest god, yet still a child" (*Und.*, 385); *cf.* Lucian's *Gods, 2.* Moreover, at *Chl.* 97, Cupid resents being treated as a child and being omitted from the councils of the gods.

Moschus, 1, and later mythologies (*e.g., Fasti*, 4. 1; *Met.*, 1. 463; 5. 365; *Aen.*, 1. 664) make Venus the mother of Cupid, as does J. at *C.R.*, I, i, 218; II, i, 250; IV, i, 292, 293; V, iii, 340; *Po.*, IV, i, 447; *Vo.*, I, i, 161; *N.I.*, III, ii, 370, 371; *Be.*, 34; *Hue*, 88; 90 footnote; 93; 95; 97; 101; *Tilt*, 214-219; *Christmas*, 262, 263; *Lethe*, 278; *T.V.*, 17; *Chl.*, 97; *L.W.Bol.*, 136; 138; *For.*, 243; 261; *Und.*, 297; 377; 420. Venus' statement at *Christmas, l.c.*, that Vulcan is the father of Cupid is possibly derived from the marital relationship of Vulcan and Venus; *cf. Anacreontea, 28.* 1-7. At *Al.*, II, i, 46; *Tilt*, 215, 216; 219; *For.*, 243, Mars and Venus, symbolizing valour and beauty, are acknowledged as Cupid's parents (Cicero's *De N.D.*, 3. 23. 59; 60).

Cupid's attributes are the familiar torch and bow and arrow identified with the little winged deity by Moschus, 1, by Ovid (*Met.*, 1. 463-471; 10. 311, 312; *Amores*, 1. 1. 21-26; 2. 9. 5; 3. 9. 7-10) and by others. J.'s passages including these attributes are *C.R.*, I, i, 216; 217; 220; II, i, 250; IV, i, 284; 303; V, ii, 330; iii, 348-350; 351; 353; *Po.*, I, i, 377; IV, i, 447; *Se.*, II, i, 41; *Vo.*, II, ii, 215; *D.A.*, II, ii, 64; *S.S.*, I, ii, 249, 250; III, ii, 282, 283; *Case*, II, iii, 334; *Be.*, 28; 31; 35; *Ba.*, 76; *Hue*, 89; 91-93; *L.F.*, 185; 205-208; *Tilt*, 214-218; *Christmas*, 260; 266; *Lethe*, 278; *G.M.*, 363; 373; *T.V.*, 17; *F.I.*, 63; *L.T.*, 89; *Chl.*, 98; *L.W.Bol.*, 136-138; *For.*, 243; 264; *Und.*, 294, 295; 297, 298; 302;

309; 362; 377; *M.P.*, 357. Referring to the almost irresistible golden arrow of Cupid at *Case* and *Tilt, l.c.,* J. seems to have in mind Ovid's arrow which kindles love, *"auratum est et cuspide fulget acuta"* (*Met.*, 1. 470). This arrow Cupid uses upon his own mother (*Be.*, 35; *Hue*, 91; *L.F.*, 186), according to Moschus, 1. 21.

The blindness of Cupid—an unclassical notion—is spoken of at *C.R.*, I, i, 216; II, i, 237, 238; *Po.*, IV, i, 447; *Case*, III, iii, 355; *Be.*, 34; *Hy.*, 56; *Hue*, 90; *L.F.*, 185; *G.M.*, 373; *T.V.*, 16; *Epi.*, 217, 218; *For.*, 264; *Und.*, 294; 312; 362; 377. As evidence that Cupid's blindness was presented before the Elizabethan period, Root points to Chaucer's *House of Fame,* 138, etc., and Gower's *Conf. Am.*, 4. 1456; 5. 1417, etc.

Whalley, in his edition of *Hue*, p. 302, indicates the substantial indebtedness of J. to Moschus, 1, for the characterization of Cupid at *Hue*, 90, as an "almost naked, wanton, blind," cruel, and little boy (see Introduction of this Dictionary). Ovid (*Amores*, 1. 10. 15, 16) and others also describe Cupid as an unclothed child, a characteristic which J. uses at *L.F.*, 207; *Tilt*, 214; *Lethe*, 278. The notion that Venus has lost Cupid (*Po.*, IV, i, 447; *Hue*, 89, 90; 92; *Christmas*, 262), a borrowing from Moschus, *l.c.,* is intensified by Venus' statement that in his absence, she "is undone" (89). This thought reflects Vergil's address of Venus to her son, *"nate, meae vires, mea magna potentia, solus"* (*Aen.*, 1. 664) and Ovid's similar address, *"arma manusque meae, mea, nate, potentia"* (*Met.*, 5. 365). At *Chl.*, 98, however, it is declared that Cupid is yet under her command, just as he seems to be in Lucian's *Gods*, 11. From that dialogue is derived, too, the suggestion for clipping Cupid's wings (*Hue*, 90).

Among Cupid's exploits enumerated, *ibid.,* are his making the sun turn, for which J. cites Lucian's *Gods* (12), his occasioning that "Neptune in the waters burn'd," which

probably should be related to an episode like that related
by Lucian in *Sea-Gods,* 6, his causing hell to feel greater
heat, for which J. refers to Claudian's *R.P.,* (1. 26, 27), and
his rearing his trophies high "from the center of the sky,"
for which J. recalls "an elegant Greek epigram. *Phil. Poe.,*"
which proves to be Phillipus in *The Greek Anthology,* 16.
215. These trophies of Cupid, J. explains, are Jove's thunder,
Phoebus' arrows, Hercules' club, etc.; they are also mentioned
at *Hue,* 95.

Another exploit of Cupid is recounted by himself in *C.R.,*
I, i, 217, 218: "We . . . have made the whole body of divinity tremble at the twang of our bow, and enforced Saturnius
himself to lay by his curled front, thunder, and three-fork'd
fires, and put on a masking suit, too light for a reveller of
eighteen to be seen in." That Cupid could thus sway the
gods is made clear even by Hesiod (*Theogony,* 120-122),
and that Jove was the especial mark of his archery is close
to Lucian's *Gods,* 2. Again, at *Hue,* 93 (see Introduction
of this Dictionary) Venus notices how unusually frolicsome
Cupid seems to be. She asks if he has achieved a new con-
quest such as hitting Minerva or the Muses with his arrows,
or renewing the love of Rhea and Atys, or arranging Selene's
again visiting Endymion, or bringing Hercules again to
spin for Omphale, or tempting Jove again to disguise himself and to leave his thunder. J. says that these, Cupid's
conquests, are recounted by Lucian in *Gods,* 12 and 19; he
overlooks the fact that the story about Hercules is from 13,
and that it does not speak of Cupid. Venus' question to
Cupid is derived from Claudian's *Epithalamium,* 111-116.
For Mercury's account of his having heaved Cupid's "heels
up into the air" (*C.R.,* I, i, 218), see MERCURY.

At *Hue,* 92, Cupid is accompanied by "Sports and pretty
Lightnesses . . . under the titles of Joci and Risus; and are
said to wait on Venus, as she is the prefect of marriage."
In support of this, J. cites Horace's *Odes,* 1. 2. (33, 34);

cf. also 1. 19. 1; and 4. 1. 5. The Sports also appear at *Hue,* 101, and *T.V.,* 15.

Again, at *Volp.,* I, i, 160; *Be.,* 27; 31-35; *Hue,* 89; *N.T.,* 35; *L.T.,* 88, J. presents numerous Cupids, or Erotes, and at *Be.,* 31, and *Hy.,* 62, he cites as a precedent not only Propertius' *Elegies,* 2. 29, Statius' *"in Epit. Fulcra,"* (*Silvae,* 1. 2. 54), Claudian's *"in Epith. Pennati,"* (Shorter Poems, 25. 10; 110-123), and Sidonius Apollinaris (11. 42; 14. ep. 4), but "especially *Phil. in Icon. Amor.,* whom I have particularly followed in this description" (*Be.*). Philostratus' *Imagines,* 1. 6, presents, like *Be.,* a multitude of Cupids playing amid an apple harvest. J. comments, however, that these are "chaste Loves that attend a more divine beauty than that of Love's common parent" (*Be.,* 34, 35); hence they are not blind, or wanton, "or straying." This agrees with Philostratus' assertion that Aphrodite has made the nymphs the mothers of the Cupids in the picture he describes. Also see VENUS. Cupid as the deity of marriage is found at *Hue,* 88, probably because he is the son of Venus, *q.v.*

In *C.R.,* V, iii, 342-344, Cupid, disguising himself as "Anteros, or Love's enemy," describes himself as "more fit for the court of Cynthia than the arbours of Cytherea." Later (*ibid.,* 350) Mercury reminds Cupid that his arrows are not affecting their marks, possibly because Cupid has so transformed himself. Again, in *L.R.,* 205, Robin Goodfellow, revealing the masquing of Plutus as Cupid, says, "No; it is not he, nor his brother Anti-Cupid, the love of virtue." At *Tilt,* 220, however, Anteros, like Cupid a son of Mars and Venus, is called "reciprocal affection," and at *L.W.Bol.,* 136-139, Anteros is Cupid's double, born when Themis advised Venus and the Graces that Eros' nature

> ne'er will prosper, if he have not one
> Sent after him to play with.

In both *Tilt* and *L.W.Bol.* one of the Loves serves the husband and his counterpart waits on the wife.

Cicero (*De N.D.*, 3. 23. 59, 60) states merely that Mars and Venus are the parents of Cupid, *"qui idem est Anteros,"* born out of wedlock.

Only sundry ideas remain for consideration. For *Hue,* 89, see PSYCHE; for Cupid's raillery of Mercury at *C.R.*, I, i, 215, and at *Lethe,* 277, 278, see MERCURY. Cupid's praising his own wit (*C.R.*, II, i, 237, 238) may be accounted for by Aphrodite's final remark in Lucian's *Gods,* 12 : "Masterful boy! always the last word!" The association of the Graces with Cupid and his mother (*S.S.*, I, ii, 248; *Hue,* 89-93; *L.F.*, 193, 194; *L.R.*, 207; *Tilt,* 218; and *L.W.Bol.*, 137) resembles *Anacreontea,* 44. 6-11, but see VENUS. From *Anacreontea,* 55. 4-8, may have come the suggestion for Cupid's garland (*Und.*, 366). The hand of Cupid (*Hue,* 94) is referred to in Lucian's *Gods,* 19. The antagonism between Cupid and Cynthia (*C.R.*, V, iii, 340) is explained in CYNTHIA.

A couplet (*L.F.*, 185) reads:

> Come, Sir Tyrant, lordly Love,
> You that rule the gods above.

This notion of Cupid as a tyrant and a lord is medieval in origin (*cf.* "throne of Love" at *Tilt,* 214, and "lord Love" at *Und.*, 398). Likewise medieval is the court of Love (*N.I.*, III, ii, 394 ff.) where Love and his mother are personified, but neither is referred to by the classical names; the discussion, moreover, is purely philosophical.

In making Plenty and Want the parents of Love (*L.T.*, 87) J. must have recalled, as Whalley points out, the similar passage in Plato's *Symposium* (203 B-D). Many of the epithets employed by J., as "giddy Cupid" (*C.R.*, V, iii, 340), "the wag" (*Hue,* 90), and "my little straggler" (*Hue,* 93), accord with the tenor of *Anacreontea, passim,* and

Moschus' *Idyls,* 1. "Light honey-bee" (*C.R.,* V, iii, 351) also reflects *Anacreontea,* 35, and Theocritus, 19.

For Cupid's baths (*C.R.,* V, ii, 330; *Hue,* 91; *G.M.,* 373; *Und.,* 298; 363) see VENUS. No sources are known for his bathing in the streams of ladies' blood (*L.F.,* 192), or for "the wheel of love" (*L.T.,* 86; 88), which probably reflects Ixion's suffering, or for the power of the Fates over love (*Lethe,* 276) though this is hinted by Vergil (*Aen.,* 6. 440-466), by Tibullus, 1. 1. 69, and by Lucian (*Charon,* 15, 16, and *Voyage to the Lower World,* 3). From the latter work, 6 and 14, J. may have taken the suggestion for the effect that love has upon some individuals (*Lethe,* 273-277); certainly this section of *Lethe* is in the spirit of the *Voyage.*

The allusion to Cupid's chariot "and both the doves and swans I have borrowed from my mother to draw it" (*Tilt,* 218) is close to Ovid's *Amores,* 1. 2. 23-26, and Love's arming (*Tilt,* 215) seems related to *Amores,* 1. 9. 1-20. From *Pausanias,* 6. 23. 5, comes, possibly, J.'s introduction of the palm at *Tilt,* 219, 220, and at *L.W.Bol.,* 136-138. The representation of Plutus disguised as Cupid and the statement that Cupid ruled the world during the Golden Age (*L.R.,* 199-205) reflect rather generally Tibullus, 2. 3. 29-36; 49, 50. For the effect that Cupid has upon Hell (*Chl.,* 98-104), see HELL. For *S.N.,* IV, i, 253, see AMBROSIA.

CURTIUS. *Ca.,* II, i, 233.

This reference—legendary rather than mythological—recalls Livy's story (7. 6) of Marcus Curtius, a Roman youth who, when the forum fell in and the soothsayers declared that the nation to perpetuate itself must sacrifice its greatest strength, mounted his horse and in his full armour plunged into the chasm because he claimed that the strength of Rome was in its arms and valour. Valerius Maximus, 5. 6. 2, is probably J.'s source.

CYBELE. *Qu.,* 30 footnote.

J. comments that the dancing of the witches is similar to the dancing "which Pliny observes in the priests of Cybele, *Nat. Hist.* lib. xxviii. cap. 2."

CYCLOPES. *Po.,* IV, iii, 456; *Ca.,* I, i, 195; *Hue,* 95; 97, 98; *Ob.,* 174 and footnote; *M.V.,* 233, 234; *L.W.Bol.,* 135; *Epi.,* 236; *Und.,* 372; *Canaan,* 348.

J.'s Cyclopes are chiefly those of later story who assist Vulcan at his forge on Mount Aetna (*Aen.,* 8. 440)— Brontes, Steropes, and Pyracmon, named, as J. says, in *Aen.,* (8. 424, 425). *Ob.,* however, alludes to the story related by earlier writers of Ulysses' being captured by the Cyclope, Polyphemus; to effect his release, Ulysses plied Polyphemus with wine, and then burned out his only eye. J. says that he had Euripides' *Cyclops* (443-664) in mind, but his footnote, *"ubi Satiri Ulyssi auxilio sint ad amburendum oculum Cyclopis,"* is not clear, for the satyrs were too frightened to participate in blinding Polyphemus. Homer does not introduce the satyrs, but explains how "sly Ulysses stole in a sheep-skin" past Polyphemus and out of the cave (*Epi.*) by concealing himself and his companions under the bodies of the sheep, while Polyphemus felt only their backs. Both Euripides and Homer tell how, when the satyrs or Cyclopes asked Polyphemus about who injured him, he answered, *"Outis"* (Nobody), this being the name that Ulysses used when Polyphemus took him captive (see ULYSSES). The meat of the Cyclopes (*Canaan*) is human (Euripides' *Cyclops,* 126-128; 241-249). For their armour-making, see VULCAN.

CYCNUS. *Ode,* 353-357.

Cycnus, because of the destruction of his relative, Phaëton, went lamenting through the world, and was eventually transformed into a swan (*Met.,* 2. 366-380). This version of the Cycnus myth is probably J.'s basis, but here the swan has become black. "And Phoebus' love cause of his blackness is" (*Ode,* 354). *Cf.* Apollo's ire which caused the raven, once white, to become black (*Met.,* 2. 531-541; 631, 632). Now Phoebus conducts Cycnus to Hippocrene, then to "the clear Dircaean fount" (*q.v.*), then to "the pale Pyrene and the forked Mount" (Parnassus, as *e.g., Culex,* 15, 16), and finally, Phoebus "from Zephyr's rape would close him with his beams." See ZEPHYR. Because of Love, whom he once gaily celebrated, Cycnus is now "daily dying"; hence the sweetness of his song. The bird's flight through J.'s contemporary world is followed by an allusion that is not clear: "In heaven the sign of old Eridanus" (357). This sign may be the epitaph which the Naiads made for Phaëton (*Met.,* 2. 325-328), or it may be the amber for which the Eridanus is celebrated (*e.g.,* Lucian's *Gods,* 25).

CYLLARUS. *Und.,* 428.
See DIOSCURI.

CYLLENE. *Pen.,* 461.
See MAIA.

CYLLENIUS. *L.T.,* 92.
See MAIA.

CYNTHIA.
See DIANA.

CYNTHIUS. *Und.,* 371.
This is a title of Apollo, *q.v.,* who was born at the foot of Mount Cynthus in Delos.

CYPARISSUS. *Sat.,* 441.
J.'s description of the appearance of the prince, "That is Cyparissus' face!" is close to *Met.,* 10. 120, where Ovid says of Cyparissus, *"Ceae pulcherrime gentis."*

CYPRIS.
See VENUS.

CYTHEREA.
See VENUS.

DAEDALUS. *P.R.*, 306-309; *L.T.*, 88.

The dance in *P.R.* is directed by Daedalus, who instructs the participants to "interweave the curious knot" symbolic of the conflict that once occurred between Virtue and Pleasure over Hercules; their creation of this dance, Daedalus says, "the labyrinth of beauty is." Ovid (*Met.*, 8. 157-168) relates that Daedalus constructed a labyrinth in which Minos confined the Minotaur, *q.v.*, as do likewise Diodorus, 4. 77, Hyginus' *L.F.*, 40, and Apollodorus, 3. 1. 4; 3. 15. 8.

DAMON AND PHINTIAS. *Epic.*, IV, ii, 444; *B.F.*, V, iii, 479, 480; 484, 485; 494, 495.

Properly speaking, the story of the unselfish friendship of Damon and Phintias (this name has been corrupted to Pythias) is not mythological. Their mutual faith and brotherly affection are demonstrated by Valerius Maximus, 4. 7, Plutarch (*Moralia,* 93 E), and Cicero (*De Officiis,* 3. 10. 45). When Phintias was condemned to death, Damon volunteered to sacrifice his own life as bond for Phintias' temporary release, but when the latter returned to face death, the tyrant Dionysius pardoned him because of his fidelity to Damon.

DANAË. *Ca.*, II, i, 223; *Al.*, II, i, 48, 49; IV, i, 112, 113. *Cf.* ACRISIUS.

See ACRISIUS. *Al.* mentions only "Jove's shower."

DANAUS. *Chl.*, 99.

All but one of the fifty daughters of Danaus were condemned in the lower world to pour water into "bottomless tubs" because they had murdered their cousin-husbands, the sons of Aegyptus. J. could have learned of their punishment from *Met.*, 4. 462, 463; *Heroides,* 14. 1-78; Horace's *Odes,* 3. 11. 23-33; and Tibullus, 1. 3. 79, 80.

DAPHNE. *P.A.*, 42; *Epi.*, 153; 226.
See APOLLO.

DARKNESS. *Und.*, 373.
See NIGHT.

DAY, *V.D.*, 295; *Se.*, I, i, 23.
These, the only passages where Day is presented in a somewhat mythological manner, seem to accord with Hesiod's notion at *Theogony*, 124, and 748-757. Hesiod, however, personifies Day as feminine, but J. uses the masculine pronoun. See AURORA.

DEATH. *Po.*, Apologetical Dialogue, 509; *Ca.*, V, v, 323; *S.S.*, I, ii, 249, 250; *Case*, I, ii, 321; IV, ii, 361; *Bl.*, 11; *Epi.*, 221; *Und.*, 324; 58, 59; *M.P.*, 326.
Of all J.'s references to Death, only the above seem worth consideration as mythological, and even some of them may well be no more than Elizabethan personifications. The "Thanatos" and "Mors" of classical myths are never exhaustively described, but in Euripides' *Alcestis*, 223-225, there is mention of "Death's hand," as in *Ca.*, *S.S.*, and *Und.* Other characteristics of Death in J.'s work suggest the usual delineations of the Eumenides, as, for example, Euripides' description of their wings and his "swart-hued Eumenides" (*Orestes*, 316-321); cf. *Po.*, *Ca.*, and *Case*. Osgood recounts that at *P.L.*, 2. 672, Death is armed with a dart although in *Alcestis* (74; 76) Euripides speaks of his sword; there seems to be no classic precedent for the dart. Perhaps the only source for this attribute of Death in Milton and J. is J.'s playful invention of a comparison of Death's equipment with Cupid's (*S.S.*); and in *Lethe*, 273-277, J. does portray the almost fatal effect that love works upon some whom it affects. See CUPID. There is small likelihood that "death's harbinger," and death's being "pale and blue" and cold, and being at strife with Time are anything but Elizabethan; cf., however, "*pallida Mors*" of Horace's *Odes*, 1. 4. 13.

DECII. *Ca.,* II, i, 233.

Publius Decius Mus, a Roman consul, dedicated himself to the Manes and to Earth in order that the Romans might gain a victory over the Latins (Livy, 8. 9), and it is said that his son, when he was consul, did likewise. *Cf.* Valerius Maximus, 5. 6. 5, 6, which is probably J.'s source.

DELIA. *C.R.,* IV, i, 274; *Po.,* IV, i, 447; *B.F.,* V, iii, 487; *Und.,* 375.

These citations, excepting perhaps *B.F.,* for which see DIANA, recall the Delia whom Tibullus addressed in his verses.

DELOS. *Be.,* 26 footnotes; *N.T.,* 28, 29; 33.

J. makes Neptune the god who came to Latona's aid when she was about to deliver Apollo and Cynthia. Neptune caused Delos, an island floating under the sea, to emerge and to become stationary. Of all the classic versions of this myth, only Lucian's (*Sea-Gods,* 10) names Neptune as Latona's benefactor. At *N.T.,* 33, Delos is used merely to land the masquers, and is then withdrawn, the chorus singing meanwhile that "no envious stepdame's rage" has been responsible for Albion's (the English prince's) travels; obviously, here J. thinks of the jealous wrath of Here, who frightened the earth and necessitated Neptune's raising Delos. Her ire is related in the *H.H. to Delian Apollo,* 3. 95-101, and *Met.,* 6. 184-187; 332-338; *cf.* Ovid's *"noverca"* (336) with J.'s "step-dame."

DELPHI. *Und.,* 371.

Delphi is the place of the oracle of Apollo and Themis. See THEMIS.

DESTINY.

See FATES.

DEUCALION. *Bl.*, 13; *M.V.*, 239.

J. recalls only "old Deucalion's days" and that Deucalion "had the philosopher's stone, and threw it over his shoulder." The story of Deucalion's re-peopling the earth with men, and of his wife's, Pyrrha's, creating women by throwing stones over their shoulders after a deluge had devastated the land is told by Apollodorus, I. 7. 2; Ovid in *Met.*, I. 348-415; Hyginus in *L.F.*, 153; and others.

DIANA. *C.R.*, Dedication, 203; I, i, 219; 220; 223; IV, i, 302; V, ii, 311; 336-338; V, iii, 339-356; *Se.*, IV, i, 102; V, x, 143; *B.F.*, V, iii, 487; *K.J.E.*, 429; *Sat.*, 446; 449; *Bl.*, 17; *Hy.*, 69; *Hue*, 90; *T.V.*, 18, 19; *Epi.*, 208; *Und.*, 329; 373. See also HECATE.

Diana, or Phoebe, or Cynthia (a surname derived from Mount Cynthus in Delos, *q.v.*), is, like her brother Apollo, a deity of several parts. Their parents and birth are discussed in APOLLO and in DELOS. Diana is preeminently a goddess of chastity (*e.g.*, *Od.*, 18. 202; 20. 71) and of the hunt (*e.g.*, *Od.*, 6. 102-105; *Il.*, 21. 470; *Aen.*, I. 498, 499; *Met.*, 2. 441, 442). The supposed antagonism of Venus and Cupid to Diana is found at *Met.*, 5. 374-376. Diana's hunting equipment consists of her spear and her bow and arrows (*e.g.*, *H.H. to Artemis*, 28. 1-10; *Met.*, 3. 116). See also ACTAEON, CALLISTO, CEPHALUS, and HIPPOLYTUS.

In time Selene, the moon goddess, became fused with the concept of Artemis and Diana (*e.g.*, Aeschylus' *Fragments*, 171; *Aen.*, 10. 215, 216; *Met.*, 15. 196-198; Cicero's *De N.D.*, 2. 27. 68). Cicero also explains why Diana is invoked in childbirth (*ibid.*, 2. 19. 50; 2. 27. 68, 69) and why the tides are influenced by the moon (*ibid.*, 2. 7. 19). Generally the colour that the moon goddess casts upon the earth is described as golden (*e.g.*, *H.H. to Selene*, 32. 5, 6); J.'s allusion to her "silver chair" or car, and his description of Hecate as "the silver moon" (*Be.*, 27 and footnote) may perhaps be explained by his citing Euripides' rather similar designation in *Helen*, (569), or by recalling *Heroides*, 18. 71 : *"fulges radiis argentea puris."* Cynthia's chariot is included in accounts of her as the lunar deity in the *H.H. to Selene,* 32. 9, 10; *Aen.,* 10. 215, 216; and elsewhere. See also ENDY-MION.

That the beauty of Diana is remarkable is shown, for instance, in the *H.H. to Py. Apollo,* 3. 197-199, and in *Heroides,* 18. 69: *"a Veneris facie non est prior ulla tuaque."* There is, indeed, small wonder that Queen Elizabeth was complimented when the poets termed her Cynthia, especially since the latter is honoured as a queen in the classics (*e.g., Il.,* 21. 470, and *H.H. to Selene,* 32. 5). Mercury is Cynthia's brother because Jove is the father of both in all accounts, but her declaration that Mercury is "next Jove beloved of us" (*C.R.,* V, iii, 353; 356) seems to have no classical precedent. In the masques in *C.R.,* Cynthia's characteristics are not mythological. For passages about Cynthia and Niobe, see NIOBE.

By Hecate, J. seems to mean only Diana in his references at *Qu.,* 122, and *T.V.,* 14. Elsewhere his thoughts of her are more in the classic manner. As Gifford vaguely suggests, *S.S.,* II, ii, 264, 265, is a borrowing from Theocritus (2. 10-13): "So shine me fair, sweet Moon; for to thee, still Goddess, is my song, to thee and that Hecat infernal who makes e'en the whelps to shiver on her goings to and fro where these tombs be and the red blood lies." J. renders this:

> Where'er you spy
> This browder'd belt with characters, 'tis I.
> A Gypsan lady, and a right beldame,
> Wrought it by moonshine for me, and star-light,
> Upon your grannam's grave, that very night
> We earth'd her in the shades; when our dame Hecate
> Made it her going night over the kirk-yard,
> With all the barking parish-tikes set at her.

"Trivia" (*C.R.,* V, iii, 355) and "thou, three-formed star" (*Qu.,* 123) may be explained by J.'s footnote at the latter place giving *Aen.,* 4. (511) as his source; cf. *Heroides,* 12. 79: *"per triplicis vultus . . . Dianae,"* and *Fasti,* 1. 141, 142: *"ora vides Hecates in tres vertentia partes."* In the same footnote J. supports his having Trivia (or Hecate) invoked in matters of witchcraft by these precedents: Theocritus, 2. (14); Seneca's *Medea,* (750-842) ; and Lucan, (6. 700, 701).

DICE. *Panegyre,* 434.
See THEMIS.

DIDO. *C.R.,* II, i, 252; *T.T.,* III, ii, 172; V, ii, 214.
Dido's beauty is dwelt upon in *Aen.,* 1. 496: *"forma pulcherrima Dido."* For Juno's solicitude for Dido, the "brave Carthage queen," see *Aen.,* 1. 12-22; 441-447; etc.

DIOMEDES. *N.I.,* I, i, 325.
J.'s citation of "Tydides' fortitude, as Homer wrought" it indicates that he had *Il.* in mind (*e.g.,* 5. 1-887).

DIONYSUS. *Ob.,* 169 footnote.
"Dionysius" (J.'s spelling) is mentioned but once as an alternative to Bacchus, *q.v.*

DIOSCURI. *Und.,* 131. See also citations under CASTOR, POLLUX, and TYNDARIDES.
J. seems familiar with many ramifications of the Castor-Pollux myth. When he terms them Dioscuri (sons of Zeus), he adopts the Zeus-Leda parentage presented in *H.H. to the Dioscuri,* 17. 2; Euripides' *Orestes,* 1689; and Theocritus, 22.1; see also LEDA. But when he calls them Tyndarides, he accepts Homer's declaration they are the sons of Tyndareus and Leda (*Od.,* 11. 298-300). A third version makes Castor the son of Tyndareus and therefore mortal, while Pollux is the son of Zeus and consequently immortal (Apollodorus, 3. 10. 7; Pindar's *Nemean,* 10. 79-90). When Castor died,

Zeus granted Pollux's request that they be permitted to spend their days alternately in the heavens and in the lower world so that they might not be separated (Apollodorus, 3. 11. 2; *Od.*, 11. 303, 304; Pindar's *Nemean,* 10. 55-60, and *Py.,* 11. 61-64; Lucian's *Gods,* 26; *Aen.,* 6. 121; *Fasti,* 5. 719; Hyginus' *L.F.,* 80, and *De A.,* 2. 22). J. certainly has this last version in mind in his ode on the friendship, broken by death, of Cary and Morison (*Und.,* 13). The legend that the Tyndarides were "heav'd" up to become the Gemini (*For.,* 269) is found in Hyginus' *De A.,* 2. 22, *Fasti,* 5. 693-720, and *Met.,* 8. 372.

Castor has always been famed for his horsemanship, and Pollux for his wrestling (*Il.,* 3. 237; *Od.,* 11. 300; Hesiod's *Fragments,* 93; *Met.,* 8. 301, 302). J.'s comparison of the Earl of Newcastle with "Castor mounted on Cyllarus" reflects Ovid's *"Castore dignus erit"* (*Met.,* 12. 401), which, however, concerns the *centaur* Cyllarus. At *N.I.,* I, i, 313, J. mentions "Pollux' mystery, to fence"; Apollodorus, 2. 4. 9, seems to be the only source mentioning this characteristic.

Pollux and Castor were "of men the best" (*T.V.,* 19), an idea possibly received from Hesiod, *l.c.,* but also implied in numerous other stories. The ability of the two in battle is obvious from their being among the heroes of the Argonaut expedition (Apollodorus, 1. 9. 16; Apollonius Rhodius, 1. 146-150), during which Pollux, in a boxing contest, slew Amycus, the giant king who had refused the travellers the right to draw water in his land (Apollonius, 2. 1-163; Theocritus, 22. 27-134). During this expedition, too, they captured Aphidna (Diodorus, 4. 63; Plutarch's "Theseus," 31. 2-33. 2; Pausanias, 1. 17. 5; 2. 22. 6; 3. 18. 4, 5; Apollodorus, 1. 23; Herodotus, 9. 73; Strabo, 9. 1. 17) and finally they combated Idas and Lynceus (Apollodorus, 3. 11. 2; Theocritus, 22. 137-213; Hyginus' *L.F.,* 80; Pindar's *Nemean,* 10. 60-64; *Fasti,* 5. 705-714). "Their nobler loves" (*T.V.,* 19) are their cousins, who although they are betrothed to Idas and Lynceus, were stolen by the Dioscuri (Theocritus and Hyginus, *l.c.; Fasti,* 5. 699-704; and Pausanias, 3. 17. 3; 4. 31. 9).

J.'s mentioning the Dioscuri's prowess in the hunt reflects the account of their accompanying Meleager in his hunt for the boar which was devastating his father's fields (*Met.,* 8. 299-302; 372-377). The playful allusions to the Dioscuri as sea-deities and as lights "on the main yard" (*N.T.,* 37; *Epi.,* 235) are reminiscent of the *H.H. to the Dioscuri,* 33. 6-17; Lucian's *Gods,* 26; Horace's *Odes,* 1. 12. 27-32; 1. 3. 2; and *Fasti,* 5. 720. Gifford comments upon J.'s exactness in conforming to Gellius' assertion that Roman men never swore by Castor, and Roman women never by Hercules. It is true that J. observes this custom in *Ca.,* II, i, 224, 225; 228; but he violates it at *Se.,* IV, v, 106.

DIRCE. *M.P.,* 453.

J. speaks of

> The clear *Dircaean* fount
> Where *Pindar* swam.

This agrees with Pindar's *Isthmian,* 6. 74, 75: "I shall give him to drink of the pure water of Dirce, which the deep-zoned daughters of golden-robed Memory made to gush forth beside the noble gates of the walls of Cadmus." The ordinary myth, (*e.g.,* Apollodorus, 3. 5. 5; Pausanias, 2. 6. 1-4; 9. 25. 3; Hyginus' *L.F.,* 8) asserts that Dirce and her husband Lycus imprisoned Antiope, but one day, her bonds falling from her, she sought her sons, who slew Lycus and threw the lifeless body of Dirce into a fountain after they had tied her to a bull.

DORIS. *N.T.,* 34.

Hesiod (*Theogony,* 350) names Doris as a daughter of Oceanus and Tethys (*cf. ibid.,* 337), and wife of Nereus (*ibid.,* 240, 241). Homer asserts that there is another Doris, the daughter of Nereus and the first Doris (*Il.,* 18. 37-45).

The significance of J.'s "Doris, dry your tears" is not clear. He may be thinking of the grief which Doris would feel for her daughter Galatea, *q.v.*, or he may be thinking of Lucian's declaration (*Sea-Gods,* 12) that the second Doris wept for the fate of Danaë. Both of these possibilities, however, are unsatisfactory.

DOULOSIS. *K.J.E.,* 420.

Doulosis is merely a personification by J. of Servitude; it seems to have no mythological source.

DRYADS. *Pen.,* 461; *P.A.,* 46; *For.,* 244.

See NYMPHS.

EACUS.

See AEACUS.

EARTH. *V.D.,* 292, 293; *P.R.,* 302; 305; *Au.,* 427; *Chl.,* 96; *Epi.,* 164; *Und.,* 392; 19, 20.

J. seems to think of Earth chiefly as "our common mother," from whom Spring is born (*V.D., Chl.,* and *Und.*). This accords with the *H.H. to Earth,* 30. 1; 13-15, and it also reflects *Il.,* 14. 347-349: "Beneath them the divine earth made fresh-sprung grass to grow, and dewy lotus, and crocus, and hyacinth, thick and soft." The conflict which raged between Earth and Heaven (*Theogony,* 126-187) is brought to mind by the Gods' decree that the combatants shall live at peace (*Chl.*). See also GIANTS. With "teeming earth" (*Und.*) cf. *H.H. to Earth,* 30. 16, and *Il.,* 14. 301. No source is known for "proud earth" in *V.D.* Hercules' exclamation, "Breeds earth more monsters yet?" (*P.R.*), is based upon the belief that Earth was the mother of Antaeus, *q.v.;* whenever Antaeus "touched the earth so it was that he waxed stronger, wherefore some said that he was a son of Earth" (Apollodorus, 2. 5. 11; Lucan, 4. 589-653). The *Au.* and *Epi.* citations are of doubtful mythological significance.

ECHO. *C.R.*, I, i, 220-224; *Pen.*, 462-464; *Ob.*, 168; *P.A.*, 48; *Und.*, 17.

Ovid's account of Echo and Narcissus is J.'s principal source. Thus he alludes to "Juno's spite" and to Saturnia's being abroad (*C.R.*), reflecting *Met.*, 3. 359-369, where Juno deprives Echo of speech because her conversation has interfered with the goddess' wrath towards the nymphs whose company Jove enjoyed. Shortly thereafter Echo became enamoured of Narcissus, whose beauty led him to love himself when he discovered his image in a fountain; so deeply does he yearn to know the person reflected that his grief over being frustrated causes his death (*Met.*, 3. 370-510). The youths and nymphs—all admirers of Narcissus, though he, in his self-love, had rejected all their endeavours to win his companionship—come to bury him, but find, instead of his corpse, a *"croceum . . . florem"* with white petals (*Met.*, 3. 509; *cf. C.R.*). Jove allows Echo to become articulate in *C.R.*, that she may better express her grief for the death of Narcissus. Ovid portrays Echo as a mountain nymph (*cf. Met.*, 3. 400; *"inde latet silvis, nulloque in monte videtur"*) as does J., who also mentions her living in a "cavern of the earth" (*cf. Met.*, 3. 394: *"vivit in antris"*). J. recalls that it was Cynthia's self-love that made her so cruel to Actaeon, *q.v.*, and that it was Niobe's self-love that caused Phoebe's vengeance. See NIOBE.

J.'s statement at *P.A.* that Echo was "Beloved of Pan the valleys queen" reflects Moschus, 5: "Pan loved his neighbour Echo." No source is known for "Echo the truest oracle on ground." The introduction of Echoes in *Bl.* and *Be.* has not been recorded because they have no mythological value.

EIRENE. *K.J.E.*, 418-421; 424, 425; *Panegyre*, 433, 434; *Sat.*, 451.

Eirene, or Irene, or Pax is an Hour, the daughter of Themis, and personifies the blessings of peace (*Theogony*, 901-903). J. gives the Roman concept of Pax: "she was placed aloft in a cant, her attire white, semined with stars, her hair loose and large: a wreath of olive on her head, on her shoulder a silver dove: in her left hand she held an olive branch, with an handful of ripe ears, in the other a crown of laurel, as notes of victory and plenty" (*K.J.E.*). She is so represented on Roman coins, and by Tibullus, 1. 10. 45-49; 67, 68; also *cf.* "*Pax alma*" of 67 with "sweet peace" (*K.J.E.*, 424). The "bright state" of Peace also agrees with Tibullus. Those associated with Irene in *K.J.E.* reflect broadly the "*Fides et Pax et Honor Pudorque*" and others of Horace's *C.S.*, 53-60. At *K.J.E.*, 421,

NULLA SALUS BELLO:

PACEM TE POSCIMUS OMNES

is not "*Aen.*, 1. 11," but 11. 362. See also HOURS.

ELECTRA. *K.J.E.*, 428-431, and footnotes; *Be.*, 29 footnote.

J. thoroughly documents all of the sources from which he gained information about Electra and the Pleiades. That the names of the Pleiades are Alcyone, Celaeno, Taygete, Asterope, Merope, Maia, and Electra, and that they "are also said to be the souls" of Venus, Saturn, Luna, Jupiter, Mars, Mercury, and the sun, Helios, respectively, J. learned from Proclus' Commentary upon Hesiod's *Works*, 381. From Ovid's *Fasti*, 4. (169, 170; 177, 178 quoted) and from Rufus Festus Aviens' *Carmina*, (2. 576-578; 582, 583 all quoted) he learned that Electra is seldom visible, and from the latter, too (*ibid.*, 2. 585-587), he recalls Electra's grief over the fall of Troy. In addition to Aviens (*ibid.*, 2. 589-594), J. quotes an anonymous source for making Electra a comet, and he explains that after the defeat of Troy, Electra fled from her sisters "unto the Artic circle, here" by quoting Hyginus (*De A.*, 2. 21).

When he states that Electra is the mother of Iris, the rainbow, J. cites Aristotle's *Meteorology*, (3. 2), but they are, of course, not personified there. That the "roseate wings, in compass of a bow" are a sign of the arrival of Electra is supported by Valerius Flaccus' *Argonautica,* 1. (655, 656). "Mithra's coach" is from Statius' *Thebais,* 1. (720), and Martianus Capella's *De Nuptiis Philologiae et Mercurii,* 3. (this should be 2. 191). Justifying his use of a comet in a happy sense, J. quotes from Pliny's *N.H.,* 2. 25, the account of the comet which reigned over "Augustus' state." Electra's "serenest face" is properly hers, for her name is a compound of the Greek words for sun and serene, according to J. See also SERENITAS.

ELEUTHERIA. *K.J.E.,* 419; 424. *Cf.* LIBERTY.

The word Eleutheria designates the Greek festival of liberty, celebrated in honour of Zeus Eleutherius every fifth year after the battle of Plataea. J. uses the word, however, in preference to *Libertas*—the Roman personification of freedom. Her gowns are always ornate when she is portrayed on Roman coins, and she sometimes bears a dagger and the cap of Liberty. *Cf.* J.'s "in her right hand she bare a club, on her left a hat, the characters of freedom and power." For the festival of Eleutheria, see Pausanias, 9. 2. 5, 6, and Plutarch's "Aristides," 21. 1-5.

ELYSIUM. *E.M.O.,* II, i, 47; *Po.,* I, i, 389; *N.I.,* II, ii, 339-341; *C.A.,* V, i, 379; *Be.,* 27; 37; *G.A.R.,* 251; *Lethe,* 274.

The most comprehensive treatment of Elysium is found in *C.A.*; it is a place of "odorous and enflower'd fields" where "blessed ghosts do walk." There is a suggestion in *G.A.R.* that those "in Elysian bowers" have been spared death, "and went away from earth, as if but tam'd with sleep." Both Homer (*Od.,* 24. 13, 14) and Pindar (*Ol.,* 2. 68-74) describe Elysium as the flowery abode whither the phantoms of virtuous men were directed, and Hesiod (*Works,* 166-169) implies their exemption from death. *Cf.* FORTUNATE ISLANDS.

EMPUSA. *Und.,* 329.

Empusa is a monster with cannibalistic tendencies, according to the belief of the Greeks (Aristophanes' *Frogs,* 293; *Ecclesiazusae,* 1056).

ENDYMION. *Hue,* 93 footnote; *Ob.,* 174-176; *N.N.W.,* 342; *T.V.,* 14.

The love of the moon (J. does not mention Selene) for Endymion was so great that she nightly left her car to visit him as he slept in the open near his flocks (Theocritus, 20. 37-39; Pausanias, 5. 1. 4; Apollonius Rhodius' *Argo.,* 4. 54-58; Hyginus' *L.F.,* 271). The *Hue* allusion, J. says, is from Lucian (*Gods,* 12), and the recollection that Endymion went to the moon "by rapture in sleep, or a dream" (*N.N.W.*) reflects Theocritus, 3. 49, 50; Plato's *Phaedo,* 17. 72 C; Apollodorus, 1. 7. 5; and others. With *T.V. cf.* HECATE.

ENVY. *Po.,* Prologue, 369-372; Apol. Dia., 510; *Se.,* II, iv, 56; *Panegyre,* 435; *Sat.,* 448; 451; *G.A.R.,* 247; *N.N.W.,* 348; *T.V.,* 7; *Und.,* 323; 355; 366; 385; 49, 50.

J.'s presentation of Envy in the Prologue of *Po.* agrees very closely with *Met.,* 760-805, where she is described as dripping venom, living in darkness, and surrounded by snakes which she consumes. Ovid says, "Her eyes are all awry, her teeth are foul with mould" (776). "Her festering hand" and her "pestilential, poisonous breath" infect those whom she chooses as her victims. Envy's aversion to light may be accounted for by the fact that she is the child of Night (Cicero's *De N.D.,* 3. 17. 44; Claudian's *Against Rufinus,* 1. 32, 33). Also *cf.* Hesiod's description of Envy (*Works,* 195, 196).

ENYALIUS. *K.J.E.,* 418.

Enyalius is a epithet of Mars, which J. may have found in *Il.,* especially 13. 518-522; 20. 69, or from Pindar (*e.g., Ol.,* 13. 105, 106). The lines quoted here are those of Silius Italicus (11. 595-597), as J. says.

Enyo. *Ca.,* V, vi, 333.

In this passage J. seems to ascribe to "fierce Enyo" the spirit of madness in warfare, in contrast to Pallas' representing the prudence and justice which are essential to successful battling. This interpretation of their respective characters is implied when Homer says of Venus: "she was a weakling goddess, and not one of those that lord it in the battle of warriors,—no Athene she, nor Enyo, sacker of cities" (*Il.,* 5. 330-333).

Eous. *Bl.,* 14.

Catullus, 62. 35, uses Eous as the name of the morning star, alternating it with Hesperus, the evening star. *Cf. Aen.,* 3. 588. Eous, probably from the Greek *Eos,* then, is equivalent to Phosphorus, and signifies the eastern part of the world, as Hesperus does the western.

Epidaurian Serpent. *B.F.,* II, i, 380.

See LYNCEUS.

Erebus. *Po.,* III, i, 433.

It is impossible to determine whether J. has in mind the personified Erebus, child of Chaos (*Theogony,* 123; *Aen.,* 4. 509-511; Cicero's *De N.D.,* 3. 17. 44), or whether he simply thinks of "princely Erebus" as parallel to "king Pluto's hell" as many have thought of it (*e.g., Od.,* 11. 37; *Geor.,* 4. 471, 472; *Met.,* 14. 403-405).

Erechtheus. *Be.,* 26 footnote.

See ORITHYIA.

Eridanus. *M.P.,* 357.

See CYCNUS.

Eros. *L.W.Bol.,* 136-138.

See CUPID.

ERYCINA. *Volp.*, III, vi, 251.

Erycina is a surname of Venus derived from her being worshipped on Mount Eryx in Sicily (*Fasti,* 4. 871-876; *Heroides,* 15. 57, 58; etc.). For her affair with Mars, see VENUS.

ERYNNIS (ERINYES). *Qu.,* 131.

The Erinyes are described as dark by both Aeschylus (*Eumenides,* 50-52) and Euripides (*Orestes,* 317-322). They are here related to witchcraft, but in classic sources they are avengers of crime.

EUCLIA (EUCLEIA). *L.T.,* 90.

Euclia personifies "a fair glory." Perhaps J. remembers the Corinth festival in honor of Artemis, which was called Eucleia (Xenophon's *Hellenica,* 4. 4. 2).

EUNOMIA. *Panegyre,* 434.

See HOURS.

EUPHEMUS. *L.T.,* 85-89.

J.'s Euphemus does not seem to have anything in common with any of the mythological characters of the same name. The latter are: (1) The son of Apollo and Mecionice (Hesiod's *Great Eoiae,* 6); (2) The son of Poseidon and Europa. This Euphemus, returning on the *Argo,* received a clod of earth which would have insured his descendants' becoming rulers of Libya, but lost it (Pindar's *Py.,* 4. 43-53; 251-259; Apollonius Rhodius, 1. 179-184; 4. 1546-1563; 1731-1764; Herodotus, 4. 150; Hyginus' *L.F.,* 14)); (3) "The son of Ceas' son Troezenus, nurtured by Zeus" and "captain of the Ciconian spearmen" (*Il.* 2. 846, 847).

EUPHORBUS. *Volp.,* I, i, 171.

See AETHALIDES.

EUPHROSYNE. *K.J.E.,* 406.

See GRACES.

EUROPA. *Epic.*, III, i, 381 ; *Volp.*, III, vi, 251 ; *Ca.*, II, i, 223.

J. only mentions the union of Zeus and Europa, the former taking upon himself the guise of a bull to deceive her. See *Met.*, 2. 836-875 ; 6. 103-107 ; *Fasti*, 5. 603-618 ; Moschus, 2. 72-166 ; Diodorus, 5. 78 ; Lucian's *Sea-Gods*, 15 ; Hyginus' *L.F.*, 178.

FAME.

In classical literature Fame is a *"dea foeda"* (*Aen.*, 4. 195) who spreads rumour through the world. Her house is situated upon a high hill in J.'s *Chl.*, 103, as it is in *Met.*, 12. 43 : *"summaque domum . . . in arce,"* and it is "built all of sounding brass" in *Qu.*, 143, paralleling *Met.*, 12. 46 : *"tota est ex aere sonanti."* Describing Inigo Jones' execution of the house for *Qu.*, 139, 140, J. remarks that the designer, with Chaucer's *House of Fame* (3) in mind, placed "statues of the most excellent poets . . . and those great heroes, which these poets had celebrated . . . in massy gold. . . . Underneath, were figured land-battles, sea-fights, triumphs, loves, sacrifices, and all magnificent subjects of honour, in brass, and heightened with silver."

Occupying this house, J. continues (*Qu.*, 107 ; 131 ; 142 ; 143 ; also *cf. For.*, 381 ; *Und.*, 41-43), is "good Fame"—not Infamy. Fame is the child of Virtue, begotten when Terror died ; the only likely precedent for this parentage seems to be, as Gifford suggests at *Chl.*, 104, Tacitus' *"Contemptu famae contemni virtutem."* Although Gifford gives no clue to the passage in which these words may be found, it has been located in *Annals*, 4. 38. 5. The attire of Fame is "white, with white wings, having a collar of gold about her neck, and a heart hanging at it . . . the note of a good Fame. In her right hand she bore a trumpet, in her left an olive branch : . . . her feet on the ground, and her head in the clouds."

The basis of this characterization, J. asserts, is Cesare Ripa's *Iconologia* (inaccessible). The inspiration of the collar and heart, he mentions, is from Orus Apollo's (Horapollo's) *Hieroglyphics* (2. 4): "The HEART OF A MAN SUS-PENDED BY THE WINDPIPE signifies the *mouth of a good man.*" From *Aen.*, 4. (177): "*ingrediturque solo et caput inter nubila condit,*" comes the concept of Fame's feet being on the earth while her head is in the clouds, a thought also introduced at *Chl.*, 105, and *Exp.*, 110. Fame's voice or trumpet is mentioned frequently: *S.S.*, I, ii, 250, 251; *K.J.E.*, 415; *T.V.*, 6; *N.T.*, 27; *Chl.*, 103; *Epi.*, 209; *For.*, 265; *Und.*, 326; 365; 41-43; and it is compared to thunder at *Pen.*, 460, and *Qu.*, 143, recalling *Met.*, 12. 51, 52, where the noises in the House "*extrema tonitura reddunt.*" The wings of Fame are also alluded to at *Henry's Ba.*, 160; *N.N.W.*, 347; *Chl.*, 104; cf. *Aen.*, 4. 180; 7. 104; 11. 139.

With "whispering Fame" (*Se.*, II, ii, 47) cf. *Met.*, 12. 61, and with the opposites to good Fame (*Qu.*, 107) cf. *Met.*, 12. 59-61. The chariots, eagles, griffins, and lions which J. uses at *Qu.*, 142, 143, seem to have their origin only in J.'s creativeness, as his explanations of their significance indicate. Ovid (*Met.*, 12. 41-63) personifies Fame in the sense of Rumour alert to all things transpiring on land and sea and "*in caelo*"; cf. *S.N.*, III, i, 227; *Qu.*, 131; *T.V.*, 6; and *For.*, 255. Fame as an Elizabethan concept is found at *M.L.*, IV, iii, 86; *T.T.*, V, v, 233; *C.A.*, III, iii, 351, 352; *Panegyre*, 435; *Qu.*, 145; *N.N.W.*, 348; *T.V.*, 4-18; *Chl.*, 105; *L.W.-Bol.*, 130; and such allusions as "golden Fame" (*Chl.*, 104), "fair Fame" (*Und.*, 49, 50), "Fame's fingers" (*Und.*, 41-43), and "her file" (*Qu.*, 131) are scarcely mythological.

FATES.

In *J. and A.*, 477-481, the Fates or Parcae or Destinies are addressed as "Daughters of Night and Secrecy," as Hesiod (*Theogony*, 213-218) implies without naming Secrecy, but at *Qu.,* 104, they are termed the daughters of Necessity, as Plato (*Republic,* 10. 617 B, C) asserts. Both Hesiod and Plato (*l.c.*) also state that the names of the Fates are Clotho, Lachesis, and Atropos (*J. and A.,* 477-481; and CLOTHO). The spindle from which they take the thread of man's life is mentioned in *Il.,* 24. 209; 219; *Od.,* 7. 196; *Aen.,* 10. 814, 815; and Lucian's *Charon,* 15, 16. In the *Latin Anthology,* 1. 792, it is said that *"Clotho colum baiulat, Lachesis trahit, Atropos occat."* J. refers to the spindle, thread, and shears of the Fates at *C.R.,* II, i, 252; *Po.,* Apol. Dia., 512; *Se.,* V, vii, 130; *Volp.,* V, ii, 291; *Al.,* III, ii, 89; *J. and A.,* 477-481; *Ba.,* 78; *Lethe,* 275; *Epi.,* 165; 185. Suggesting that the Fates have been especially kind to someone, J. says (*Hue,* 94; *L.W.Bol.,* 139; *Und.,* 425; *M.P.,* 335) that they have spun "round and even threads, and of their whitest wool"; this recalls Statius' *Silvae,* 1. 2. 24, 25. For the rolls and the book of the Fates (*K.J.E.,* 412; *J. and A.,* 477-481) see CLOTHO.

The association of the Fates with death at *Se.,* III, i, 64; *G.A.R.,* 249; *Lethe,* 275; 279; and *Epi.,* 222, recalls their using the shears; cf. *Met.,* 8. 451-455. Gifford has remarked that J., lamenting the untimely passing of "Salathiel Pavy, a Child of Queen Elizabeth's Chapel" (*Epi.,* 221-223), has copied Martial's *Epigrams,* 10. 53, in writing that the Parcae believed this child was old because he had accomplished so much during his brief life. The presence of the Fates in *Lethe,* 273-276, and the declaration that Love possesses no power over them accord closely with Lucian's *Voyage,* for which see CUPID. Twice (*Se.,* V, iv, 122, 123; *Epi.,* 222) does J. call the Fates cruel.

At *J. and A.,* 477-481, *Au.,* 427, and *F.I.,* 76, the Fates are said to depend upon Jove. Such domain is implied in the *Orphic Hymns,* 14 and especially 19, the latter being a supplication to Jove to grant a peaceful end to life. Homer also implies this at *Il.,* 16. 431-438; cf. *Aen.,* 3. 375, 376. But at

Au., 426, and *For.*, 276, it is reported that the Fates conceal some things even from the gods; cf. *Il.*, 19. 87; *Od.*, 22. 413; *Aen.*, 3. 379, 380; *Met.*, 15. 779-782. The sources for "the muffled Fates" and "their own full store" (*E.M.O.*, II, ii, 73) are unknown. Probably J.'s "O, the whore Fortune, and her bawds the Fates" (*Ca.*, V, vi, 330) is only in the Elizabethan convention. The Fates are responsible for peace at *K.J.E.*, 426, and at *Au.*, 425, possibly because they are sometimes said to be the arbiters of life. General references to the Fates are *E.M.O.*, V, iii, 191; *Po.*, IV, i, 445, 446; *Se.*, IV, v, 103; V, i, 111; 112; *Volp.*, I, i, 86; II, i, 196; *Al.*, IV, i, 129; *Ca.*, IV, iii, 292; V, v, 322; *S.N.*, III, i, 235; *Case*, III, iii, 354; IV, iv, 368; *Panegyre*, 434; 437; *Be.*, 36; *Hue*, 94; *Henry's Ba.*, 152-154; *Epi.*, 146; 158; 186; 207; 213; and *Und.*, 417.

In addition to these rather definitely mythological allusions to the Fates, J. frequently speaks of Fate and Destiny in a philosophical sense, and while these have a precedent in Hesiod's *Theogony*, 211, and elsewhere, they have not been recorded because they may be only personifications of the Elizabethan notion of the appointed lots of men. Vergil (*Eclog.*, 4. 46, 47) likewise distinguishes between the Parcae and Destiny.

FAUNS. *Ca.*, II, i, 223; *For.*, 245.

The *Ca.* citation describing the Fauns as imperious, saucy, rude, and boisterous is not unlike Horace's *Art of Poetry*, 244-247: "The Fauns . . . should, methinks, beware of behaving as though born at the crossways and almost as dwelling in the Forum, playing at times the young bloods with their mawkish verses, or cracking their bawdy and shameless jokes." In associating the "lighter fauns" with "ruddy satyrs" at *For.* J. is following the tradition, as *e.g., Met.*, 6. 392, 393.

Favonius. *Al.,* II, i, 45; 49; *Pen.,* 460-464; *V.D.,* 290-294; *F.I.,* 77; *Chl.,* 96, 97.

Favonius, or Zephyr, is described traditionally as the gentle wind of spring. For J.'s borrowing from Claudian's *R.P.,* 2. 73-75; 88-100, see Introduction of this Dictionary. For the association of Flora and flowers with Favonius, see also CHLORIS. It is customary to regard Favonius as a gentle wind (*e.g., Od.,* 4. 566-568; *Geor.,* 1. 43; *Ciris,* 25). The music of this wind seems to result only from its sound, and the characterization of Zephyr as a plump boy seems without precedent.

Flora. *S.N.,* IV, i, 253, 254; *Pen.,* 460-464; *V.D.,* 294; *Epi.,* 208.

See CHLORIS.

Follies. *L.F.,* 191-193.

See SPHINX.

Fortunate Islands. *E.M.O.,* IV, vi, 153; Epilogue, 198; *Pen.,* 460; *F.I.,* 61-81.

The Fortunate Islands are not mythological, properly speaking. So designated are the islands to which the souls of the blessed were transported. In *Od.,* 4. 561-569, the abode of these souls is the Elysian plain, but in Hesiod's *Works,* 169-171, "they live untouched by sorrow in the islands of the blessed along the shore of deep swirling Ocean." Pindar (*Ol.,* 2. 67-74) also mentions these islands. Macaria, *q.v.,* is the poetical name for several of the Grecian isles. When J. uses Fortunate Islands, however, he has England in mind, just as Camden in *Britannia,* p. iii, describes England and places it among the Islands of the Blessed. *Cf.* ELYSIUM.

Fortune.

It is not always possible to distinguish, even in the classics, whether a reference is to the mythological personification of the Greek Tyche or the Latin Fortuna, or to a merely

philosophical aspect of chance or fortuitous circumstance.
In Elizabethan literature this difficulty is even greater.

Plato (*Laws,* 4. 709 A) states that "human affairs are
nearly all matters of pure chance," and Pausanias (4. 30. 5)
declares Tyche to be "the mightiest of gods in human affairs." Conforming to these opinions, the Chorus in *Ca.*
asks:

> Can nothing great, or at the height,
> Remain so long, but its own weight
> Will ruin it? or is't blind chance,
> That still desires new states to advance,
> And quit the old? else why must Rome
> Be by itself now overcome? (*Ca.,* I, i, 211.)

Close to this concept of powerful Chance are these passages: *E.M.I.,* I, i, 22; *E.M.O.,* II, ii, 73; *Po.,* V, i, 472;
473; 512 (Apologetical Dialogue); *Se.,* IV, i, 89; IV, v, 99;
V, x, 151; *Epic.,* III, ii, 391; *Ca.,* II, i, 226; *B.F.,* II, i, 406;
D.A., I, iii, 30, 31; *Case,* IV, v, 375, 376; *Au.,* 425; *Epi.,*
179; *Und.,* 359; *M.P.,* 328.

Plutarch (*De Fortuna Roma,* 1. 2, and "Theseus and
Romulus," 3. 1, 2) asserts that the calamities falling upon
men are caused by Fortune or by a lack of virtue. Seneca
(*De Constantia Sapientis,* 5. 4), however, says: *"Nihil eripit
fortuna, nisi quod dedit: uirtutem autem non dat."* These
passages illustrate the struggle between Tyche and Virtue
which J. alludes to at *Po.,* V, i, 473; 477; *Se.,* III, i, 64; 73;
III, iii, 88; *N.I.,* IV, iii, 390; *P.R.,* 310; *Ba.,* 160; *Epi.,* 202;
Und., 414, 415. Cf. Horace's *Odes,* 3. 29. 49-56, and Cicero's
De N.D., 3. 24. 61. For this reason the manliness of Crites
is esteemed by Phoebus although not by Fortune (*C.R.,* V, iii,
341, 342), and practically the same thought occurs at *E.M.O.,*
I, i, 36.

Allied to this notion is the malignant and unjust influence
of Chance when she operates in human matters, as the following citations demonstrate: *E.M.O.,* II, ii, 73 ("fortune's

spite") ; II, ii, 77 ("blind Fortune still/Bestows her gifts on
such as cannot use them") ; *C.R.*, II, i, 350; *Se.*, III, ii, 83;
V, iv, 122; V, x, 145; 151; *Al.*, Dedication, 5; Prologue,
10; *N.I.*, I, i, 315; *G.M.*, 371. Under this.aspect of malicious
Fortune one should probably include the passages containing
the Elizabethan allusions to her as "giglot," etc.: *E.M.O.*,
I, i, 39; *Ca.*, V, vi, 330; *Se.*, V, iv, 120; *N.I.*, II, ii, 341;
T.T., II, i, 159; *Und.*, 406.

J. frequently introduces the blindness of Fortune: *E.M.O.*,
I, i, 36; II, ii, 77; *C.R.*, Induction, 206; *Se.*, II, ii, 49; IV,
i, 89; V, iv, 120; *Ca.*, I, i, 211; IV, iii, 292; *Al.*, III, ii, 107;
N.I., II, ii, 341; *T.T.*, II, i, 159; *K.J.E.*, 426; *Und.*, 352;
415. This concept J. could have known from Cicero's *Laelius*,
15, Pliny's *N.H.*, 2. 7, and even Chaucer's *Fortune*, 50. Fortune's wheel, introduced at *Ba.*, 160, 161; *Se.*, V, x, 144;
Case, III, iii, 354; *G.M.*, 363; *Und.*, 334, is found in Tibullus, I. 5. 70, Cicero's *Against Piso*, 10. 22; Horace's *Odes*,
3. 10. 10, and Seneca's *Agamemnon*, 71, 72. Chaucer, *l.c.*,
46, also should be considered. The hope that Fortune, "wings
deplumed," will be fettered at the feet of the king and queen
(*L.W.Bol.*, 139) reflects Horace's *Odes*, 1. 34. 14-16: "Fortune with shrill whirring of wings. . . ."

Love and Fortune have their blindness in common. Both
are introduced at *D.A.*, I, iii, 30, 31; *G.M.*, 369; and *Und.*,
362, as helpful "t'assist the spirits that dare." Gifford is
probably correct in his declaration in *Und.* that this is an
enlargement of the proverbs, *"Fortes Fortuna juvat,"* and
"Faint heart ne'er won fair lady." At *Case*, IV, v, 375, 376;
V, iv, 391, Venus and Fortune are invoked with the same
thought in mind; cf. *Fasti*, 4. 133-162, where both goddesses
are lauded for their benefits to women in love. *"Fortuna non
mutat genus"* (*Case*, III, iii, 354) is quoted from Horace's
Epodes, 4. 6. "O Fortune my friend, and not *Fortune my
foe*" (*Case*, IV, iv, 369) alludes to the old ballad, "Fortune
my foe." As the deity of plenty, Fortune stands behind the

benediction that the Genius wishes the King in *K.J.E.*, 426, and also behind *Po.*, V, i, 473; *Se.*, III, i, 63, 64; *cf.* Pausanias, 4. 30. 6, where a statue of Fortune "carrying in one hand the horn of Amaltheia" is described.

The following passages seem without classical precedent: the hands of Fortune (*Se.*, III, i, 73; *Epic.*, II, ii, 368); the dice of Fortune (*Ca.*, V, vi, 329); the treasure-laden mules of Fortune (*E.M.O.*, II, i, 62); the playful reference to Fortune, a dog (*E.M.O.*, II, ii, 73) whose thread is cut by the Fates (*C.R.*, II, i, 252); the strife between Fortune and wit (*E.M.O.*, I, i, 37; *Se.*, V, x, 145; *Al.*, Dedication, 5; *S.S.*, Prologue, 235); the cooperation of Fortune and Nature (*Epic.*, III, ii, 391; *J. and A.*, 480, 481); the hope that Fortune would be the bondwoman of the state's Genius (*L.W.Wel.*, 130); and other miscellaneous thoughts at *E.M.I.*, IV, vii, 127 (oath); *Se.*, I, i, 30; V, vi, 128; V, x, 147; *Al.*, III, iii, 107; 110; *N.I.*, I, i, 315; and *Case*, IV, iv, 369. "Fortune holds out these to you, as rewards" (*Ca.*, I, i, 205) is Sallust's *"Fortuna omnia ea victoribus praemia posuit"* (*Bellum Catilinae*, 20. 15). The mention of "the goddess" at *Se.*, I, ii, 35, is an allusion to Fortuna equestris at Antium, the story of which Tacitus, *Annales*, 3. 71, relates.

The use of Fortune in *Se.* agrees with what has been said in the third paragraph of this article upon the relation of the goddess and virtue. Sejanus not only keeps a "grateful image" of Fortune in his home (*Se.*, V, i, 113) as Dio's *Roman History*, 58. 7. 2, declares, but he sacrifices to her for the happy outcome of his traitorous designs (*Se.*, V, iv, 118-120) as Dio (*ibid.*, 58. 7. 3) states. The details of the rites, being ceremonious acts of worship rather than evidences of Fortune's powers and the myths allied with them, do not fall within the scope of this study, except where they are elsewhere mentioned for such other testimony as they present incidentally. The climax of Sejanus' sacrifice—Fortune's turning her head from him—is related by Dio, *l.c.*, but seems to have no paral-

lel in non-historical sources that speak of Fortune. Sejanus'
angry condemnation of Fortune for the uncertainty of her
favours may reflect Seneca's *"Fortuna varia"* (*Medea, 287*)
or Pliny's *"incerta"* (*N.H., 2. 7*). The statement that the
Roman people were taking oaths by Sejanus' Fortune (*Se.,*
IV, v, 106) is derived from Dio, *l.c., 58. 2. 8; 6. 2.*

FURIES.

J. in naming only two Furies—Alecto (*Qu., 114* footnote)
and Megaera (*Qu., 122* footnote)—admittedly follows Claudian in *Against Rufinus, 1. 26; 74.* The Furies' arms, either
whips or firebrands, are introduced, probably from Claudian's
R.P., 2. 215, 216, at *Se.,* I, i, 24; III, i, 61; *B.F.,* II, i, 399,
400; *Qu.,* 122; and *M.P.,* 362; Vergil alludes to their whips
at *Aen.,* 6. 570-572, and to their firebrands at *Culex,* 246,
while Ovid mentions the latter several times (*e.g., Met.,* 4.
481, 482; 10. 313, 314; 349-351). Perhaps the precedent
for J.'s associating the Furies with death and war (*Se.,* V,
iii, 115; *Ca.,* V, v, 323; V, vi, 332) is to be found in *Aen.,*
7. 445-455.

At *E.M.O.,* 12, the concept of "black, ravenous ruin,
with her sail-stretched wings" suggests the concept of the
Furies in Euripides' *Orestes,* 317-322, and in the later poets
(*e.g., Aen.,* 3. 225-258; 7. 561). The union of the Furies
with Nemesis at *M.P.,* 362, at least implies their rôles as
the avengers of the crimes committed by men; so they are
portrayed in *Il.,* 19. 259, 260; Euripides' *Orestes,* 28-38;
255-265; and *Aen.,* 6. 566-574. These passages also justify
J.'s uniting the Furies with certain aspects of Hades at *Se.,*
II, ii, 51; *Ca.,* I, i, 192; III, ii, 247; *Lethe,* 274; *Chl.,* 98;
99; *Epi.,* 233; 234; 237. For the guilt of the Furies (*Ca.,*
IV, ii, 278) see ATE. Other general citations to the Furies
are *E.M.I.,* III, i, 61; *Po.,* To the Reader, 514; *Se.,* V, x,
146; 148; *Volp.,* III, ii, 232; *Epic.,* IV, i, 406; 417; *Al.,* I,
i, 15; *Tilt,* 214; and *Epi.,* 160.

GALATEA. *N.T.,* 34.

Hesiod (*Theogony,* 250) makes Galatea, a sea-nymph, the daughter of Doris, *q.v.* Telling of her thwarted love for Acis, whom the Cyclops, Polyphemus, killed, Galatea is interrupted by tears (*Met.,* 13. 738-897). Her story is also related by Theocritus, 6 and 11, and by Philoxenus ("Cyclops" in *Deipnon*). Gifford's observation that the wooing speech of Lorel in *S.S.,* II, i, 261-263, is based upon the Cyclops' lament in Theocritus, 11. (19-48) deserves notice.

GANYMEDE. *E.M.O.,* IV, iv, 132; *C.R.,* I, i, 217; *Po.,* IV, iii, 454-456; *Epi.,* 157.

Homer speaks of "godlike Ganymedes that was born the fairest of mortal men; wherefor the gods caught him up on high to be cupbearer to Zeus by reason of his beauty that he might dwell with the immortals" (*Il.,* 20. 232-235; *H.H. to Aphrodite,* 5. 202-206). Among the later writers following this tradition are Ovid (*Met.,* 10. 155-161) who alludes to Ganymede's serving nectar to Jove; Apollodorus, 3. 12. 2; Martial (*Epigrams,* 9. 25); and Cicero (*De N.D.,* 1. 40. 112). Juno's jealousy of Ganymede in *Po.* and the immoral implication, as well as Ganymede's being mentioned along with a goat, in *Epi.* cause one to recall Lucian's *Gods,* 4 and 20; also *cf. Met.,* 10. 160, 161. Mercury's handling of the "nectar when Ganymede's away" (*C.R.*) is suggested by *Gods,* 24.

GARGAPHIE. *C.R.,* Induction, 207; I, i, 219.

See ACTAEON.

GENIUS.

The Romans assigned Genii not only to themselves but to their homes, their state, and their actions. Thus in *K.J.E.,* 404-426, the *Genius Urbis,* or guardian of London since it was founded, recalls the statue of the *Genius Populi Romani* who was personified in the Forum as a bearded man holding the cornucopiae—and it may be added that the Genius in *J. and A.*, 477-481, holds the cornucopiae. The *Genius Urbis* in appearance is "rich, reverend, and antique: his hair long and white, crowned with a wreath of plane-tree, which is said to be *arbor genialis*; his mantle of purple, and buskins of that colour: he held in one hand a goblet, in the other a branch full of little twigs, to signify increase and indulgence." J. probably wrought this description from numerous sources; many pictures of the Genius include a garland for his head, and he holds a cup for wine (*cf.* Horace's *Epistles*, 2. 1. 144). J. also specifies Camden's *Britannia*, 368 (inaccessible). *Cf. J. and A.* with the *K.J.E.* passage. The notion that the best aides of the Genius are the personifications of the army and of the council of the nation is derived, he says, from Seneca's *Octavia*, act 2 (443, 444 quoted). There seems to be no classical authority for the six daughters of the Genius in *K.J.E.*

As Juno preserves from harm the woman in marriage, so the Genius serves the man (*Hy.*, 53; 68 and footnotes; *L.T.*, 91), and J. recalls Servius' comment on the *Aen.*, 6. (603), and Festus' *"Genialis Lectus"* and *"Genium."* The idea of the Genius of the grounds (*M.V.*, 237; *G.A.R.*, 252), as well as allusions to the Genii of books at *Und.*, 322; 335; and 371, is similar to *Aen.*, 5. 95; 7. 136: *Genius loci.* A passage at *M.L.*, III, iv, 68, 69, states that one of the valours of man is infused "by our genii, or good spirits"; indeed, no great action is ever accomplished *"Sine divino aliquo afflatu."* This recalls Apuleius' *De Deo Socratis*, p. 142, that the Genius is responsible for all the good desires of man, and it also recalls Servius' comment on *Aen.*, 6. 743, that man has two spirits, *"unus est qui hortatur ad bona, alter qui depravit ad mala."* Other allusions to the Genius are *C.R.*, III, iii, 271; *Po.*, Apologetical Dialogue, 508; *Ca.*, IV, iii, 292; *Case*, I, ii, 313; I, iii, 325; *L.W.Wel.*, 130; *For.*, 278; and *Und.*, 424, 425.

GIANTS. *Se.,* IV, v, 99; *Ca.,* III, i, 242; III, v, 270; V, vi, 333; *G.A.R.,* 249.

J. in referring to the Giants' war against the gods during the Iron Age, *q.v.,* seems to adhere closely to Claudian's *Gigantomachia.* Thus in *G.A.R.* the Iron Age, anticipating victory over good, urges various evils:

> We are the masters of the skies,
> Where all the wealth, height, power lies,
>   The sceptre, and the thunder
> Which of you would not in a war
> Attempt the price of any scar,
>   To keep your own states even?
> But here, which of you is that he,
> Would not himself the weapon be,
>   To ruin Jove and heaven?

With this *cf.* Claudian's speech of Earth, the mother of the Giants, to her children, inciting them to battle and offering them her own parts for weapons: "Here are seas and mountains, limbs of my body, but care not for that. Use them as weapons. Never would I hesitate to be a weapon for the destruction of Jove. Go forth and conquer; throw the heaven into confusion, tear down the towers of the sky. Let Typhoeus seize the thunderbolt and the sceptre" (52. 29-32).

But Pallas, in *G.A.R.,* by showing her shield to the evils, conquers them (*cf. Il.,* 5. 737-742, and *Met.,* 4. 790-803, which state that Pallas' aegis was adorned with the Gorgon's head); somewhat similar is *Ca.:*

> And . . . in that rebellion 'gainst the gods,
> Minerva holding forth Medusa's head,
> One of the giant-brethren felt himself
> Grow marble at the killing sight, and now
> Almost made stone, began to inquire, what flint,
> What rock it was, that crept through all his limbs,
> And ere he could think more, was that he feared.

Again *cf.* Claudian's account of the battle: "Minerva rushed forward presenting her breast whereon glittered the

Gorgon's head. The sight of this, she knew, was enough: she needed not to use a spear. One look sufficed. Pallas [a giant] drew no nearer, rage as he might, for he was the first to be changed into a rock. When, at a distance from his foe, without a wound, he found himself rooted to the ground, and felt the murderous visage turn him, little by little, to stone (and all but stone he was) he called out, 'What is happening to me? What is this ice that creeps o'er my limbs? What is this numbness that holds me prisoner in these marble fetters?' Scarce had he uttered these few words when he was what he feared . . ." (52. 91-101). Pindar (*Pythian,* 10. 46-48) and Apollodorus, 2. 4. 3, also declare that the Gorgon's head on Athene's shield turned beholders to stone. See also PHLEGRA.

GLAUCUS. *L.T.*, 88.

Glaucus, as J. says, is a sea-deity. One finds him so mentioned in various sources, among which are Apollonius Rhodius' *Argonautica,* 1. 1310; Pausanias, 9. 22. 7; Athenaeus, 7. 296 A-F; Euripides' *Orestes,* 362-364 (where he is said to be the son of Nereus, who is also named in *L.T.*); Plato's *Republic,* 10. 611 D; *Met.,* 13. 904-14. 69 (Palaemon and Proteus are named at 13. 918, 919, as in *L.T.*); *Aen.,* 5. 823 (where Palaemon is also named); and Claudian, 10. 156-158 (with Palaemon and Nereus).

GODS.

Among J.'s myriad allusions to the Gods—expressions of confidence in their virtue, justice, mercy, and immortality, assertions of gratitude, expletives, oaths, blasphemies, declarations of defiance or indifference to them—few are noteworthy. To *K.J.E.,* 414, he appends a footnote calling attention to the practice of Homer in describing outstanding mortals as god-like. One finds the phrases which J. quotes in *Il.,* 1. (7; 264). From *Il.,* 1. 533-604, too, J. received the suggestion for the burlesque banquet of the Gods at *Po.,*

IV, iii, 452-459, although such an affair was conducted by
Augustus Caesar himself (Suetonius' *Augustus, 70*) ; see
Whalley's footnote quoted by Gifford, p. 456, and Herford
and Simpson, vol. 1, p. 438. With *Au.,* 427, where Apollo
returns to his seat in "the Senate of the Gods," *cf. Il.,* 8. 1-3.
Other references to the Gods have been incidentally discussed
under various articles (*e.g.,* for Cupid's awing the Gods at
L.F., 185, see CUPID).

GOLDEN AGE. *Volp.,* I, i, 166, 167; *K.J.E.,* 425; *G.A.R.,*
247-254; *T.V.,* 14; *Epi.,* 177; *For.,* 250; 267; *cf.* SATURN.

J.'s vision of the restoration of the Golden Age in the
place of the Iron Age has precedent in *Eclogues,* 4. 4-45,
where Vergil, too, invites Astraea, the goddess of justice,
once more to take up her place among mankind. It will be
recalled that Astraea (J.'s "Astrea"), fleeing the earth when
men became wicked (*Met.,* 1. 149, 150; Juvenal, 6. 19; Hyginus' *De A.,* 2. 25), became Virgo, a star. In making Saturn
or Time (Cronos) the ruler of the Golden Age and prede-
cessor of Jove, J. is following the usual account (*e.g.,* Hesiod's *Works,* 109-120; *Met.,* 1. 89-112; Tibullus, 1. 3. 35-50).
From these last-named sources he also derives not only the
suggestion that Whalley and Gifford have indicated in the
footnote to *G.A.R.,* 251, but likewise the entire passage.

Thus J. writes of the poets of the Golden Age—"CHAU-
CER, GOWER, LIDGATE, SPENSER"—this passage:

> Then see you yonder souls, set far within the shade,
> That in Elysian bowers the blessed seats do keep,
> That for their living good, now semi-gods are made,
> And went away from earth, as if but tam'd with sleep?
> These we must join to wake; for these are of the strain
> That justice dare defend, and will the age sustain.
> Cho. Awake, awake, for whom these times were kept,
> O wake, wake, wake, as you had never slept!
> Make haste and put on air, to be their guard,
> Whom once but to defend, is still reward.

Cf. Hesiod's "But after the earth had covered this genera-
tion—they are called pure spirits dwelling on the earth, and
are kindly, delivering from harm, and guardians of mortal
men; for they roam everywhere over the earth, clothed in
mist and keep watch on judgements and cruel deeds, givers
of wealth . . ." (*Works,* 121-125). Again, J., describing the
Golden Age to be, writes:

> .The earth unplough'd shall yield her crop,
> Pure honey from the oak shall drop,
> The fountain shall run milk.

And Ovid says, "The earth herself, without compulsion,
untouched by hoe or plowshare, of herself gave all things
needful. . . . Streams of milk . . . flowed, and yellow honey
was distilled from the verdant oak" (*Met.,* 1. 101, 102; 111,
112). Pallas is not ordinarily associated with the Golden
Age, but perhaps J. is thinking of her virginity (*e.g., H.H.
to Aphrodite,* 5. 8, 9; *Aen.,* 2. 31; *Met.,* 4. 799; *Amores,*
1. 7. 18).

GOLDEN BOUGH. *Epi.,* 234.
See AVERNUS.

GOLDEN CHAIN. *Hy.,* 60 and footnote; *G.A.R.,* 247; *For.,*
264.

In his footnote, J. recalls the references to the Golden
Chain in *Il.,* 8. (19-26), in Plato's *Thaeatetus,* (153 C), and
in Macrobius' *Commentarius,* 1. 14. (15.16). To Macrobius,
J. is indebted for the thought not only in *Hy.* (where he acknowledges it), but also in *For.,* where he metaphorically
describes true love:

> It is a golden chain let down from heaven,
> Whose links are bright and even,
> That falls like sleep on lovers, and combines
> The soft, and sweetest minds
> In equal knots.

Macrobius' philosophical explanation of the Golden Chain
and its links gave J. this notion: "To which strength and
evenness of connexion, I have not absurdly likened this
uniting of Humours and Affections by the sacred Powers
of marriage."

GOLDEN FLEECE. *Henry's Ba.,* 155.
See JASON.

GORGON. *E.M.O.,* V, vii, 193; *Epic.,* II, ii, 366; III, ii, 404;
Qu., 131 and footnote; *Epi.,* 235.
In *Qu.* Heroic Virtue, accoutred as Perseus, says:

> I did not borrow Hermes' wings, nor ask
> His crooked sword, nor put on Pluto's casque,
> Nor on mine arm advanced with Pallas' shield,
> (By which, my face avers'd, in open field
> I slew the Gorgon) for an empty name:
> When Virtue cut off Terror, he gat Fame.

J.'s footnote upon his sources does not even suggest how
skilfully he has blended his material. Hesiod in *Shield* (226,
227), speaking of Perseus, says, "Upon the head of the hero
lay the dread cap of Hades," and later (236, 237), "And
upon the awful heads of the Gorgons great Fear was quak-
ing." See also *Il.,* 5. 844, 845. Apollodorus, 2. (4. 2, 3)
states that Perseus procured winged sandals from the Graeae.
"They had also the cap of Hades. . . . So he . . . fitted the
sandals to his ankles, and put the cap on his head. Wearing
it, he saw whom he pleased, but was not seen by others. And
having received also from Hermes an adamantine sickle he
flew to the ocean and caught the Gorgons asleep. . . . Now
Medusa alone was mortal. . . . So Perseus stood over them
as they slept, and while Athena guided his hand and he
looked with averted gaze on a brazen shield, in which he
beheld the image of the Gorgon, he beheaded her. When
her head was cut off, there sprang from the Gorgon the
winged horse Pegasus and Chrysaor." Upon his return, "he

gave back the sandals . . . and the cap to Hermes, but the Gorgon's head he gave to Athena."

Apollodorus, 2. 5. 12, also relates that when Hermes visited Hades, he drew his sword against the Gorgon, but that being only a phantom, she could hurt no one; this seems to throw light upon *Canaan,* 347, where the report of a new prodigy caused people to cry,

> For want of great Alcides' aid,
> And stood like people who have seen Medusa's head.

For this and other allusions to the sight of Medusa's head's turning men to marble, see GIANTS.

GRACES. *S.N.,* III, i, 239, 240; IV, i, 253; *S.S.,* I, ii, 248; *Hue,* 88-93; *L.F.,* 193-196; *L.R.,* 207; 208; *Tilt,* 218; 220; *G.A.R.,* 253; *G.M.,* 375; 403; *T.V.,* 17; *N.T.,* 35; *M.O.,* 53; *F.I.,* 78; *L.T.,* 91; *L.W.Bol.,* 137; *Epi.,* 208; *Und.,* 300; 351; 403; 420; 19, 20; 53; *M.P.,* 338.

J.'s treatment of the Graces is mostly conventional. They are three in number—Aglaia, Thalia, and Euphrosyne—and are of exceptional beauty, as Hesiod declares at *Theogony,* 907-911. They associate particularly with the Hours, the Muses, and Venus, and they likewise dance in a lovely manner (*H.H. to Py. Apollo,* 3. 189-196; *to Athena,* 27. 15; *Theogony,* 52; 63, 64). They are present as Venus' maidens, and they also attend some marriages (*Met.,* 6. 428, 429; Claudian, 10. 99-110; 202, 203). They are thought of in connection with the spring of the year, with flowers, and with Bacchus, and usually they wear a floral garland on their heads (*Anacreontea,* 44; 55; *Fasti,* 5. 207-220). When J. states that they, like truth, are best when unadorned, he may be thinking of Servius' comment on *Aen.,* 1. 720, or of Pausanias, 9. 35. 6. There seems to be no direct source for the statement that the Graces were the nurses of Cupid, though, of course, they were available to Venus for such service. The allusions to Euphrosyne and Aglaia at *K.J.E.,*

406, and *C.R.*, V, ii, 342, though undoubtedly inspired by the names and characteristics of the Graces, are not to them.

GYGES. *N.I.*, I, i, 321.

Gyges, a shepherd, descended into a chasm in the earth, where he discovered, among other things, an immense corpse wearing a golden ring. Later he realized that this ring, when turned one way, rendered him invisible, and he used this knowledge to murder the Lydian king, whom he succeeded on the throne (Plato's *Republic*, 2. 359 C-360 B; Cicero's *De Officiis*, 3. 9. 38). Another version, in which Gyges' ring is not mentioned, is related by Herodotus, 1. 8-14.

HARMONY. *Be.*, 31; *T.V.*, 17; *N.T.*, 33; *F.I.*, 77.

J.'s allusions to Harmony, for the most part, are in the spirit of *H.H. to Py. Apollo*, 3. 194-196, quoted under IDA. For Harmony's "crown of gold, having in it seven jewels equally set" (*Be.*) J. points to Cesare Ripa's *Iconologia* (inaccessible) and Macrobius' *Commentarius*, 2. (1.3).

HARPY. *D.A.*, III, i, 78; *S.N.*, II, i, 203; *Tilt*, 218; *Epi.*, 235; *Und.*, 383.

Harpies are horrible bird-like creatures with "maiden faces" and "clawed hands," according to *Aen.*, 3. 210-257; *cf.* "hookhanded" of *Und.* The allusion to "ugly centaurs," and "Gorgonian scolds, and Harpies" in *Epi.* recalls Martial's

> *Non hic centauros, non gorgonas, harpyiasque*
> *Invenies.*

> *Epigrams*, 10. 4. 9, 10.

J. quotes these lines for his motto for *Se.*

HEBE. *S.N.*, IV, i, 253; *Be.*, 31; *Ob.*, 170 footnote.

Hebe is the daughter of Zeus and Here, and the wife of Hercules (*Od.*, 11. 601-604; *Theogony*, 921-923; 950-953; Apollodorus, 1. 3. 1; 2. 7. 7). Pindar calls her "fairest of goddesses" (*Nemean*, 10. 18), and Ovid associates her with youth (*Met.*, 9. 397-417) as does Cicero (*De N.D.*, 1. 40.

112: *"Iuventas"* is Hebe who served as cup-bearer to the gods). With the *Ob.* comment that Hebe was *"semper virens"* cf. *Fasti*, 6. 66: *"et in voltu signa vigoris erant."*

HECATE. *S.S.*, II, ii, 264, 265; *Be.*, 27 and footnote; *Qu.*, 122, 123 and footnote; *T.V.*, 14.
See DIANA.

HECTOR. *Po.*, IV, i, 445.
J.'s citation of Hector as outstanding among citizens should be associated with the character of Hector at *Il.*, 6. 403; 24. 729, 730; *Aen.*, 2. 281; and elsewhere.

HELEN. *C.R.*, II, i, 252; *Po.*, IV, i, 445; *Volp.*, II, ii, 214; *S.N.*, IV, i, 254; *F.I.*, 74, 75; *For.*, 268; *Und.*, 374.
J. seems to be serious only upon the subject of Helen's beauty, which Homer emphasizes (*e.g., Il.*, 3. 154-157; 171). She is Menelaus' wife (*Po.*), and was present at the fall of Troy (*Volp.; cf. Il.*, 3. 39-54; *Od.*, 8. 492-520; *Aen.*, 2. 567-603). The story of the powder given by Apollo to Venus and by her to Helen seems to have no precedent.

HELICON.
See MUSES.

HELL. *Se.*, II, ii, 45; IV, iii, 95; *Ca.*, I, i, 192; 211; III, i, 237; III, ii, 247; III, iii, 260; V, i, 308; *Chl.*, 98-104; *Epi.*, 233-239.
J.'s Hell probably is Tartarus rather than Hades. Those who inhabit Hades are disembodied spirits (*e.g., Od.*, 11. 204-222), and those in Tartarus expiate the crimes of their earthly existence. Thus in *Chl.*, when Cupid, angered by the treatment accorded him by the older gods, flees to Hell, the effect of his presence upon Pluto and Proserpine brings about surcease of torment for Tantalus, Ixion, Tityus, and others— a lengthy borrowing from Claudian's *R.P.*, 2. 333-342. See various articles on the above subjects and on the personages

and rivers mentioned in *Epi*. The locating of Hell far under the earth agrees with *Theogony*, 713-731, and the description of it at *Ca.*, V, vi, 327, is a translation of Sallust's *War with Catiline*, 52. 13. For the presence of the Furies in Hell, see FURIES.

HERCULES.

Of all the deities in J.'s pantheon, his preferences seem to be Venus and Cupid (the patrons of love) and Hercules. This observation is strengthened by a reading of the Charis poem (*Und.*, 294, 295) where J. represents himself as picking up the bow and arrow dropped by Cupid at the sight of Charis; but J., alas, was turned to stone himself by Charis' glance, and there he stood,

> Cupid's statue with a beard;
> Or else one that play'd his ape,
> In a Hercules his shape.

This passage recalls Odysseus' account of Hercules in Hades: "He like dark night, with his bow bare and with arrow on the string, glared about him terribly, like one in act to shoot" (*Od.*, 11. 606-608), and Bacchylides, 5. 71-80, where there is also an image of Hercules with bow and arrow.

Of the labours of Hercules, J. seems concerned with only four. At *Po.*, III, i, 418, and *Canaan,* 348, there is a suggestion of Hercules' encounter with the Lernaean hydra which, according to various sources, had from one to one hundred heads and which sprouted two heads for each one that Hercules ruined (Euripides' *Hercules Furens,* 419-421; Diodorus, 4. 11; Pausanias, 2. 37. 4; etc.; *Aen.*, 8. 299, 300; *Met.*, 9. 68-74; Hyginus' *L.F.*, 30; and others). J. alludes indefinitely to Hercules' cleaning the Augean stables (Theocritus, 25. 7-152; Apollodorus, 2. 5. 5; Diodorus, 4. 13; Pausanias, 5. 1. 9; Hyginus' *L.F.*, 30; and others).

At *P.R.*, 302-305, Hercules' winning the Hesperian apples and receiving a crown from Mercury are thought of (see

ANTAEUS and ATLAS). While *en route* to perform this feat, Hercules frightened the sun into offering him a large bowl to transport him across the ocean. This is the cup to which J. refers at *P.R.,* 302. Whalley correctly connects this experience of Hercules with the story in Macrobius' *Saturnaliorum Conviviorum,* 5. 21. (16), and in Quintus Curtius Rufus, 10. 4. (18). On Hercules' use of the cup see also Apollodorus, 2. 5. 10, and Athenaeus, 11. 469 D-470 D.

The third labour of Hercules in J. is found at *Epi.,* 232-234—Hercules' visit to Hades. J. offers no explanation of this; his source probably was one or more of the following accounts: *Il.,* 8. 366-369; *Od.,* 11. 623-625; Euripides' *Hercules Furens,* 23-25; 1276-1278; Diodorus, 4. 25, 26; Hyginus' *L.F.,* 30; Seneca's *Hercules Furens,* 46-63; and others. Hercules' labours are mentioned in a general manner at *E.M.O.,* IV, iv, 142; *C.R.,* V, ii, 336; *Ca.,* III, i, 237; *B.F.,* V, iii, 505; *S.N.,* III, ii, 242; *Bl.,* 10; *Epi.,* 234; and *For.,* 260. His strength and travels, which are associated with his labours, are the subject of *E.M.O.,* III, i, 105; *C.R.,* I, i, 217; *Po.,* III, i, 418; *Ca.,* IV, ii, 288; *T.T.,* III, iv, 179; and *Epi.,* 239.

The pillars of Hercules (*Hy.,* 72, 73; *P.R.,* 306; *Exp.,* 114) are mentioned by Pindar (*Ol.,* 3. 43-45; *Nemean,* 3. 19-26; *Isthmian,* 4. 11-13), by Athenaeus, 7. 315 C; by Apollodorus, 2. 5. 10; by Strabo, 3. 5. 5; by Pliny, *N.H.,* 3. 4; Martianus Capella, 6. 624; and others. They are generally thought of as commemorating Hercules' journey to Lybia. Allusions to Hercules' spinning or to his distaff (*Hue,* 93; *Christmas,* 266; *Wales,* 323, 324) recall the service he performed for Omphale, so that he might regain his health. J.'s source is probably Lucian (see CUPID), but Ovid (*Heroides,* 9. 73-80), Statius (*Thebais,* 10. 646-649), and Seneca (*Hercules Oetaeus,* 371-373) also relate the episode.

In *Hy.,* 48; 54, the bride is said to wear a girdle of white wool fastened with the Herculean knot; J. calls attention to

Pliny's comment on the wool at *N.H.,* 8. 48, and Festus' *De Verborum Significatu,* "*Cingulo,*" on the knot. Of the several possible interpretations of the meaning of the Herculean knot in the marriage rites, J. chooses to believe with Festus that it represents the seventy children of Hercules; this knot "the husband at night untied, in sign of good fortune, that he might be happy in propagation of issue, as Hercules was." Apollodorus, who names sixty-seven of Hercules' children (2. 7. 7, 8), says that Hercules consorted on fifty successive nights with the fifty daughters of Thespius (2. 4. 10); this throws some light upon Mammon's lustful speech at *Al.,* II, i, 52. In explanation of "the French Hercules" who exercises power over language (*Volp.,* IV, ii, 272, 273), Gifford gives a footnote: "The *Gallic* or *Celtic Hercules* (says Upton) was the symbol of eloquence. Lucian has a treatise on this *French Hercules,* surnamed Ogmius." See Lucian's *Hercules,* 1; 4.

Hercules' victories over Antaeus and Comus (*P.R.,* 302-310) prove that his choice is still for Virtue rather than for Pleasure, just as it was in his young manhood (Xenophon's *Memorabilia,* 2. 1. 21-34). The mention of Hercules at *E.M.O.,* The Stage, 13, has been shown by Gifford to be from Juvenal, (2. 19. 20).

For J.'s footnotes at *Hy.,* 55, stating that Juno, the step-mother, nursed Hercules, see JUNO and BACCHUS. These imply, moreover, the Zeus-Alcmena parentage of Hercules, as Hesiod (*Theogony,* 943, 944) and Homer (*Il.,* 19. 95-99) say. Hercules' club is referred to at *C.R.,* IV, i, 294; *Se.,* IV, v, 102; *Volp.,* IV, ii, 272, 273; *Hue,* 90 footnote; *Wales,* 323, 324; and *Epi.,* 234. For *Hue,* see CUPID: trophies; *cf.* also Apollodorus, 2. 4. 11.

At *Po.,* III, i, 418, occurs mention of

Alcides' shirt,
Tearing my flesh and sinews.

This recalls the garment which Deianira, Hercules' wife, treated with the blood of the centaur, Nessus, who had told her that it was a love charm. When Hercules wore the garment, it "clung to his body, so that his flesh was torn away with it" (Apollodorus, 2. 7. 7). See also *Met.*, 9. 157-210; Sophocles' *Trachiniae*, 756-771; Seneca's *Hercules Oetaeus*, 784-841. Because of his suffering, Hercules had built a pyre (*Met.*, 9. 229-272; Apollodorus, *l.c.*) upon which he lay for the flames to consume his body. Being the son of Zeus, he was translated to the sky where he became a star (*S.N.*, III, ii, 242; *For.*, 269); see Euripides' *Heraclidae*, 854-856; Hyginus' *De A.*, 2. 22; 42.

Oaths occur at *E.M.I.*, III, ii, 85; *C.R.*, II, i, 241; IV, i, 300; V, ii, 327; and *Ca.*, II, i, 225; see DIOSCURI. There seems to be no precedent for Hercules' "black eye" at *P.R.*, 305, although Philostratus mentions his eyes several times in *Imagines*. General allusions to Hercules are to be found at *C.R.*, IV, i, 297; *Po.*, V, i, 492; *Henry's Ba.*, 163; and *Und.*, 295.

HERMAPHRODITE. *Epic.*, IV, ii, 446; *S.N.*, I, i, 161, 162.

Strictly speaking, J. does not refer to the myth of Hermaphrodite; rather, he uses the notion of bi-sexuality which is the consequence of the myth (*e.g.*, *Met.*, 4. 285-388; Diodorus Siculus, 4. 6).

HERMES.
See MERCURY.

HERMIONE. *S.N.*, IV, i, 253, 254.

Hermione, the daughter of Helen and Menelaus, "had the beauty of golden Aphrodite" (*Od.*, 4. 12-14).

HERO. *B.F.*, V, iii, 479, 480; V, iii, 483-485; 495.

J. burlesques the myth of Hero, a priestess of Aphrodite, who set a light each evening so that Leander might swim across the Hellespont to visit her. In *B.F.* the fatal outcome of the romance is not included. The early versions of the story are Ovid's *Heroides,* 18 and 19; Vergil's *Geor.,* 3. 258-263; and Musaeus' *De Amore Herois et Leandri.* Gifford points out that J. uses phrases from Marlowe's *Hero and Leander.*

HESPERIDES. *E.M.I.,* I, i, 17; III, ii, 70; *E.M.O.,* II, i, 63; IV, vi, 153; *Al.,* II, i, 48, 49; *N.I.,* III, ii, 363; *P.R.,* 305, 306; *Wales,* 330; *N.T.,* 27.

See ATLAS.

HESPERUS. *Bl.,* 14; *Be.,* 24; *Hy.,* 57; 61, 62; 66; *Hue,* 88; 94; 97; 100-102; *P.R.,* 305, 306; *G.M.,* 367; *Epi.,* 197.

In a footnote to *Hy.,* 61, 62, J. explains that "the bright Idalian star" is *"Stella Veneris,* or *Venus,* which when it goes before the sun, is called Phosphorus, or Lucifer; when it follows, Hesperus, or Noctifer." Sources which J. names are Catullus (62, which mentions Noctifer at 7, and Hesperus as the marriage star at 20-30); Cicero's *De N.D.,* 2. (20. 53, which J.'s note practically translates); Martianus Capella's *De Nuptiis,* 8. (this should be 9. 902); and Claudian's *De Nuptiis Honorii Fescennina* (Fescennine Verses, 4. 1, 2, quoted). For the *Bl.* allusion, see EOUS. The *P.R.* passage is symbolic of the king,

> Of Hesperus, the glory of the west,
> The brightest star that from his shining crest
> Lights all on this side the Atlantic seas.

Cf. articles on LUCIFER, NOCTIFER, PHOSPHORUS, and VESPER.

HIMERUS. *Be.,* 33 footnote.

J. distinguishes between Himerus and Eros: "Himerus, . . . which is *Desiderium post aspectum:* and more than *Eros,* which is only *Cupido, ex aspectu amare."* According to Hesiod, Himerus is a companion of the Muses and Graces (*Theogony,* 64, 65).

HINGES OF WORLD. *Ca.,* III, i, 241; V, i, 273; *Qu.,* 116.

The ancients believed that the heavens turn upon the North Pole and that the lower part of the universe turns upon another hinge (Ovid's *Epistulae ex Ponto,* 2. 10. 45-48). The four winds were also thought of as operating upon hinges (Servius on *Aen.,* 1. 85: *"cardinales quattuor venti sunt . . ."*).

HIPPOCRENE.
See MUSES.

HIPPOLYTUS. *Ca.,* IV, v, 298; *T.V.,* 18.

When Hippolytus rejected the advances of his step-mother, she falsely accused him to his father, who banished him. In exile a sea-monster terrified his horses; they, running madly, dragged him to death. Aesculapius then restored Hippolytus to life, and Diana thereafter protected him. The myth is found in Euripides' and in Seneca's *Hippolytus, passim,* and in *Met.,* 15. 495-546; *cf. Fasti,* 3. 261-268; 6. 737-756; and *Aen.,* 7. 761-780. Both Ovid and Vergil relate that Diana sheltered Hippolytus in a woody grove.

HONOUR. *Qu.,* 140.

Among the ornaments on the House of Fame, Inigo Jones, J. says, placed statues of Honour and Virtue. Cicero (*De N.D.,* 2. 23. 61) mentions both as being treated as deities; they also are found on Roman coins. Other allusions to Honour are but personifications.

HOURS. *S.N.,* IV, i, 253; *N.I.,* I, i, 325; *Panegyre,* 433-435; *Two Kings,* 471; *Hy.,* 57, 58; *V.D.,* 289, 290; *L.T.,* 91; *Chl.,* 102; *Und.,* 19.

The Hours—Dike (Justice), Eunomia (Order), and Irene (Peace)—are named by Hesiod in *Theogony,* 901-903, as the daughters of Themis and Zeus. Contrary to Whalley's note to *Two Kings,* however, not Hesiod but Homer says that they stand at the portals of heaven (*Il.,* 5. 749-751; also

Fasti, 1. 125). J.'s "gold-hair'd Hour" in *V.D.* recalls that the Hours are described as "rich-haired" in Hesiod's *Works,* 74, 75, and as "gold-filleted" twice in *H.H. to Aphrodite,* 6. 5-13. This hymn, too, is probably J.'s basis for asserting that the Hours nursed Venus (*L.T.*); *cf. S.N.* The dancing of the Hours in this hymn can also be connected with the pleasures mentioned in *V.D.* The union of the Hours with flowers is found in *Works,* 74, 75; *Cypria,* 6, and *Fasti,* 5. 217, 218. There is a similarity between the descent of Peace "that keeps the gate of heaven, and turns the year" and is "the opener of the new year" (*V.D.*) and Janus' speech in *Fasti,* 1. 120-124. In Theocritus, 15. 101-105, the Hours are thought of as Seasons or the passing of time; *cf. Two Kings.* In the classics the Hours do not seem to be thought of as generous, but Lotspeich quotes Natalis Comes' *Mythologiae,* 4. 16: *"rerum omnium abundantia."* Nothing associating the Hours with marriage or birth or music has been located; perhaps J. did not intend these to be mythological allusions. See EIRENE.

HYDRA. *Po.,* III, i, 418; *Al.,* IV, iv, 145; *Ca.,* III, i, 237; IV, ii, 290, 291; *Epi.,* 235; *Canaan,* 347-349.

See HERCULES. The hydra in *Canaan* is not, of course, mythological except in inspiration.

HYMEN.

At *Hy.,* 47-52, J. writes: "Entered HYMEN (the god of marriage) in a saffron-colour'd robe, his under vestures white, his socks yellow, a yellow veil on his left arm, his head crowned with roses and majoram, in his right hand a torch of pine tree." J. instances Catullus, 61. 6-15, as the chief source of his description, but adds that allusions to the veil may also be found in Pliny's *N.H.,* 21. 8, to the pine torch in Vergil's *Ciris,* (439), and Ovid's *Fasti,* 2. (558), and to the thorn torch in Pliny's *N.H.,* 16. 18, and Festus' *"Patrimi."* *Cf.* Ovid's picture of Hymen *"croceo velatus amictu"* (*Met.,*

10. 1). As the god of perfection in marriage, similar to Juno, Hymen is presented at *Hy.,* 58-67 (the thought that Venus, the deity of love, can do nothing without Hymen or Juno unless she arouses shame is from Catullus, 61. 61-64), and at *Hue,* 93-102 (Catullus, 61. 66, 67, also suggests Hymen as a patron of propagation). The suggestion that Hymen has stolen the bride from her mother, J. connects with *Fasti,* (3. 179-228), and *"Catui."* (probably Catullus, 61. 56-59; 62. 20-25); both seem to recall "Romulus, who, by force, gat wives for him and his, from the Sabines," as Plutarch ("Romulus," 14, 15) and Livy, 1. 9-13, relate. General references to Hymen occur at *Epic.,* III, ii, 396; *Ba.,* 80; 83; *Tilt,* 219, 220; *L.T.,* 91; *L.W.Bol.,* 139; and *M.P.,* 339. As Whalley points out, the speeches at *Ba.,* 78-80, are almost literally translated from Catullus, 62. 39-58.

HYPSIPYLE. *Qu.,* 111 footnote.

J.'s incidental and rather inaccurate quotation from Hypsipyle's epistle to Jason is, of course, from Ovid's *Heroides,* 6. (91, 92).

ICARIUS. *Ob.,* 170 footnote.

See PENELOPE.

IDA. *Po.,* I, i, 376; *V.D.,* 294; *T.V.,* 17; *Epi.,* 208.

"The old Idalian brawls," wherein Venus danced with the Graces and other companions, are reminiscent of *Cypria,* 6: "The bright-coiffed goddesses, the Nymphs and Graces, and golden Aphrodite too, . . . sang sweetly on the mount of many-fountained Ida," and of *H.H. to Py. Apollo,* 3. 194-196: "Meanwhile the rich-tressed Graces and cheerful Seasons dance with Harmonia and Hebe and Aphrodite."

IDMON. *Au.,* 421 and footnote.

Idmon is the son of Apollo, but Asterie is not named as his mother in the source which J. offers: Valerius Flaccus'

Argo., I. (228-233). She is named, however, in Pherecydes' *Fragments,* 70.

IDOMEN. *For.,* 269.

Idomen, whom J. merely names among the heroes "that Homer brought to Troy," is frequently mentioned (*e.g., Il.,* 2. 405; 7. 165; *Od.,* 14. 237).

INSULAE FORTUNAE. *E.M.O.,* IV, vi, 153; Epilogue, 198.
See FORTUNATE ISLANDS.

IO PAEAN. *Pen.,* 464.

A paean is a song of praise in honour of Apollo (*e.g., Il.,* 1. 472-474) or a song of victory (*e.g., Il.,* 22. 391). Io (the wanderer) suggests that here the birds are singing a gladsome song for distinguished travellers—the king and queen.

IRENE. *Panegyre,* 434.
See EIRENE.

IRIS. *Po., IV,* i, 446; *K.J.E.,* 429; *Panegyre,* 435, 436; *Hy.,* 56; *V.D.,* 291; *Chl.,* 101-104; *Expostulation,* 110.

For the significant material in *K.J.E.,* see ELECTRA, and for *V.D.,* see FAVONIUS. The other notices of Iris are explained by the general treatment of the goddess of the rainbow (*e.g., Aen.,* 4. 700-702; *Met.,* 1. 270, 271). Various writers, *e.g.,* Homer (*Il.,* 15. 183, 184; etc.) and Ovid (*Met., l.c.*) say that Iris is *"nuntia Iunonis"*; with this *cf. Chl.* and *Expostulation.* The fourth to seventh entries in *Chl.* may be simply a development of *Met.,* 1. 262-269.

IRON AGE. *G.A.R.,* 247-249.

J.'s personification of the Iron Age seems to be his own device. Hesiod (*Works,* 169c-201) and Ovid (*Met.,* 1. 127-163) relate the afflictions that men suffered and the crimes that they became guilty of during this era in the evolution of mankind. Ovid also declares that during the Iron Age the Giants warred upon heaven; *cf.* GIANTS for the similarity between the speech delivered by the Iron Age and that by Earth in Claudian.

Ixion. *Po.,* IV, iii, 462; *Chl.,* 98.

Ixion's crime—his infatuation for Juno—led to his embracing a cloud to which Juno had given her form, and subsequently the cloud gave birth to Centaurus, from whom the Centaurs descended. As Whalley says, J. alludes to this in *Po.*:

> O, who shall follow Virtue and embrace her,
> When her false bosom is found naught but air?
> And yet of those embraces centaurs spring.

For sources of this myth, see Pindar and others under CENTAUR, and *cf.* Lucian's *Gods,* 6.

Either because of his crime or because he boasted of it, Ixion was bound to a rotating wheel in Tartarus, the prison of Hades; but when Love visits in Hades, "Ixion is loosed from his wheel" (*Chl.*). Undoubtedly *R.P.,* 2. 335-337, was in J.'s mind, for Claudian relates that when Pluto, in love, brought Proserpine to his realm, *"non rota suspensum praeceps Ixiona torquet,"* and *"solvitur Ixion."* Orpheus' visit to Hades produced a similar effect: *"atque Ixioni vento rota constitit orbis"* (*Geor.,* 4. 484), and *"stupuitque Ixionis orbis"* (*Met.,* 10. 42).

Janus. *E.M.O.,* I, i, 38; III, i, 105; *C.R.,* I, i, 215; V, ii, 323; *Po.,* I, i, 383; III, i, 413; 420; *K.J.E.,* 416-418; 423; 424 and footnote; 427; *Be.,* 24; *Und.,* 36.

The setting for *K.J.E.,* a temple of Janus reminiscent of his temple at Rome, presented the god's head with four faces and the legend, *Jano quadrifronti sacrum,* which, J. says, is from Bassus on Macrobius' *Saturnalia,* 1. 9. (13), and suggests that Janus "respecteth all climates, and fills all parts of the world with his majesty," *"et lingua pariter locutus omni"* being quoted from Martial's *Epigrams,* 8. 2. (5). Or it suggests that "the four elements . . . brake out of him, being

Chaos," as Ovid states in *Fasti,* 1. (103-106). Or, as J. prefers, it suggests "the year, which . . . is divided into four
seasons." For this, J. advises, "Lege Marlianum, lib. 4, cap.
8. *Alb. in deorum,*" but Marlianus' *Topographia* has not
been accessible. The last words in J.'s note indicate Albricius'
Commentariolum de Imaginibus Deorum. Munckerus' commentary upon Albricius' *"De Iano"* (XIV) mentions St.
Augustine's *De Civitate Dei,* 7. 4 and 7. 8, Servius on *Aen.,*
7. 607 and 12. 198, and Isidorus' *Origines,* 8. 11 as speaking
of Janus Quadrifrons. The symbolism in these sources is
identical with J.'s. *Cf.* "four-faced Janus" and "his vernal
look" at *K.J.E.,* 424. Or, as J. also prefers, "Quadrifrons"
suggests "the beginnings and ends of things," from Cicero's
De N.D., 2. (27. 67); or lastly, it suggests that Janus con-
trols *"caelum, mare, nubila, terras"* from Ovid's *Fasti,* 1.
(117-120).

Around Janus' head on J.'s temple there is a gold wreath
inscribed *"Tot vultus mihi nec satis putavi,"* also adapted
from Martial's *Epigrams,* 8. 2. (3), to signify that Janus'
four faces were insufficient "to behold the greatness and glory
of that day" when James I arrived in London. Under the
head J. placed *"et modo sacrificio Clusius ore vocor"* from
Fasti, 1. (130) to recall that the gates of Janus' temple were
open during wars, but were closed during peace; now since
the advent of James I was a guarantee of peace, Janus was
termed "Clusius"—his title in times of peace, "Patulcius"
being his title in times of war. *Cf. Fasti,* 1. 129; 277-282.

Po., implying that Janus has but two faces, recalls *"Iane
biceps"* of *Fasti,* 1. 65; 89-92; etc. Similarly, *Und.,* stating
that "Janus opens the new year," suggests *"anni . . . origo,"*
ibid., 1. 65; and *Be.,* asserting that Janus is "shutting up
wars, proclaiming peace," reflects *ibid.,* 1. 120-124. The fact
that "January" is derived from Janus (*Be.*) is also mentioned,
ibid., 1. 43, 44.

JAPETUS. (JAPHET). *Und.,* 369.
See PROMETHEUS.

JASON. *Po.,* I, i, 377; *Ca.,* III, iii, 264, 265 ("dragon's teeth") ; *Al.,* II, i, 48, 49; *For.,* 269; *Canaan,* 348.

Jason was ordered to procure the golden fleece in Colchis, and for this purpose he had built his ship, the *Argo.* Aeëtes, the ruler of Colchis, promised to give Jason the fleece, provided the latter would harness two fierce bulls and then sow dragon's teeth in Mars' field. Medea, Aeëtes' daughter, after making Jason agree to marry her, told him how by a magic ointment he might overcome the bulls and also kill the armed men who she knew would spring from the dragon's teeth. All that Medea directed him to do, Jason did, and when the newly created men gathered, he threw stones at them so that they fought with one another. This allowed him to attack and kill them. The usual sources for this myth are Apollonius Rhodius' *Argo.,* 3. 400-4. 182; Valerius Flaccus' *Argo.,* 5. 177-8. 468; Apollodorus, 1. 9. 23; *Met.,* 7. 5-148. J. however, curiously mentions Varro (*Po.*), who is supposed to have written an *Argonautica,* probably a translation of Rhodius', but only fragments of it remain. The specifications in *Al.* also agree with Apollonius. The question, "who placed Jason's Argo in the sky?" in *For.,* seems to allude to the fact that *"Minerva in sideralem circulum retulit"* (Hyginus' *L.F.,* 14; *De A.,* 2. 37).

JOVE.
See JUPITER.

JUNO.
In *Hy.,* 46, the scene is an altar "to marriage, or Union; over which Juno was president: to whom there was the like altar erected, at Rome, as she was called Juga Juno, in the street, which thence was named Jugarius. See *Fest.*; and at which altar, the rite was to join the married pair with bands of silk, in sign of future concord." For an explanation of

J.'s source, see "Juga" in the following paragraphs. Then (*Hy.*, 55-59) the scene began to change, *"and the air clearing, in the top thereof was discovered Juno, sitting in a throne, supported by two beautiful peacocks; her attire rich and like a queen, a white diadem on her head, from whence descended a veil, and that bound with a fascia of several colour'd silks, set with all sorts of jewels, and raised in the top with lilies and roses: in her right hand she held a sceptre, in the other a timbrel, at her golden feet the hide of a lion was placed: round about her sat the spirits of the air in several colours, making music: above her the region of fire . . . was seen to whirl circularly . . . : beneath her the rainbow, Iris, and on two sides, eight ladies attired richly, and alike, in the most celestial colours, who represented her powers, as she is the governess of marriage."*

J.'s footnotes on the foregoing quotation, and his allusions to similar characteristics of Juno in his other works, follow: He identifies Juno with the air, following Macrobius' *Commentarius*, 1. 17. (15), and Martianus Capella's *De Nuptiis*, (probably 2. 168: *"atheria Juno"* although J. writes *"Aeria"*). Juno's peacocks (also at *Hy.*, 71; *Chl.*, 101-104; *Expostulation*, 110; and *Epi.*, 208) "in respect to their colours and temperament, so like the air," J. mistakenly says, are Ovid's in *Ars Amandi*, but his passage is an adaptation of *De Medicamine*, 33, and in *Met.*, 2. (531, 532), also quoted. As in *Hy.*, *l.c.*, and in *Po.*, IV, iii, 455, "she was called *Regina Juno* with the Latins because she was *soror et conjux Jovis, deorum et hominum regis*" (J. offers no further source, but see *e.g.*, *Met.*, 1. 620, 621; 2. 512; *Aen.*, 1. 9. *Theogony*, 921-923, by implication makes her a queen, and "queenly" is an Homeric epithet, as at *e.g.*, *Il.*, 14. 300; *H.H. to Hera*, 12). Apuleius in *De Asino Aureo*, 10. (30), mentions Juno's diadem.

"The several colour'd silks" imply "the several mutations of the air, as showers, dew, serenity, force of winds, clouds,

tempests, snow, hail, lightning, thunder, all which had their
noises signified in her timbrel: the faculty of causing these
being ascribed to her by *Virg. AEneid.* lib. iv." Here J.
quotes *Aen.*, 4. 120; 122, but omits 121. He further asserts
that "lilies were sacred to Juno, as being made white with
her milk that fell on the earth, when Jove took Hercules
away, whom by stealth he had laid to her breast: the rose
was also called Junonia." For this statement no source has
been discovered, but Hyginus (*De A.*, 2. 43) accounts thus
for the milky way. The lion's hide recalls that "so she was
figured at Argos, as a step-mother, insulting on the spoils of
her two privigini, Bacchus and Hercules." No more definite
source for this has been found, but *cf.* BACCHUS and
HERCULES. In making Juno "the governess of marriage,"
J. quotes *Aen.*, 4. (59) and (166, 167; here the word-order
is at fault, but see comment on Juno's mixing air with fire,
below); J. also quotes Ovid's *Heroides, 2.* (41, but J.'s
"terris" should be *"toris"*).

To J.'s comments above, it may be added that Juno's veil
is mentioned by Homer (*Il.*, 14. 184, 185: "And with a veil
over all did the bright goddess veil herself, a fair veil, all
glistering, and white was it as the sun"). Homer (*l.c.*, 186)
alludes to Juno's feet as "shining"; *cf.* J.'s "golden." J. re-
views his description of the *Hy.* setting in an essay at the end.
The reader finds the picture of Juno in this essay (*Hy.*, 72,
73) substantially the same as the one quoted above, but it is
noteworthy that in the second version, Juno's throne is
golden, as Homer describes it at *Il.*, 1. 611. In both descriptions and also at *Chl.*, 101-104, and at *Expostulation,* 110,
Iris, the rainbow, is with Juno; see IRIS.

Continuing with *Hy.*, 55-59, the reader learns that eight
of Juno's "noblest Powers" or faculties "that govern nuptial
mysteries" descend, "their habits . . . after some statues of
Juno, no less airy than glorious." These personify the surnames of Juno: Curis, Unxia, Juga, Gamelia, Iterduca,

Domiduca, Cinxia, and Telia. Again J. documents his material: "Curis," the surname of Juno among the Sabines before the Romans adopted it, signified that the hair of the bride was dressed with a spear "which had struck in the body of a slain sword-player"; J. quotes four reasons which Festus (*De Significatione, "Celibari"*) offers: "*Ut quemadmodum illa conjuncta fuerit cum corpore gladiatoris, sic ipsa cum viro sit; vel quia matronae Junonis curitis in tutelâ sit, quae ita appellabatur à ferenda hasta; vel quòd fortes viros genituras ominetur; vel quod nuptiali jure imperio viri subjicitur nubens, quia hasta summa armorum, et imperii est, &c.*" Plutarch in *Moralia,* "Roman Questions," (87), confirms much of what Festus says, but in *Lives* under "Romulus" (15. 5) he attributes the practice of dressing the bride's hair with a spear point to the fact "that the first marriage was attended with war and fighting" (see HYMEN). In addition to Festus and Plutarch, J. quotes *Fasti, 2.* (560): "*Comat virgineas hasta recurva comas.*"

"Unxia," J. continues, indicates that "with the Romans . . . before the new-married brides entered the houses of their husbands, they adorned the posts of the gates with woollen tawdries, or fillets, and anointed them with oils, or the fat of wolves and boars; being superstitiously possesst that such ointments had the virtue of expelling evils from the family: and that thence they were called *Uxores, quasi Unxores.*" This information J. has from Martianus' *De Nuptiis,* 2. (149), and Servius on *Aen.,* 4. (probably 166). *Cf.* J.'s incidental comment in "Cinxia," below, from Arnobius.

"Juga" recalls "the yoke which was imposed in matrimony," according to Servius on *Aen.,* (4. 59), but Festus (*De Significatione, "Juges"* and *"Jugarius"*) gives two other possibilities: "*quòd Juges sunt ejusdem Jugi Pares, unde et Conjuges,*" or because the altar of Juno was "*in Vico Jugario.*" "Gamelia," another of Juno's surnames, signifies that in sacrificing to her, "they took away the gall, and threw it behind the altar; intimating, that (after marriage) there should be no bitterness, nor hatred between the joined couple, which might divide or separate them. See *Plutarch. Connub. Prae."* (Plutarch's *Moralia,* 141 F). Also *cf.* Servius, below, on "Telia."

"Iterduca" is another of Juno's titles among the Romans, as J., following Martianus' *De Nuptiis,* 2. (149), says, *"quòd ad sponsi ædes sponsas comitabatur."* "Domiduca," Martianus *(l.c.),* J. says, was given to Juno *"quòd ad optatas domus duceret."* Martianus *(l.c.)* also explains that "Cinxia" indicates that Juno is "the defendress of maids," and as Festus (*De Significatione,* "Cinxiae") says: *"Cinxiae Junonis nomen sanctum habebatur in nuptiis, quòd initio conjugis solutio erat cinguli, quo nova nupta erat cincta."* Arnobius in *Adversus Gentes,* 3. (25) says: *"Unctionibus superest Unxia. Cingulorum Cinxia replicationi."*

"Telia," the last designation, J. says, "signifies Perfecta, . . . with *Jul. Pol.,* lib. iii. *Onomast."* Julius Pollux, 3. (38), states that *"Telia"* is derived from the Greek for marriage and for married people (*cf.* Pausanias, 9. 2. 7). J. adds, "Servius interprets it the same with Gamelia *AEneid* iv. *ad verb. Et Junone secunda."* Servius on *Aen.,* 4. (45) says: "IUNONE SECUNDA *vel* quae praeest coniugiis, *quae pronuba appellatur* . . ."—a comment scarcely satisfactory. J. asserts that he agrees more completely with the Scholiast on Pindar's *Nemean,* 10. (3), saying, "Nuptials are therefore called τέλειοι, because they affect perfection of life, and do note that maturity which should be in matrimony. For before nuptials, she is called *Juno* παρθένος, that is, *Virgo*; after nuptials, τέλεια, which is, *Adulta,* or *Perfecta."*

J. quotes *Aen.,* 4. (166-168) to support Hymen's words to the bride at *Hy.,* 62:

thrice hath Juno mixt her air
With fire, to summon your repair.

At *Hy.,* 68, the part played by Juno over the women in pro-
creation is suggested—a notion frequent enough (*e.g., Il.,*
14. 205-207; Plutarch's *Moralia,* 143 D; *Met.,* 6. 428: *"pronuba Iuno"; Aen.,* 4. 166). Juno's power over childbirth
(*Ob.,* 175: "Midwife Juno") can be attributed to the fact
that that goddess of travail, Eileithyia, or Ilithyia, or Lucina,
q.v., is the daughter of Zeus and Juno (*Theogony,* 921-923;
Il., 11. 269-271, where "daughters" is used; *H.H. to Delian
Apollo,* 3. 97-116; Apollodorus, 1. 3. 1). As the deity of
marriage, Juno is also mentioned at *L.T.,* 91.

"Saturnia" (*C.R.,* I, i, 222; *Po.,* IV, iii, 459) indicates
that Juno is the daughter of Saturn (*e.g., Aen.,* 1. 23; *Met.,*
1. 612). When, during a domestic quarrel, Jove mentions
Juno's jealousy of Thetis (*Po.,* IV, iii, 455, 456), there is a
reflection of a similar dispute in which Thetis figures at *Il.,*
1. 536-611 (see also THETIS); and both *Po.* and *Il.* suggest that the gods may all oppose Jupiter, until, as Gifford
observes, Vulcan makes peace by offering to both Jove and
Juno generous quantities of drink. Vulcan here addresses
both Jove and Juno as his parents, but see VULCAN. That
Mars is a son of Juno (*Po.,* IV, iii, 454) is asserted at
Theogony, 922; *Il.,* 5. 890-893; Apollodorus, 1. 3. 1; and
Fasti, 5. 255-258.

Jove's threat to "cudgel" Juno and to throw her from
Olympus during their quarrel in *Po., l.c.,* reflects his threat
to scourge her and again to hang her from Olympus (*Il.,* 15.
16-20; Apollodorus, 1. 3. 5; 2. 7. 1). The beauty of Juno is
instanced at *Po., l.c.,* where the allusion to her lips seems
without precedent. For her jealousy of Ganymede, see
GANYMEDE. At *S.N.,* IV, i, 253, where J. introduces the
beauty of Juno's arms, he awakens the memory of the
Homeric epithet, "white-armed" (*e.g., Il.,* 1. 595; *H.H. to
Delian Apollo,* 3. 95). For the allusion at *Und.,* 298, to
Juno's vying with Venus and Minerva in a beauty contest,
see VENUS. Similarly, for Juno's power over Aeolus, see

AEOLUS. No source has been found to explain the allusion to Juno's disguises at *Ca.,* I, i, 196, or to her fingers at *Tilt,* 215. General citations occur at *C.R.,* IV, i, 278; *Po.,* IV, i, 440; 443; *Se.,* II, iv, 57; V, x, 143; *Ca.,* II, i, 215; 224 (oath); *T.T.,* III, ii, 172; *F.M.,* I, i, 297.

JUPITER.

The most sweeping of J.'s characterizations of Jupiter occurs in the following passage:

> Apol. *My arts are only to obey.*
> Jove. *And mine to sway.*
> *Jove is that one, whom first, midst, last, you call,*
> *The power that governs, and conserveth all;*
> *Earth, sea, and air, are subject to our check,*
> *And fate with heaven, moving at our beck.*
> *Till Jove it ratify,*
> *It is no augury,*
> *Though utter'd by the mouth of Destiny (Au., 427).*

To the word "sway" J. appends a footnote: *"Vide Orpheum in hym. de omnip. Jovis."* It seems quite likely that J. here has some thought in his mind of the Christian concept of Deity, rather than the pagan, for ordinarily the realm of Jove is heaven only (*e.g., Il.,* 15. 190-193), and J. observes this at *Hy.,* 56, where appears "Jupiter standing in the top (figuring the heaven) brandishing his thunder" while Juno sits beneath; see also Horace's *Odes,* 1. 26, and *Geor.,* 1. 416-422. The subjection of the Fates to Jupiter (*J. and A.,* 477-481; *Au., l.c.;* and *F.I.,* 76) is discussed under FATES.

At *F.I.,* 63-65, Saturn is said to be the father of Jupiter, as report Hesiod at *Theogony,* 453-458; Diodorus, 5. 70; and Apollodorus, 1. 1. 5, 6. A footnote at *Ob.,* 170, recalls Apollo's celebrating in music the victory of Jove over Saturn, to support which J. quotes Tibullus' *Elegia,* 2. (5. 7-10). For Jove's sister and wife, see JUNO, and for his loves see MAIA, VENUS, THETIS, LEDA, PASIPHAÊ, CALLISTO, EUROPA, ACRISIUS (for Danaë), and GANY-

MEDE. Jove's disguises (*Ca.*, I, i, 96; *Hue*, 63) may be associated with *Met.*, 6. 103-114, where they are enumerated, and with some of the articles listed above. See also CUPID. His loves among the stars (*Po.*, IV, iii, 456; *Epic.*, III, i, 390) are made at least partially clear under CALLISTO and ARIADNE. For his children in J.'s pantheon see APOLLO, MERCURY, DIOSCURI, PALLAS, CYNTHIA, VE-NUS, and VULCAN. His parentage of Mars, *q.v.*, is seemingly indicated by the passage from *Ca.* quoted under REMUS.

When Jove wishes to confirm or promise something (*Po.*, IV, iii, 456; *Au.*, 428 and footnote), he nods his head; the *Au.* footnote, however, is unsatisfactory: *"Mos Jovis, annuendo votis et firmandis omnibus. Apud Homer. 7c."* Homer discusses this custom at *Il.*, I. 524-527. No literary source for Jove's beard (*C.R.*, II, i, 237; *Se.*, IV, v, 99) has been located, but his "black-lidded eye" (*l.c.*) parallels *Il.*, 1. 528. That Jove is "the king of gods" (*Po.*, V, i, 489) is a classic idea, as *e.g.*, *Met.*, 2. 280: *"summe deum."* At *G.A.R.*, 247-254, he is said to desire that justice and righteousness exist among men—a thought found at *Il.*, 16. 384-388. See also GOLDEN AGE. *C.R.*, I, i, 224, and the statement at *G.A.R.*, 254, that his "power is everywhere" reflect such phrases as *"pater omnipotens"* of *Met.*, 2. 401, and *Aen.*, 7. 770.

Jove's weapon against his enemies is lightning. Hesiod (*Theogony*, 503-506; 689-710) and Ovid (*Met.*, 2. 308-313), for example, relate Jove's hurling his lightning against the Titans and against Phaëton, respectively. J. mentions Jove's lightning many times: *C.R.*, I, i, 218; *Po.*, IV, iii, 456; V, i, 489; 496; *Se.*, IV, v, 102; 104, 105; *Ca.*, II, i, 223; III, ii, 244; *Hy.*, 56; 73; *Hue*, 90 footnote, and 93 (see CUPID); *Qu.*, 122; *G.A.R.*, 249; *Au.*, 427; *Canaan*, 348. Cf. *Fasti*, 2. 69, 70. No source has been located for the claim that Neptune believed that Jove's lightning had taken his palace (*Henry's Ba.,* 159), but the statement that Mercury took Jove's sceptre with his lightning (*C.R.,* I, i, 218) is from Lucian's *Gods,* 7. The sceptre is another symbol of Jove's might. For J.'s citations (*C.R., l.c., Po.,* IV, ii, 451; IV, vi, 469; and *G.A.R.,* 249), see *Met.,* 1. 178; 2. 847; and others.

Cicero's address to Jupiter (*Ca.,* IV, ii, 288) is a transla-tion of Cicero's *Oration against Catiline,* 1. 13. The setting of *Ca.,* IV, ii, and V, vi, in the temple of Jupiter Stator ac-cords with Livy, 1. 12, and *Fasti,* 6. 793, 794; this is also mentioned at *Ca.,* IV, ii, 274. Gifford's remark that a passage involving Jupiter at *L.R.,* 207, is from "one of Lucian's Dialogues" can be verified at *Timon,* 20. Astronomical and chiromantic allusions are *Al.,* I, i, 39; *S.S.,* III, ii, 281; and *G.M.,* 365. For *Ca.,* III, i, 242, and *Und.,* 369, see PROME-THEUS; for *Al.,* IV, i, 117, see AESCULAPIUS; for *Ca.,* IV, v, 299, see CAPANEUS; for *Au.,* 422 and 427, see APOLLO; for *For.,* 259, see AMBROSIA; for *Und.,* 400 and 404, see VULCAN; for *Hy.,* 55 footnote see JUNO; for *C.R.,* I, i, 220, see ECHO.

General allusions to Jove—prayers, expressions of grati-tude, oaths, etc.—occur at *E.M.I.,* III, i, 61; IV, vii, 126; *E.M.O.,* V, vii, 197; *C.R.,* I, i, 216-218; 222; 234; II, i, 241; 252; III, i, 258; III, iii, 268; IV, i, 273; V, ii, 311; 316; 324; 326; 327; V, iii, 340; 347; 349; 350; 356; *Po.,* I, i, 374; 386; 391; II, i, 405; III, i, 409; 411; 415; 416; 418; 420; 423; 424; 428; 433; 435; IV, i, 440; 442; 443; 445, 446; 448; IV, ii, 451; IV, iii, 453; 461; IV, iv, 464; V, i, 474, 475; 486; 500; 503; Apol. Dia., 508; *Se.,* I, i, 23; 26; I, ii, 33; II, ii, 45; 50; III, i, 63; 66; 71; III, iii, 86; IV, iii, 93; 94; IV, v, 101; V, iv, 120; 123; V, x, 143; *Al.,* I, i, 33; V, iii, 178; *Ca.,* II, i, 215; IV, iv, 294; V, i, 308; *B.F.,* II, i, 396; *Satyr,* 451; *Pen.,* 410; *Hy.,* 52; *M.V.,* 237; *N.T.,* 23; *Chl.,* 95, 96; *Epi.,* 239.

LACHESIS. *J. and A.,* 477-481.
See FATES.

LAIS. *Ca.,* II, i, 228.

When Fulvia "draws her knife" against the advances of Curius, he exclaims, "Will Lais turn a Lucrece?" Fulvia answers:

> Hold off your ravisher's hands, I pierce your heart
> else.
> I'll not be put to kill myself, as she did,
> For you, sweet Tarquin.

In history there are two courtesans by the name of Lais, the more noted being spoken of by Athenaeus, 13. 54, 55, and Claudian (*Against Eutropius,* 1. 90-97). Lucrece, on the other hand, was the wife of Collatinus who stabbed herself to death after she had been violated by a son of L. Tarquinius Superbus (Livy, 1. 57-59).

LAMIA. *Chl.,* 99; *Und.,* 329.

Lamia—sometimes plural—is a child-stealing monster of "the full Grecian store," and the term is also used of women who allured young men. See Diodorus, 20. 41; Horace's *Art of Poetry,* 340; and Aristophanes' *Wasps,* 1177. J.'s authority for placing the Lamiae in Hades (*Chl.*) does not come from any of the usual sources.

LAPITHES. *N.I.,* IV, iii, 380.
See CENTAURS.

LARES. *Ca.,* I, i, 205; *S.N.,* IV, i, 261; *Case,* I, iii, 326; V, i, 378; *Satyr,* 445, 446; *J. and A.,* 477-481.

J. refers to the private or family Lares (Pliny's *N.H.,* 213; *Fasti,* 2. 617-634; 5. 129-136), and to a "Lararium, or seat of the household gods, where both the Lares and Penates were painted." Before this Lararium offerings of food and wine were placed (*Fasti,* 2. 634). The *S.N.* allusion to a dog being the Lares of Pennyboy recalls *Fasti,* 5. 137-142, where

Ovid compares the alertness, etc., of the Lares with that of dogs.

LATONA. *C.R.,* I, i, 223, 224; *N.T.,* 28.
  In *C.R.* Echo complains,

> But here, O here, the fountain of self-love
> In which Latona, and her careless nymphs,
> Regardless of my sorrows, bathe themselves
> In hourly pleasures.

This is a curious allusion to the treatment which Latona accorded Niobe, *q.v.,* and J.'s suggestion that self-love was her motive is highly appropriate in a drama upon this humour. For *N.T.,* see DELOS.

LEDA. *Ca.,* II, i, 223; *S.N.,* IV, i, 253, 254; *Ode,* 357.
  Taking the form of a swan upon himself, Jove consorted with Leda (Vergil's *Ciris,* 489; Euripides' *Helen* 17-21; Apollodorus, 3. 10. 7; Lucian's *Gods,* 20; *Charidemus,* 7; Hyginus' *L.F.,* 77). This seems sufficient evidence to justify J.'s allusion to Leda's beauty in *S.N.* In *Ode* he speaks of

> Leda's white adulterer's place
  Among the stars.

Hyginus' *De A.,* 2. 8, seems to be the only source for this notion.

LEMNOS. *M.V.,* 234; *Und.,* 404.
  When Jove expelled him from heaven, Vulcan fell into Lemnos (*Il.,* 1. 592, 593).

LERNA. *Canaan,* 348.
  See HERCULES.

LETHE. *Lethe,* 273, 274; 276; 279.
  Lethe is the river of forgetfulness tasted by the deceased (Lucian's *Of Mourning,* 5; Plato's *Republic,* 10. 621A; *Aen.,* 6. 713-715; Claudian's *R.P.,* 1. 282, 283).

LEUCOTHOE. *N.T.*, 37.

When Odysseus was beset by furious winds, "the daughter of Cadmus, Ino of the fair ankles, saw him, even Leucothea, who of old was a mortal of human speech, but now in the deeps of the sea has won a share of honour from the gods" (*Od.*, 5. 333-353; 458-462), and she gave him a veil to bear him to shore. Ovid gives two accounts of Ino's being made a sea-deity (*Fasti*, 6. 485-550; *Met.*, 4. 512-542).

LIBERTY. *S.N.*, I, i, 162. *Cf.* ELEUTHERIA.

Liberty—the personification of freedom—was worshipped by the Romans, but here she is only invoked; consequently the mythological value of the passage is to be questioned. See Cicero's *De N.D.*, 2. 23. 61.

LIBURNIAN PORTERS. *Se.*, V, x, 132.

Gifford cites Juvenal's *Satires*, 3. 239-241, to explain the use of Liburnians to bear opulent Romans about in the *lectica*.

LINUS. *Be.*, 27; *Au.*, 421 and footnotes; 425; *F.I.*, 78.

In his footnote on this early poet and singer J. says, *"Linus, Apollinis et Terpsichores filius. Paus."* Pausanias gives the following genealogies: One Linus is the son of Apollo and Psmathe (2. 19. 8); another "Linus the poet" is the son of Amphiaraus and Urania (9. 19. 5). Apparently J. has confused the two, possibly because Vergil in his *Eclog.* (4. 55-57, quoted) says that *"formosus Apollo"* is the father of Linus—and because Urania, like Terpsichore, is a Muse.

LOCUSTA. *Volp.*, III, vi, 245.

Cunningham quotes Upton: "Locusta, an infamous woman skilful in poisoning, who assisted Nero in destroying Britannicus, and Agrippina in poisoning Claudius. In the same sense Juvenal, 1. 71:

> Instituitque rudes melior *Locusta* propinquas."

It may be added that Tacitus in *Annales,* 12. 66; 13. 15, relates the story of Locusta. Therefore, *"Locust* is not the mischievous insect so named," but is a clever allusion to Locusta.

LOLLIA PAULINA. *Volp.,* III, vi, 249.

Upton, Whalley, and Gifford have commented upon J.'s borrowing this passage about the splendour of Lollia Paulina's jewels from Pliny's *N.H.,* 9. 58.

LOVE.

Where Love is mythological, see CUPID.

LUCIFER. *Hy.,* 61, 62.

See HESPERUS.

LUCINA. *For.,* 269.

Lucina is the Latin goddess of childbirth (*Fasti,* 3. 255-258; Horace's *Carmen Saeculare,* 13-20), as Eileithyia is the Greek (see JUNO). Catullus, 34. 13-16, identifies Lucina with Juno, Trivia, and Luna, and Ovid at *Fasti,* 6. 39, 40, offers a second explanation for Lucina, implying that the word is derived from *luces,* which can be translated by the word "days."

LUCRECE. *Po.,* IV, i, 445; *Ca.,* II, i, 228.

See LAIS.

LYAEUS. *Po.,* III, i, 407; *Ob.,* 171 and footnote; *Und.,* 419.

See BACCHUS.

LYCAEUM. *P.A.,* 46; 49.

Pan is connected with two Arcadian mounts—Lycaeus and Maenalus—by Theocritus, 1. 123, 124, and Vergil (*Geor.,* 1. 16, 17).

LYNCEUS. *E.M.O.,* IV, iv, 134; *Se.,* IV, v, 107; *B.F.,* II, i, 380.

Lynceus was an Argonaut reputed to be keen-sighted (Apollonius Rhodius' *Argo.,* 1. 151-155; Pindar's *Nemean,*

10. 60-64). J. writes in *B.F.*: "Fain would I meet the Linceus now, that eagle's eye, that piercing Epidaurian serpent (as my Quintus Horace calls him)." Horace mentions Lynceus in *Satires*, 1. 2. 90, 91; *Epistles*, 1. 1. 27, 28; and he speaks of the sharpness of vision of the eagle and the Epidaurian serpent at *Satires*, 1. 3. 26, 27. Aesculapius, moreover, took upon himself the form of a serpent when he travelled from Epidaurus to relieve Latium of a plague (*Met.*, 15. 641-744; Valerius Maximus, 1. 8. 2; Pausanias, 3. 23. 6, 7; Livy's *Summary*, 11).

MACARIA. *F.I.*, 76; 77; 78.
　See FORTUNATE ISLES.

MACHAON. *M.L.*, V, v, 102.
　See AESCULAPIUS.

MAENALUS. *P.A.*, 49.
　See LYCAEUS.

MAIA. *C.R.*, V, ii, 338; *K.J.E.*, 428-431; *Pen.*, 460-464; *J. and A.*, 477-481; *Epi.*, 208.
　Maia and Zeus are the parents of Mercury born on Cyllene, as report *H.H. to Hermes*, 4. 1-12; *Theogony*, 938, 939; *Fasti*, 5. 85-88; Apollodorus, 3. 10. 2; and others. The fact that May, the month of flowers, is named after Maia (*Fasti*, 5. 103) may explain the *Epi.* passage. For *K.J.E.*, see ELECTRA.

MARS.
　At *Po.*, IV, iii, 454, Mars is said to be the son of Juno, *q.v.*, and he is frequently mentioned as the lover of Venus, *q.v.* He is the father of Cupid, *q.v.*, of Penthesilea, *q.v.*, and of Romulus and Remus, *q.v.* His attempt to arouse Juno against Jupiter (*Po.*, IV, iii, 454) reflects the rebuke which Jove administers to him at *Il.*, 5. 888-895. Classically Mars is the bloody god of war (*e.g.*, Hesiod's *Shield*, 191-196; *Il.*,

5. 889-893; *Fasti,* 3. 12), and his weapon—a spear or a sword—is often alluded to (*e.g., Il.,* 5. 594, 595; *Fasti,* 3. 85, 86). J. so introduces Mars at *Ca.,* I, i, 193; *Se.,* IV, v, 102; *K.J.E.,* 418; 424; *Be.,* 24; *Ba.,* 81, 82; *Henry's Ba.,* 154, 155; 157; *Ob.,* 170; *Tilt,* 216; *P.A.,* 42. Cupid's charge at *C.R.,* I, i, 215, that Mercury stole Mars' sword is found in Lucian's *Gods,* 7.

Allusions to "great father Mars" (*Ca.,* II, i, 232; V, i, 308) result from his being taken as the father and protector of Rome (*Fasti,* 3. 71-85). At *Ob.,* 170 and footnote, J. mentions the beauty of Mars before "his armour rung"; "he was then lovely, as being not yet stained with blood. . . ." The Greek epithet, χρυσοπήληξ Ἄρης, in this footnote occurs in Aeschylus' *Seven against Thebes,* 106; J. construes it *"quasi aureum flagellum (vel rectius auream galeam) habens."* The second supposition, of course, is correct. *Cf.* Seneca's *Medea,* 63, 64.

At *K.J.E.,* 421-426 and footnotes, occurs the description of the Flamen Martialis in "a long crimson robe to witness his nobility, his tippet and sleeves white, as reflecting on purity in his religion, a rich mantle of gold with a train to express the dignity of his function. Upon his head a hat of delicate wool, whose top ended in a cone, and was thence called *apex,* according to that of Lucan, lib. I, [604] *Attolensque apicem generoso vertice flamen.* This apex was covered with a fine set of yarn, which they named apiculum, and was sustained with a bowed twig of pomegranate tree; it was also in the hot time of summer to be bound with ribands, and thrown behind them, as Scaliger teacheth. In his hand he bore a golden censer with perfume, and censing about the altar, (having first kindled his fire on the top,) . . . ."

J. supports this quotation in his footnotes: The Flamen is "one of the three Flamines that, as some think, Numa Pompilius instituted; but we rather, with Varro, take him of Romulus's institution, whereof there were only two, he, and Dialis; to whom he was next in dignity. He was always created out of the nobility, and did perform the rites of Mars, who was thought the father of Romulus." Here J. is mistaken, for Varro, (7. 45), makes Numa the originator of *all* Flamines. For the wool in the Flamen's hat, J. instances *"Scaliger in conject. in Var.* saith, *Totus pileus, vel potius velamenta, flammeum dicebatur, unde flamines dicti."* This passage will probably be found in Scaliger's *Coniectanea* to Varro's *De Lingua Latina* at 5. 84 (inaccessible). Varro (5. 84, not 4., as J., imperfectly quoting, says) also speaks of the yarn: *"Flamines, quod in Latio capite velato erant semper, ac caput cinctum habebant filo, flamines dicti."* The pomegranate tree in the Flamen's "attire was called *Stroppus,* in their wives' *Inarculum,"* J. says. His source, which he does not reveal, probably is Scaliger, *l.c.* See also the comment of Pliny (*N.H.,* 21. 2. 2), Festus on *"albogalerus"* and *"inarculum,"* and Gellius, 10. 15. The ribands are from Scaliger, *ibid.,* J. says, quoting at some length.

The Flamen tells the Genius of the City that he has been awakened by "the present tumult of this day"—"the Ides of March" and the feast "of Anna styled Parenna, Mars' guest." See ANNA PARENNA. The Genius, in dismissing the Flamen and his rites, refers to his use of "masculine gums" in the sacrifice to the god, and J. quotes Vergil's *Eclog.,* 8. (65), Arnobius, 7. (28), and Pliny's *N.H.,* 12. 14. (61). He cites, moreover, 34. 11. (26) in Pliny. Commenting upon Romulus' assigning the first month of the year to Mars, J. says: *"Varr. Fest. in frag. Martius. . . ."* See Varro, (6. 33) and Festus, *l.c.* He likewise quotes *Fasti,* 3. (75-77), and cites Macrobius' *Saturnalia,* 1. 12. (5) and *"Solin. in Polyhist. cap. 3:'Quod hoc mense mercedes exsolverint magistris, quas completas annus deberi fecisse, &c.'";* the only passage in Solinus which J. could have had in mind, however, seems to be chap. 1, p. 3: *"Romani initio annum decem mensibus computaverunt a Martio auspicantes. . . ."*

J. also introduces a footnote on "Salian rites" (*Au.,* 423), saying in part: *"Salius ὑμνωδὸς, vet. gloss. et Pacuv.* Pro imperio sic Salisubsulus vestro excubet Mars. *et Virg. AEneid.* lib. viii." Pacuvius' *Fragments,* however, yield no information, but J. quotes *Aen.,* 8. (285, 286).

No source has been located in the classics for Mars' fondness for drink (*Po.,* IV, iii, 454-456), or for his interest in Ganymede (*l.c.*). His field, in which Jason, *q.v.,* found the golden fleece, is mentioned by Apollonius Rhodius in *Argo.,* 2. 1268, 1269; 4. 162-166; Apollodorus, 1. 9. 16; and *Met.,* 7. 101. Another field of Mars—probably Campus Martius—is the setting for *Ca.,* III, i. No sources are known for the "rosin of Mars" (*M.V.,* 239) or for Mars giving Vulcan a lantern for a crown (*Und.,* 400). Astronomical and chiromantic allusions are *S.S.,* III, ii, 281, and *Canaan,* 348; and *G.M.,* 375, respectively. Oaths occur at *Po.,* III, i, 424; *Se.,* V, v, 125; and *Ca.,* I, i, 200. General allusions to Mars are *Se.,* V, x, 143, and *Ca.,* IV, v, 300.

MEDEA. *Epic.,* IV, i, 413; *Al.,* II, i, 48, 49; *Qu.,* 111 footnote; 120 footnote; 122 footnote; 126 footnote; 127 footnote; *M.V.,* 236.

The story of Medea's assistance to Jason, *q.v.,* has been told. Specifically, her magic preparation is mentioned by Apollonius Rhodius at *Argo.,* 3. 844-868; Apollodorus, 1. 9. 23; *Met.,* 7. 98, 99; 149-155. Ovid tells, furthermore, that when Jason returned to his home with Medea as his wife, he besought her to use her magic to lengthen his father's (Aeson's, *q.v.*) life (*Met.,* 7. 159-293). To this episode J. alludes in the footnote to *Qu.,* 111, where he quotes *Met.,* 7. (243-245), and to *Qu.,* 122, where he gives attention to Medea's boast of her power (*Met.,* 7. 192-249). He also recalls the contents of her potion, quoting *Met.,* 7. (269), at *Qu.,* 120 footnote. That J., moreover, was familiar with Seneca's *Medea* is shown by his notes to *Qu.,* 126 and 127 on *"ramus . . . tristis"* (804, 805) and on *"sacro . . . cultro"* (805-808). Medea's kettle (*M.V.*) is dwelt upon at *Met.,* 7. 262, 263.

MEDUSA. *Epic.,* III, ii, 404; *Ca.,* V, vi, 333; *Canaan,* 347. See GORGON.

MEGAERA. *Qu.,* 122 footnote. See FURIES.

MELPOMENE. *Po.,* IV, i, 446; *Ca.,* IV, iv, 365.

Melpomene is not characterized. Her name is used here to denote attractiveness; no hint is given that she is one of the Muses. See *Theogony,* 75-77; 915-917. Cf. MUSES (Tragic).

MEMNON. *S.N.,* III, i, 238.

"They'll sing like Memnon's statute, and be vocal" recalls the famous statue of Memnon at Thebes which daily at sunrise made a "sound one could best liken to that of a harp or lyre when a string has been broken" (Pausanias, 1. 42. 3; Pliny's *N.H.,* 36. 7. 11; Philostratus' *Apollonius,* 6. 5. 208).

MENELAUS. *Po.,* IV, i, 445; *Volp.,* I, i, 171-173.

Menelaus, in *Po.,* is suggested as a husband; *cf. e.g.,* Hesiod's *Catalogues of Women,* 67; Apollodorus, 2. 16. For *Volp.,* see AETHALIDES.

MERCURY.

Mercury is the son of Zeus and Maia at *C.R.,* V, ii, 338; *Pen.,* 460-462; 464; *J. and A.,* 477-481; *Und.,* 335; see MAIA. For the *C.R.* allusions to him as Cynthia's brother, see DIANA. Likewise he is the brother of the Muses (*For.,* 261), Jove being their father; see *Theogony,* 53-55, and Cicero's *De N.D.,* 3. 21. Cupid's "cousin Mercury" (*C.R.,* I, i, 216) indicates nothing more than that they were related;

Mars or Vulcan—whichever is Cupid's father (see CUPID)
—are both sons of Jove. Aethalides, *q.v.*, is a son of Mercury (*Volp.*, I, i, 171), and Pan is another (see PAN). For
P.R., 305, 306, where Mercury calls Atlas his grandfather,
and crowns him, see ATLAS.

As the messenger or herald of the gods, especially of Jupiter, Mercury is introduced at *C.R.*, I, i, 216; 220; *Po.*, IV,
i, 450; IV, iii, 452; 453; 459; *Se.*, V, iii, 116; *B.F.*, IV, ii,
453; *J. and A.*, 477-481; and *Chl.*, 98. This is his rôle in the
classics (*e.g.*, *Od.*, 5. 28-148; *Aen.*, 1. 297-304; 4. 222-278;
Met., 1. 668-721). In performing his duty as herald Mercury
is conveyed by winged sandals (*M.V.*, 238; *Qu.*, 131) as at
Aen., 1. 297-304; 4. 223; 259; *Met.*, 4. 756; 11. 312. Usually
he wears his petasus (*C.R.*, V, iii, 344; *For.*, 261) as at *Met.*,
1. 672, and carries his caduceus, which, at *Lethe*, 274, is
golden, as at *Od.*, 5. 87; Apollodorus, 3. 10. 2. At *C.R.*, V,
ii, 335, the caduceus is "your peaceful rod," as at Diodorus,
5. 75; *cf. Fasti*, 5. 665, 666. Again at *C.R.*, I, i, 218; *Lethe*,
277; and *L.T.*, 92, the caduceus is described as "snaky";
this, it seems, has precedent, in Martial's *Epigrams*, 7. 74,
and in tradition. The caduceus is named without qualification
at *C.R.*, V, ii, 336; *Po.*, IV, iii, 452; *J. and A.*, 477-481;
and *M.V.*, 238. Mercury's sword at *Qu.*, 131, is mentioned
by Ovid (*Met.*, 1. 717-719).

J.'s characterization of Mercury is definitely based upon
Lucian. Thus Cupid, accusing Mercury of being a thief,
says: "You did never steal Mars his sword out of the sheath,
you! nor Neptune's trident! nor Apollo's bow!" (*C.R.*, I, i,
216). Again, Mercury, threatening Cupid, says: "You have
forgot since I took your heels up into air, on the very hour
I was born, in sight of all the bench of deities, when the
silver roof of the Olympian palace rung again with applause
of the fact." And Cupid replies: "O no, I remember it freshly,
and by a particular instance; for my mother Venus, at the
same time, but stoop'd to embrace you, and, to speak by

metaphor, you borrowed a girdle of her's, as you did Jove's sceptre while he was laughing; and would have done his thunder too, but that 'twas too hot for your itching fingers. . . . I heard you but look'd in at Vulcan's forge the other day, and entreated a pair of his new tongs along with you for company" (*C.R.*, I, i, 218). These passages amount to a free translation of Lucian's *Gods, 7.*

Continuing to taunt Mercury, Cupid says: "What are you any more than my uncle Jove's pander? a lacquey that runs on errands for him, and can whisper a light message to a loose wench with some round volubility? wait mannerly at table with a trencher, warble upon a crowd a little, and fill out nectar when Ganymede's away? one that sweeps the gods' drinking-room every morning, and sets the cushions in order again, which they threw one at another's head over night; can brush the carpets, call the stools again to their places, play the crier of the court with an audible voice, and take state of a president upon you at wrestlings, pleadings, negotiations, &c. . . . You have the marshalling of all the ghosts too that pass the Stygian ferry" (*C.R.*, I, i, 216, 217). Lucian makes this passage (*Gods, 24*) a complaint of Mercury to his mother Maia against the severity of his lot.

Osgood comments at length upon Hermes' dancing with the Dryades at *Comus, 959,* and suggests as possible, although not specific sources, *H.H. to Aphrodite,* 5. 262; Aristophanes' *Themophoriazusae, 977;* Aristides' "vol. 2, p. 708, ed. Dindorf"; and *H.H. to Hermes,* 18. To these sources it may be well to add that Milton or J.—who states Pan's superiority in leading "the Naiads and Dryads forth" over Hermes at *P.A.,* 46—may have had in mind *H.H. to Pan,* 19. 2-31, where the poet writes of Pan: "Through wooded glades he wanders with dancing nymphs who foot it on sheer cliff's edge. . . . Only at evening, as he returns from the chase, he sounds his note, playing sweet and low on his pipes of reed. . . . At that hour the clear-voiced nymphs are with him and move with nimble feet, singing by some spring of dark water. . . . They sing of the blessed gods and high Olympus and choose to tell of such an one as luck-bringing Hermes above the rest, how he is the swift messenger of all the gods, and how he came to Arcadia, the land of many springs and mother of flocks, there where his sacred place is as god of Cyllene."

J., moreover, associates Mercury with Apollo and the Muses at *N.T.*, 33; *For.*, 250; *Und.*, 319; 335, and alludes to him as the god of wit and eloquence at *C.R.*, II, i, 237; V, ii, 335; *Po.*, IV, i, 450; IV, iii, 456-458; *Volp.*, IV, ii, 272, 273; *Ob.*, 170; *Tilt*, 218; *Lethe*, 278; *For.*, 261; *Epi.*, 236. The *H.H. to Hermes*, 4, states several times the friendship of Hermes and Apollo, as at 496-512; 574-576. Mercury's invention of the lyre (*For.*, 250) from a tortoise which he picked up as he was setting out to steal Apollo's cattle is further cause of his being associated with the Muses; on the lyre see *H.H. to Hermes*, 4. 22-54; 496-502; Apollodorus, 3. 10. 2; *Fasti*, 5. 667; and others. His theft of Apollo's herd won for Mercury before he was a day old the title of thief (*H.H. to Hermes*, 4. 17-408; *Met.*, 2. 676-707; and others); J. cites his dishonesty at *E.M.O.*, I, i, 35; *C.R.*, IV, i, 284; and *For.*, 261. From this undertaking Mercury also derives his reputation as a trickster, as at *C.R.*, IV, i, 303. He is likewise the god responsible for the escorting of the dead to Hades (*C.R.*, I, i, 217; V, ii, 336, 337; *Lethe*, 274-279). For his right to this office see *H.H. to Hermes*, 4. 570-573, and *Od.*, 24. 1-14; but the source given under CHARON is more likely.

Chiromantic and astronomical allusions to Mercury are *Al.*, I, i, 39, 40; *S.S.*, III, ii, 281; *G.M.*, 365; humorous allusions confusing the mythological with the chemical or cosmetic meaning of the word are *C.R.*, I, i, 216; IV, i, 303; *Po.*, IV, i, 450; *Se.*, V, iii, 116; *Al.*, I, i, 39, 40; II, i, 79, 80; *M.V.*, 233-240; and *Epi.*, 236. "Hermes Trismegistus"

(*N.T.*, 25; *F.I.*, 70; 74) is the Greek name for Thoth, an Egyptian god, and "Mercurius Britannicus" (*S.N.*, I, ii, 176) according to Gifford is the pseudonym of a journalist of J.'s times. General allusions to Mercury are *C.R.*, I, i, 217; 219; II, i, 237; V, i, 304; 305; V, iii, 346-348; 350, 351; Palinode, 357-359; *Po.*, III, i, 411; *Se.*, V, x, 143; *Ca.*, IV, v, 289, 290; *Pen.*, 468; *Tilt*, 214; *P.R.*, 307; 310; and *M.O.*, 53. See also CYLLENIUS.

MEROPE. *K.J.E.*, 428-431.
　　See ELECTRA.

MEZENTIUS. *Qu.*, 139.
　　In his essay upon *Qu.*, where he has brought together twelve queens of fable and history, his own "Bel-anna" being the last, J. says: *"How can I bring together persons of so different ages, to appear properly together? or why (which is more unnatural) with Virgil's Mezentius, I join the living with the dead?"* Vergil (*Aen.*, 8. 481-488) relates that King Mezentius executed his people by making the living embrace the dead until they expired.

MIDAS. *C.R.*, V, iii, 356; *Al.*, II, i, 49; *Und.*, 394.
　　Midas received from Bacchus the gift that he requested—that whatever his body might touch would be turned to gold. This, of course, immediately became a torment, and the god allowed Midas to bathe himself in the river Pactolus and to leave in it his golden gift (*Met.*, 11. 85-145; Hyginus' *L.F.*, 191). J. curiously digresses from these sources, however, when he writes in *C.R.*:

> And, after penance thus perform'd, you pass
> In like set order, not as Midas did,
> To wash his gold off into Tagus' stream;
> But to the well of knowledge, Helicon.

He seemingly has confused Pactolus with Tagus, another river with golden sands mentioned by Ovid at *Met.*, 2. 251.

MINERVA.

Minerva or Pallas, according to Apollodorus, 1. 3. 6, originated after Zeus had swallowed Metis: "When the time came for the birth to take place, Prometheus or, as others say, Hephaestus, smote the head of Zeus with an axe, and Athena, fully armed, leaped up from the top of his head. ..." Pindar (*Ol.,* 7. 34-38) and Lucian (*Gods,* 8) agree with J. that Vulcan performed this service for Jove, which J. refers to at *Po.,* V, i, 489 ("the issue of thy brain"); *Ca.,* V, vi, 333; *G.A.R.,* 250; *For.,* 261 ("mankind maid"); *Und.* 369; 400. Twice (*Und.,* 400 and 404) J. recalls Vulcan's desire to wed Minerva—a story oft repeated by mythologists (*e.g.,* Apollodorus, 3. 14. 6; Hyginus' *L.F.,* 166; *De A.,* 2. 13; Lucian's *Gods,* 8). Minerva's beauty is attested by her contesting with Venus and Juno; see VENUS. For Cupid's fearing to shoot Minerva (*Hue,* 93 and footnote), see CUPID. Minerva's shield, which she used in quelling the rebellion of the giants (*Ca.,* V, vi, 333; *G.A.R.,* 248, 249; 251; *Qu.,* 131), is discussed under GIANTS and GORGONS, and her weaving (*V.D.,* 291 (see FAVONIUS); *N.T.,* 36; *F.I.,* 80; *Epi.,* 198) under ARACHNE.

Minerva's association with Apollo and the Muses (*E.M.O.,* Stage, 14; *C.R.,* V, iii, 341, 342; *Po.,* III, i, 408; *N.T.,* 28; *Und.,* 378; 434) is scarcely classic; probably it is derived from her being a patroness, in her own right, of wisdom and the arts, in which she even was considered a creator or inventor (*e.g.,* Pindar's *Pythian,* 12. 6-24; *H.H. to Aphrodite,* 5. 8-15; Pausanias, 8. 36. 5; *Fasti,* 3. 833, 834; Horace's *Art of Poetry,* 385-390). J. likewise presents her as a goddess of wit (*C.R.,* III, iii, 271; *Se.,* I, ii, 30; *G.A.R.,* 251; *Und.,* 302 (this allusion to her eyes recalls the Homeric epithet "flashing-eyed" as at *Il.,* 1. 200; 5. 793; 8. 373; etc.); 327; 404). At *Au.,* 425, "Minerva's hearnshaw and her owl" are mentioned, and in an accompanying footnote J. cites *Il.,*

10. (274), adding that these are sacred to Minerva; he also speaks of the owl at *Und.*, 327. "Pallas' plumed cask" (*Epi.*, 208) seems to be referred to only by Lucian in *Gods,* 20; at *Il.*, 5. 745-747, her helmet is not plumed. For Pallas in *G.A.R.*, 247-254, see GOLDEN AGE. General allusions to her are *E.M.O.*, II, i, 52 (oath); *C.R.*, I, i, 31; *Po.*, IV, i, 443; *Se.*, V, x, 143; and *G.M.*, 379 (Gifford's footnote).

MINOS. *Po.*, III, i, 413, 414; *Epi.*, 239; *Canaan,* 348, 349.
   See AEACUS.

MINOTAUR. *C.R.*, I, i, 225; *Po.*, III, i, 428.
   The Minotaur, offspring of the enamoured Pasiphaë and a bull, "had the face of a bull, but the rest of him was human" (Apollodorus, 3. 1. 4; Plutarch's "Theseus," 15. 2; Diodorus, 4. 77; Hyginus' *L.F.*, 40; *Met.*, 8. 131-133; 155, 156).

MIRA. *Und.*, 36-38.
   Pan has no sister named Mira in mythology.

MITHRA. *K.J.E.*, 429 and footnote.
   See ELECTRA.

MOMUS. *Po.*, IV, iii, 452-458.
   J. presents Momus, "the god of reprehension," very much as does Lucian in *Hermotimus,* 20. Hesiod (*Theogony,* 214) is the first to name this deity.

MOON. *Hue.*, 93 and footnote; *Ob.*, 175; *N.N.W.*, 342.
   See ENDYMION for these citations, which seem to be the only mythological allusions to the moon in J.

MORNING.
   See AURORA.

MULCIBER. *M.V.*, 238.
   See VULCAN.

MUSAEUS. *Po.,* V, i, 502.

Here Vergil recommends the reading of Musaeus. See *Aen.,* 6. 666-676, but especially 669: *"optime vates."* Servius on *Aen.,* 6. 667, discusses Musaeus.

MUSES.

The reader of J.'s works must realize that very frequently the meaning of the word "Muse" is either "poetic inspiration" or simply "poet." This is strikingly brought out when J. writes to the memory of Lady Venetia Digby:

> 'Twere time that I dy'd too, now she is dead,
> Who was my Muse, and life of all I said;
> The spirit that I wrote with, and conceiv'd:
> All that was good or great in me, she weav'd,
> And set it forth; the rest were cobwebs fine,
> Spun out in name of some of the old Nine (*Und.,* 58).

J. also specifies that there are Nine Muses at *Christmas,* 270, and *Und.,* 354; and at *Und.,* 442-444, he names them as Hesiod does at *Theogony,* 77-79. Because Mercury is their brother (*For.,* 261), Jove must be their father; see MERCURY. See also MELPOMENE.

Hesiod likewise associates the Muses with Mount Helicon and says that they dance "in the Horse's Spring" (*Theogony,* 1, 2; 6). Similarly J. uses Helicon and Hippocrene at *E.M.O.,* II, i, 63; *C.R.,* I, i, 227; V, iii, 355; Palinode, 359; *Po.,* I, i, 374; 377; V, i, 486; *S.N.,* II, i, 204; IV, i, 251, 252; *S.S.,* Prologue, 235; *N.T.,* 25; *Epi.,* 186; *Und.,* 368; 378; 379; 396; 419; 73; *Ode,* 354. Ovid (*Met.,* 5. 254) and Pausanias, 9. 29. 1, are examples of others who follow Hesiod. The name "Hippocrene" is derived from the fact that the winged horse, Pegasus, striking the ground with his hoof, caused water to flow on Helicon—as Strabo, 8, 6. 21; Ovid (*Met.,* 5. 251-264); and Statius (*Silvae,* 2. 2. 36) relate. See citations under PEGASUS.

The concept of the "poet's horse" (*Und.*, 396; 73) is also referred to the story of Pegasus, but Osgood, following Pauly's *Real-Encyc.*, 5. 1275, points to Boiardo's *Orlando Innamorato* for the source of this notion. "Thespia" (see THESPIA), a town on the slopes of Helicon, is associated with the Muses, and "the Aonian springs" (*Und.*, 368) allude to Hippocrene; *cf. Geor.*, 3. 11: *"Aonia . . . vertice."* Hesiod (*Theogony,* 53, 54) says the Muses were born in Pieria (*Po.*, V, i, 472), and Vergil (*Culex,* 15-19) unites them not only with Pieria, but with Parnassus (*Po.*, III, i, 437; 439; *Und.*, 378) and with Castalia (*Po.*, III, i, 408). For the numerous instances where Apollo is associated with the Muses, for their singing, and for their companionship with the Graces, see APOLLO (first four paragraphs). See also MINERVA.

"The Muses priests" (*Po.*, V, i, 488; *L.F.*, 190-196 and footnote; and *For.*, 276), the "mad Thespian girls" (*E.M.I.*, III, i, 61; *Hue*, 93), and "those dull girls" (*Und.*, 73) do not seem to be mythological. J.'s references to the Comic and Tragic Muses (*Po.*, Apol. Dialogue, 520; *Epi.*, 234) give no names, and if the passages are mythological, they should be taken as evidence of J.'s familiarity with the offices of Thalia and Melpomene as expressed, *e.g.*, in some verses which have occasionally been ascribed to Vergil and have even been printed in his works: *"Melpomene tragico proclamat moesta boatu"* and *"Comica lasciva gaudet sermone Thalia."*

From what source J. received the idea of the Muses' gardens (*Se.*, To the Reader, 6) is uncertain; it may be an original description of the work of poets, or it may have been inspired by some passing description as, *e.g., Met.*, 5. 265, 266:

> *silvarum lucos circumspicit antiquarum*
> *antraque et innumeris distinctas floribus herbas.*

Or perhaps Pausanias, 9. 28 entire, is responsible for the concept. General allusions to the Muses are *E.M.I.*, I, iii, 34; *E.M.O.*, III, iii, 122 (oath); *Po.*, I, i, 389, 390; *Volp.*, Dedication, 160; *Bl.*, 14; *Hy.*, 46 footnote; *L.F.*, 190-196; *T.V.*, 6; *N.T.*, 28; 33; *L.T.*, 90; *Epi.*, 158; 197; *For.*, 244; 268; *Und.*, 320 (no explanation for the Muses' anvil); 334; 432; 38 (Phrygian harp reflects J.'s knowledge that the music of the Greeks came in part from Phrygia).

NAIADS. *P.A.*, 46; *Chl.*, 97, 98.
See NYMPHS.

NARCISSUS. *C.R.*, I, i, 220-222; *Ob.*, 168.
See ECHO.

NATURE.

The mythological value of allusions to Nature in J.'s works seems problematical. Ovid, after describing *"naturae vultus"* in the chaotic stage, continues:

> *Hanc deus et melior litem natura diremit.*
> *Met.*, 1. 5-21.

The *Orphica (Natura, 9)* makes Nature the parent of all that has been created. Cicero, without personifying Nature, makes it the generative power of the universe and comments upon how excellent its actions are (*De N.D.*, 2. 22. 57), following Zeno's teaching (Diog. Laertius, 7. 148); he likewise thinks of it "as the sustaining and governing principle of the world" (*De N.D.*, 2. 32. 82). With this Diogenes (*l.c.*) agrees, saying that Nature is "that which holds the world together, sometimes that which causes terrestrial things to spring up. Nature is defined as a force moving of itself, producing and preserving in being its offspring in accordance with seminal principles within definite periods, and effecting results homogeneous with their sources." Diogenes adds a remark about the antipathy of Nature and human craftsmanship, as do Cicero (*ibid.*, 1. 33. 92) and Ovid

(*Met.*, 3. 158, 159). The notion of the creative activity of
the earth is related to that of Nature; cf. *Met.*, 1. 416-437;
De N.D., 2. 33. 83.

J. frequently voices a reflection of some of the above concepts. At *Ca.*, III, i, 241, and *Qu.*, 127, he seems to follow
Ovid in declaring the opposition existing between Nature
and Chaos. From this the idea that Nature is responsible for
motion and for order (*M.V.*, 238-240) seems to flow, as
does also the thought of Nature's power over life (*S.S.*, I,
ii, 248; *D.A.*, IV, i, 110; *T.T.*, II, i, 153; *J. and A.*, 478-481;
M.V., 239; *Lethe*, 275; *V.D.*, 291, 292; *Epi.*, 164; 181;
186; 196; 219; 222; 226; *Und.*, 37; 55). The distinction
between Nature and art—common in Elizabethan literature
—occurs at *Epi.*, II, iii, 374; *S.S.*, III, ii, 283; *C.A.*, IV, iv,
363, 364; *Panegyre*, 437; *Bl.*, 14; *M.V.*, 233, 234; 240;
V.D., 291; *Epi.*, 186; *Und.*, 316; 319, 320; 384; 58, 59. Nature is made dependent upon God at *Und.*, 63; 64; and *M.P.*,
331, 332.

Other allusions to Nature which seem to proceed from the
views held by classic writers, but which do not accord closely
with them are *Ca.*, III, ii, 274; *S.S.*, II, ii, 264; III, ii, 281;
C.A., II, i, 327; IV, iv, 363, 364; *Ba.*, 75; *L.F.*, 194; *Tilt*,
218; *M.V.*, 238-240; *V.D.*, 291, 292; *T.V.*, 17; *N.T.*, 26;
Epi., 208; *For.*, 266; *Und.*, 336; 353; 354; 366; 389; 392;
10; 19; 24; 42; 58, 59. With *M.V.*, 241: "And Nature here
no step-dame, but a mother," cf. Claudian's *R.P.*, 3. 39, 40:

> *se iam, quae genetrix mortalibus ante fuisset,*
> *in dirae subito mores transisse novercae.*

Likewise with *G.A.R.*, 248: "Troubled Nature for her
maker fear'd," cf. Claudian's *Shorter Poems*, 52. 62: "*pro
domino Natura timet.*" It will be recalled that J. in *G.A.R.*
follows Claudian's account of the battle of the giants against
the gods; see GIANTS. The association at *M.V.*, 233; 240,
241; of the Sun and Nature, which is also stated by Ovid

(*Met.,* 1. 416-437), is confirmed by Claudian in *On Stilicho,* 22. 441-443, and when J. recalls the age of Nature and suggests that she is now lamed, his source is probably Claudian, *ibid.,* 431, 432:

> *vultu longaeva decoro*
> *ante fores Natura sedet.*

At *Und.,* 58, 59, J. writes that "sleepy or stupid Nature" would "have lost the Phoenix" if the bird had "been trusted to thee; not to itself assign'd"; but Claudian (*Shorter Poems,* 27. 62, 63) writes of the phoenix:

> *curis Natura laborat,*
> *aeternam ne perdat avem.*

NECESSITY. *N.I.,* I, i, 319; *Qu.,* 104.

The *N.I.* passage reflects the characterization of Necessity as importunate in Sophocles (*Fragments,* 256) and Aeschylus (*Prometheus Bound,* 104). For *Qu.,* see FATES.

NECTAR. *C.R.,* V, ii, 330; *Po.,* 453-458; *S.N.,* IV, i, 253; *N.I.,* II, ii, 346; *K.J.E.,* 414, 415; *Hy.,* 46; *N.T.,* 34; 37; *For.,* 259; *Und.,* 383; *M.P.,* 330.

See AMBROSIA.

NEMESIS. *Po.,* IV, i, 447; *M.P.,* 362.

Po. alludes to the lady celebrated by Tibullus, but *M.P.* recalls the mythological Nemesis, who maintains proportion and moderation among men (*Theogony,* 223; *Met.,* 3. 406; 14. 694).

NEOPTOLEMUS. *Po.,* IV, i, 445.

"Noble Neoptolemus" is praised traditionally for his valour; *cf. Il.,* 19. 327: "godlike Neoptolemus." See also *e.g., Od.,* 11. 505-537.

NEPTUNE. *C.R.,* I, i, 216; *Po.,* IV, iii, 463; *B.F.,* II, i, 397; *Bl.,* 13; 17; *Be.,* 24; 28; *Hue,* 90; *Henry's Ba.,* 159; *N.T.,* 23; 27-29; 33-38; *F.I.,* 76-81; and *L.T.,* 90.

Neptune classically is the ruler of the seas and of islands (*Il.*, 15. 187-193; Plato's *Critias*, 113 C-114 C; Apollodorus, 1. 2. 1). His palace is referred to by Homer (*Il.*, 13. 20-22), and his trident is mentioned at *Il.*, 12. 27, and *Od.*, 5. 291, 292. For the theft of the latter (*C.R.*), see MERCURY; for the effect that Love had on Neptune (*Hue*), see CUPID; for allusions to Venus (*N.T.*, 36; *F.I.*, 80; and *L.T.*, 90), see VENUS; and for Latona (*N.T.*, 28, 29; 33), see DELOS.

The numerous allusions to Albion as a son of Neptune are explained by J.'s footnote to *Bl.*, 13, as "alluding to the right of styling princes after the name of their princedoms: so is he still Albion, and Neptune's son that governs. As also his being dear to Neptune, in being so embraced by him." There is a reflection of *Il.*, 13. 23-38, in the statement that Neptune is "chief in the art of riding" (*N.T.*, 27). Another reference at *N.T.*, 37, to one ship in Neptune's fleet which is a star seems to reflect the fate of the *Argo* (see JASON). There seems to be no classic antecedent for Neptune's marble trident, or for his fearing that Jove would take his palace (*Po.* and *Henry's Ba.*, respectively).

NEREUS. *N.T.*, 38; *F.I.*, 81; *L.T.*, 88.

Hesiod (*Theogony*, 240-264), Homer (*Il.*, 18. 37-49), and Hyginus (*L.F.*, Genealogy) relate that Nereus was the father of fifty daughters, and that he is a sea-god. *Cf.* GLAUCUS and DORIS.

NESTOR. *Volp.*, III, vi, 253; *N.I.*, I, i, 313; 325.

The first *N.I.* passage clearly is an adaptation of *Il.*, 1. 247-252: Nestor "from whose tongue speech flowed sweeter than honey" and "two generations of men had he ere now seen pass away." The second passage touches upon "sage Nestor's counsels," as the tribute of Agamemnon, at *Il.*, 2. 369-374, praises the warrior's wisdom. J.'s inspiration for Nestor's hernia (*Volp.*) is unknown.

NIGHT.

A consideration of J.'s allusions to Night causes one to feel that only occasionally does J. treat the subject mythologically; other instances are but personifications. At *Ca.*, I, i, 191, and at *Und.*, 10, the offspring and the deeds of Night, respectively, are introduced, recalling Hyginus' *L.F.*, Preface, where, among others, Mors, Letum, Miseria, Petulantia, Discordia, Dolor, and Ira are listed as children of Nox, and also recalling Claudian's *Against Rufinus*, 3. 30-38. The suggestion for both Hyginus and Claudian may have been *Theogony*, 211-225.

Passages concerning "winged night" (*Ob.*, 181 ; *Hy.*, 62) may have been inspired by *Aen.*, 8. 369: *"nox ruit et fuscis tellurem amplectitur alis,"* or by other mythological personifications such as Sleep, the child of Night whom, *e.g.*, Tibullus, 2. 1. 87-90, describes: "Now Night is yoking her team; and on their mother's car follow the golden Stars, a capering troupe, while behind comes Sleep the silent, enwrapped in dusky wings, and black Visions of the night with wavering steps." Night's sceptre (*V.D.*, 284; *Und.*, 373) seems to have no precedent in classical literature, but "her chariot bespangled with stars" (*V.D.*) is mentioned in Aeschylus' *Libation-Bearers*, 660: "the car of Night," and in Claudian's *R.P.*, 2. 363: *"stellantes Nox."* References to Night as a black sorceress (*Ba.*, 75) and as humorous (*V.D.*) can scarcely be explained.

NIOBE. *C.R.*, I, i, 223; V, iii, 351, 352; 355, 356; *M.V.*, 242.

Niobe, a Phrygian mother so proud of her fourteen children that she defiantly refused to worship Latona, was atrophied into stone by the goddess after Apollo had slain all of her sons and daughters. In the first *C.R.* allusion J. has appropriately removed the petrified but still weeping Niobe to the fountain of self-love, but all of his other notices of the myth accord with *Met.*, 6. 146-315. See also *Il.*, 24. 602-617, and Apollodorus, 3. 5. 6.

NOCTIFER. *Hy.,* 61, 62.
   See HESPERUS.

NUMA POMPILIUS. *S.N.,* II, i, 196.
   The successor to Romulus as king of Rome was Numa
Pompilius, who ruled wisely and won the love of his sub-
jects. His biography has been written by Plutarch (*Lives,* 2).

NYMPHS. *E.M.O.,* II, i, 55; II, ii, 78; *S.S.,* I, ii, 247; 250;
Pen., 460-468; *Bl.,* 7; 19; *Hue,* 89; *N.T.,* 34; 36; *P.A.,* 41;
46; 48; *F.I.,* 80; *Chl.,* 97, 98; 100-104; *Epi.,* 208; *For.,* 244;
Und., 309; 368; 36-38.
   J. introduces Dryads, Naiades, Oceanides, and Nymphs
without any notable distinction among them, as *P.A.,* 48,
demonstrates:

> If yet, if yet,
> Pan's orgies you will further fit,
> See where the silver-footed fays do sit,
> The nymphs of wood and water;
> Each tree's and fountain's daughter!
> Go take them forth, it will be good
> To see them wave it like a wood,
> And others wind it like a flood.

   The nymphs are companions of Pan especially in *H.H. to
Pan,* 19. 1-26; quotations from this *H.H.* are included under
MERCURY. Homer in *Il.,* 20. 7-9, speaks of the nymphs
"that haunt the fair copses, the springs that feed the rivers,
and the grassy meadows," and in *Od.,* 6. 123, 124, uses practically the same formula. Servius on *Aen.,* 1. 500, may also
be cited for his divisions of the nymphs into their various
groups. The passages in J. associating the nymphs with spring
and with the blossoming of flowers (*Pen., Chl., P.A.*) resemble not a little Horace's *Odes,* 4. 7. 9-13. The imagery
with which J. decks the nymphs at *Chl.* and the epithet "sil-
ver-footed" (*N.T., P.A.*) may be original with J., but *cf.
Geor.,* 4. 334-352. In some passages the term "nymphs" de-

notes simply nymph-like females. In *Hue* it is applied loosely
to the Graces, and in *Bl.* and *Be.* it is in part used to designate
the daughters of the River Niger. The allusion in *S.S.* to
"those treacherous nymphs" who "pull'd in Earine" admits
of no explanation. See also OCEANUS.

OCEANIDES. *Bl.*, 7; 19.
See OCEANUS.

OCEANUS. *Bl.*, 7-17; *L.F.*, 187; *N.T.*, 34-36; *F.I.*, 79, 80;
L.T., 88.

In *Bl.* Oceanus is presented "in a human form, the colour
of his flesh blue; and showered with a robe of sea-green; his
head gray, and horned, as he is described by the ancients: his
beard of the like mixed colour: he was garlanded with alga,
or sea-grass; and in his hand, a trident." For the imagery in-
volved in this presentation, J. is possibly indebted to *Geor.*,
4. 334-352, where the nymph-daughters of Oceanus are likewise colourfully described; he appends a note to justify the
use of the horns: "The ancients induced Oceanus always with
a bull's head . . . ," and quotes Euripides' *Orestes*, (1377-
1379). To this he adds, "And rivers were so called . . . ,"
for which he cites *Geor.*, 4. (371), *Aen.*, 8. (77), Horace's
Odes, 4. 14. (25) and Euripides' *Ion*, (1261). The trident
seems to be a borrowing from the conventional portrayal of
Neptune, *q.v.* At his *Bl.* entry, Oceanus is mounted on a sea-
horse; see TRITONS.

In *L.T.*, J. incorrectly makes Oceanus the husband of
Amphitrite, *q.v.*, but in a footnote at *Bl.*, 7, he makes the
"Oceaniae" the daughters of Oceanus and Thetis, instancing
Theogony, (337; 346-366), *Geor.*, (probably 4. 334-346),
and *Orphica*, (probably 82. 4, was in J.'s mind, although
neither the Oceanides nor Thetis is mentioned). The imagery found in J.'s description of the Oceanides may have
originated in *Geor., l.c.* These nymphs are named at *Bl.*, 19,
and *Theogony*, (346-366), is given as the source; three of

the names listed, however, are found only in *Geor., l.c.,* these being Cydippe, Beroe, and Lycoris as J. spells the words. A fourth, Glauce, is named by Hesiod (*Theogony,* 244) as a Nereid, the daughter of Nereus and Doris; Glauce, therefore, would be the granddaughter of Oceanus, for Doris is among the nymphs said to be his daughters.

Another child of Oceanus in *Bl.,* 9, is Niger, since "all rivers are said to be the son of the Ocean; for, as the ancients thought, out of the vapours exhaled by the heat of the sun, rivers and fountains were begotten." J. adds that Oceanus is so considered in *Orphica,* (82. 4), and in *Il.,* 14. (244-246) where "Oceanus is celebrated *tanquam pater, et origo diis, et rebus, quia nihil sine humectatione nascitur, aut putrescit.*" To confirm his right to emphasize that Niger is separated ordinarily from the ocean, J. instances the fable of Alpheus (probably *Aen.,* 3. 694-696), that of Arethusa (*Eclog.* 10. (4, 5 quoted)), that of Nicander in *Theriaca* (174-176), and that of Plutarch in "Sulla" (20. 4, 5).

"Great Oceanus" (*Bl.,* 13) seems borrowed from *Theogony,* 20, but "divine Ocean" (*Bl.,* 10) cannot be identified. Oceanus' being "the king of streams" (*l.c.*) would seem to be the consequence of his being their father (*e.g., Il.,* 14. 246). Probably for the same reason they feast with him (*N.T.; F.I.*). For the feast of the Sun and Ocean, see APOLLO. The palace of Ocean (*N.T.; F.I.*) resembles *Il.,* 14. 311: "I depart to the house of deep-flowing Oceanus," and Aeschylus' *Prometheus Bound,* 301-304: especially "to quit the stream that bears thy name and the rock-roofed caves thou thyself hast made." *Cf.* TRITONS.

OEDIPUS. *Po.,* III, i, 426; *Se.,* III, i, 63.

The tale of how Oedipus read the riddle of the Sphinx after many had failed is related by Sophocles in *Oedipus Tyrannus,* 390-398, and by Euripides in *Phoenissae,* 45-54. His reward for this success was that he, ignorant of the truth, won his mother as his bride. When he made the dreadful discovery of his relationship, he blinded himself (Sophocles, *ibid.*, 1266-1280; Euripides, *ibid.*, 59-62).

OENONE. *Epi.,* 208.

J.'s "bright Oenone" is "drest in shepherd's tire," and is not further characterized. The story concerning her is related by Conon, 23, Parthenius (*Love Romances,* 4), Apollodorus, 3. 12. 6, and Ovid (*Heroides,* 5).

OLYMPUS. *C.R.,* I, i, 218; *Po.,* IV, iii, 456; *Se.,* V, i, 112, 113.

Olympus "is the abode of the gods that stands fast forever. Neither is it shaken by winds nor ever wet with rain, nor does snow fall upon it, but the air is outspread clear and cloudless, and over it hovers a radiant whiteness. Therein the blessed gods are glad all their days" (*Od.,* 6. 42-46). For *C.R.* details, see MERCURY; for *Po.* details, see JUNO; and for *Se.* details, see ATLAS.

OPS. *Hue,* 93 and footnote.

See ATYS and RHEA, and *cf.* CYBELE.

ORESTES. *E.M.O.,* IV, iv, 140; *Epic.,* IV, ii, 448.

J. introduces Orestes and Pylades as "the two friends." This celebrated companionship is to be found in Euripides' *Electra,* 92-94; 1249; *Orestes,* 1658, 1659; Sophocles' *Electra,* 16, 17; Hyginus' *L.F.,* 119; 122.

ORION. *Satyr,* 449.

The *Satyr* allusion to Orion's horn is mystifying. Ovid (*Fasti,* 5. 493-544) and Hyginus (*L.F.,* 195; *De A.,* 2. 34) —the standard sources of information about Orion—omit any mention of his horn; so also do Vergil, Claudian, and Pindar in incidental references to Orion. Possibly J. has confused the horn with the hunting sword of Orion (*e.g., Met.,* 8. 207; Claudian, 28. 177) or with Vergil's *"armatumque auro"* (*Aen.,* 3. 517).

ORITHYIA. *Be.,* 26 and footnote.

Orithyia is the daughter of Erechtheus, according to
Apollodorus, 3. 15. 1, to Herodotus, 7. 189, to Apollonius
Rhodius' *Argo.,* 1. 212, and to *Met.,* 6. 700, 701. When
Boreas recollects his love for Orithyia, J.'s source could have
been *Met.,* 6. 682-713, but his footnote specifies that she was
"ravished away into Thrace, as she was playing with other
virgins by the flood Ilissus: or (as some will say) by the
fountain Cephisus." Ilissus is the locale specified by Apollodorus, 3. 15. 2, by Plato in *Phaedrus,* 229 B, by Apollonius
in *Argo.,* 1. 211-223, and by Pausanias, 1. 19. 5. Cephisus is
the place designated by Choerilus, according to the scholia on
Apollonius, *ibid.,* 1. 211. See also scholia on *Od.,* 14. 533.
The "Orithya" in *Qu.,* 132 footnote, is more commonly
known as Otrera, *q.v.*

ORPHEUS. *Po.,* IV, i, 447; V, i, 502; *B.F.,* II, i, 396; *Bl.,* 13
footnote; *Be.,* 27; 33; *Au.,* 420; 425; *F.I.,* 78; *Epi.,* 229;
232; *For.,* 272; *Und.,* 327.

Orpheus is the son of Apollo and Calliope according to J.
in *Au.,* and he quotes Vergil's *Eclogues,* 4. (55-57); this
passage, however, fixes only the parentage of Calliope. Apollodorus, 1. 3. 2, names both Apollo and Calliope: "Now Calliope
bore to Oeagrus or, nominally, to Apollo, . . . another son,
Orpheus." Apollonius Rhodius' *Argo.,* 1. 23-25, and Hyginus'
L.F., 14, are among others to name Oeagrus as the father of
Orpheus. So wonderful was the music of Orpheus that he
was able to "move stocks, stones" (*For.*) and to tame beasts
(*B.F.* and *Epi.*)—versions related in Euripides' *Bacchanals,*
561-564; Apollonius, *ibid.,* 1. 26-31; Diodorus, 4. 25; Horace's *Odes,* 1. 12. 7-12; Seneca's *Hercules Oetaeus,* 1031-
1060; *Hercules Furens,* 569-576; Claudian, 31. 1-18; and
others.

OTRERA. *Qu.,* 132 footnote.

J. says that Penthesilea "was the queen of the Amazons, and succeeded Otrera, or (as some will) Orithya." Otrera is named as the mother of Penthesilea by Apollodorus, 5. 1, Tzetzes' *Scholium on Lycophron,* 997, and Hyginus' *L.F.,* 112.

PALAEMON. *L.T.,* 88.

Latin equivalent to Portunus, *q.v.*

PALES. *P.A.,* 47; *Und.,* 36-38.

The Arcadians sing that Pan can lead them "to better pastures than great Pales can." The latter is an Italian masculine deity of shepherds in Arnobius, 3. 40, and in Martianus Capella, 1. 50, and a feminine deity in Tibullus, 1. 1. 36; Festus, *"Pales"*; Vergil's *Eclogues,* 5. 35; etc.; Ovid's *Fasti,* 4. 721-782, where she is described at length. J.'s "great Pales" is Vergil's *"magna Pales"* (*Geor.,* 3. 1). The latter also rhapsodizes in the idyllic manner about the benefits which Pales confers on shepherds at *Culex,* 76-78.

PALLAS.

See MINERVA.

PAN. *S.S.,* II, i, 259, 260; *Satyr,* 441-445; *Pen.,* 464-468; *Ob.,* 170 and footnote; 173; *P.A.,* 41-43; 46, 47; 49; *For.,* 244; 250; *Und.,* 36-38.

In *Pen.* Mercury acknowledges Pan as his son begotten when Mercury, in the guise of a goat, courted Penelope. For this version, the *Ob.* footnote cites *H.H. to Pan,* (19. 34), but in this account not Penelope but Dryope bears Pan; it also cites Lucian's *Gods,* 22. (2), where J.'s details are paralleled. The same *H.H.* is the basis for J.'s characterization of the god— his "goat's feet and two horns," "his uncouth face and full beard," and his being "a noisy, merry-laughing child" (*H.H.,* 19. 2; 35-39). Similarly for Pan's musical ability, see the same *H.H.,* 14-18, and APOLLO; for his dancing with the

Naiads and Dryads, see *H.H.*, 22-24, and the quotation under MERCURY; for his hunting ability, see *H.H.*, 12-14, and SYLVANUS; and for his concern for shepherds, see *H.H.*, 5-11, and PALES, and *cf.* his traditional character (*e.g.*, Theocritus, 5. 58; 141; *Eclogues, 2.* 33: *"Pan curat ovis oviumque magistros"*). For Pan's dancing about "the fount of laughter, or Bacchus' spring," *cf.* Callistratus, 8. 20, and *Eclogues,* 5. 58, 59. Pan's mountains are Maenalus and Lycaeum, *q.v.* "Great Pan" suggests *O.H.*, 10. 1: "mighty Pan." For the Arcadians' yearly rites to Pan, see ARCADIA. The description of Pan in the *Ob.* footnote, *"Hilaris et albus, nitens Cyllenius alis,"* and its Greek epithets, χαριδοτὴς, φαῖδρος, καὶ λευκὸς are not found in the usual compilations of such terms. Pan's priests and his goat that leads the herds apparently have no mythological value. See SYRINX.

PANCHIA. *P.A.,* 42.

Panchia, an island east of Arabia, is described by Ovid at *Met.,* 10. 307-310: "Let the land of Panchia be rich in balsam, let it bear its cinnamon, its costum, its frankincense exuding from its trees, its flowers of many sorts, so long as it bears its myrrhtree, too." Claudian, like J., associates Panchia with China at 7. 211, and with the Phoenix at *R.P.,* 2. 81-85.

PANDORA. *Al.,* II, i, 48; *Und.,* 409.

Pandora, after Prometheus had stolen the fire from heaven for the benefit of mankind, was created by Vulcan and other deities at the behest of Jove who wished to revenge himself upon mankind. She was received by Epimetheus, despite Prometheus' warning, and her curiosity prompted her to uncover the "tub" containing all the ills of mankind (Hesiod's *Works,* 54-105; *Theogony,* 570-590).

PANISCI (PANISKS). *Pen.*, 462-464.

The Panisci are Pan's attendants, and associate generally with Satyrs and Sylvans (*e.g., Met.*, 14. 637-639; *Culex*, 115-117).

PARNASSUS. *Po.*, III, i, 437; 439; IV, iv, 463; *S.N.*, IV, i, 258; *K.J.E.*, 415 footnote; *Und.*, 378.

Parnassus, a mountain range in Phocis, was sacred to Apollo and the Muses (*e.g., Met.*, I. 313-317; 11. 165). For *Po.* and *Und.*, *cf.* MUSES. J. says that *K.J.E.* alludes to Luctatius' calling Parnassus *"umbilicum terrae"* (source inaccessible for verification).

PASIPHAË. *Epic.*, III, i, 390.

Pasiphaë, enamoured of a bull, subsequently bore the Minotaur. Although J. refers to *Met.*, (8. 131-137; 9. 736-743), the myth is related more satisfactorily in the other sources under MINOTAUR. Pasiphaë, of course, was Minos' queen.

PEACE. *V.D.*, 290.

Concerning Peace, see EIRENE. Here, however, the allusion to "the opener of the new year" implies the characteristics of Janus, *q.v.*

PEGASUS. *Po.*, I, i, 387; *Epic.*, III, i, 381; *S.N.*, IV, i, 251, 252; *N.I.*, III, ii, 372; *N.T.*, 25; *M.O.*, 53; *For.*, 261; *Und.*, 378; 396; 428; *Verses Placed*, 73.

See MUSES and PERSEUS. The wings of Pegasus (*Po., Und.*) are mentioned by Pindar (*Ol.*, 13. 84-86), Apollodorus, 2. 3. 2, and others.

PENATES. *Pen.*, 451; 460; *J. and A.*, 477-481; *For.*, 247; *Und.*, 52.

The Penates were household gods, as J. describes them, and were closely associated with the Lares, *q.v.* They are prominent at *Aen.*, 3. 146-178, and Cicero alludes to them (*De*

N.D., 2. 27. 68). For their javelins and their attire "after the antique manner" and for "old Penates" (*Und.*) no source has been found. There are usually but two Penates.

PENELOPE. *Po.*, IV, i, 446; *Epic.*, IV, i, 410; *Pen.*, 464-468; *Ob.*, 170 footnote; *Und.*, 423.

The character of Penelope J. emphasizes in two aspects. First, she is the mother of Pan, *q.v.*, and she is said to be the daughter of Icarius. Secondly, she is the comely and virtuous spouse of Ulysses. While he is as dead to her because of his long absence from home, she remains faithful to his parting injunction not to wed until her son became "a bearded man," despite the numerous suitors who sought her hand; this story is related throughout the *Od.* (particularly 1. 234-251; 2. 85-128; 18. 243-280; 24. 120-198). J. specifies Homer in *Und.* The *Epic.* statement that "Penelope herself cannot hold out long" against her suitors may reflect the myth that Ulysses found her unfaithful to him (Pausanias, 8. 12. 5; Servius on *Aen.*, 2. 44; and Tzetzes on *Lycophron, 771, 772*).

PENTHESILEA. *Epic.*, III, ii, 393; *Qu.*, 132 and footnote.
See ACHILLES.

PERSEUS. *Qu.*, 131-135 and 131 footnote; *T.V.*, 19; *Und.*, 428.

Perseus possessed "a brave and masculine virtue," and J. adds that his sources for the *Qu.* passage are Hesiod's *Shield*, (216-237), and Apollodorus, 2. (4. 1-5), the former seeming the more important. If J. intends that Perseus be considered as "of hunters first" (*T.V.*), he must have in mind Perseus' experience in seeking the Gorgon, as Apollodorus, *e.g.*, relates. At *Und.*, where J. writes, "You shew'd like Perseus mounted upon Pegasus," he may have been actuated by any of the following reasons: Lotspeich has indicated that only Boccaccio's *Genealogia,* 10. 27, contains this concept;

perhaps it is J.'s source. Again, he may have taken Spenser as his source; this confusion would not be unlikely, for Hesiod, *l.c.*, describes Perseus as "the horseman," and most accounts (*i.e., Theogony,* 280-286; Apollodorus, *l.c., Met.,* 4. 782-786; Hyginus' *L.F.,* 151) assert that Pegasus sprang from the blood of Medusa after Perseus had killed her. Lastly, perhaps J. has confused Perseus with Bellerophon, whom he also mentions in the *Qu.* footnote, and who did ride Pegasus.

PHAËTON. *Po.,* IV, i, 448; *Bl.,* 11 and footnote; *Canaan,* 349.

In his footnote J. instances *Met.,* 2, where "hare-brained Phaëton" asked to drive the chariot of Phoebus for a day (47, 48), "put the nether lands to rout" (210-306), and caused the complexions of the Æthiops to turn black (235, 236).

PHANTASOS (PHANT'SIE). *V.D.,* 287-293.

J. seems to use Phant'sie loosely to represent all dreams, while Ovid, his probable source, limits Phantasos to inanimate objects: *"in humum saxumque undamque trabemque"* (*Met.,* 11. 642-645).

PHAON. *Und.,* 374.

Phaon, ferrying Aphrodite, received from her, youth and beauty. Sappho, the Aeolian poetess, became enamoured of him, and after he rejected her, she threw herself from the Leucadian Rock. Lucian (*Dead,* 9. 2) gives the first of the legend, and Ovid (*Heroides,* 15) the remainder of it. J.'s immediate source, as Gifford suggests, is Horace (*Odes,* 4. 9. 10-12), but the implication in both Horace and J. that Sappho celebrated Phaon in her songs is believed to be unlikely.

PHLEGETHON. *Epi.,* 233.

Phlegethon is mentioned as one of the infernal rivers (*e.g., Met.,* 5. 543, 544; 15. 532; *Aen.,* 6. 551).

PHLEGRA. *Se.,* V, x, 142.

Phlegra is the scene of the battle between the gods and the giants, *q.v.* It is mentioned by Apollodorus, 1. 6. 1, but Claudian, 52. 4, is probably J.'s source.

PHOEBE. *K.J.E.,* 429; *Satyr,* 449; *Und.,* 373.
See DIANA.

PHOEMONOË. *Au.,* 421 and footnote.

J.'s footnote, stating that *Theogony* is his source for *"Phoemonoë filia Phoebi, quae prima carmen heroicum cecinit,"* is mistaken. Pausanias, 10. 5. 7, mentions Phoemonoë "as being the first prophetess of the god [Apollo], and the first that sang an hexameter verse," and Strabo, 9. 3. 5, makes her the first Pythian priestess.

PHOENIX. *Al.,* IV, i, 115; *N.I.,* I, i, 326; *M.V.,* 236; *P.A.,* 42; *For.,* 265; *Und.,* 26; 58, 59; *M.P.,* 325.

The phoenix, feeling itself about to expire, built its nest in a high palm, and after dissolution, found itself restored for another span of life. When J. alludes to the ashes of the bird, he seemingly follows Claudian, 22. 414-420; 27. 45-71, who says that the sun, in the process of the phoenix's metamorphosis, burns the nest; and also when he alludes to the odorous perfume of the bird, he seems to follow Claudian, 22. 420; 27. 96-100, and *Met.,* 15. 398-400. For *Und.,* 58, 59, see NATURE, where Claudian's influence is further supported. *For.* merely uses the span of the phoenix's life to suggest enduring love. The accounts speak of the bird as masculine, but throw no light on its sexual rarity (*Und.,* 26).

PHOSPHORUS. *Hy.,* 61, 62; 66; *Ob.,* 180, 181; *G.M.,* 367; *Epi.,* 185; 197.

J. introduces Phosphorus as "the herald of day" much as Cicero describes it (see HESPERUS). The *Ob.* passage, however, is like *Met.,* 2. 114, 115, in some respects.

PIETY. *Ca.*, V, vi, 332.

Pietas, the Roman deity of loyalty,

> left the field,
> Grieved for that side, that in so bad a cause
> They knew not what a crime their valour was.

Cf. Seneca's *Octavia*, 160: *"tunc sancta Pietas extulit trepidos gradus."* She also appears on coins, is discussed by Pliny (*N.H.*, 7. 121), and is referred to at *Met.*, 1. 149, and by Claudian, 3. 53; 17. 167, 168.

PIGMIES. *P.R.*, 304, 305; *Wales*, 324.

See ANTAEUS.

PLEASURE. *P.R.*, 302; 303; 305-310; *Wales*, 330.

J. uses the celebrated allegory of the two women, one personifying Pleasure, the other Virtue, as the background for the reconciliation of the two (Xenophon's *Memorabilia*, 2. 1. 21-34).

PLEIADES. *K.J.E.*, 428-430.

See ELECTRA.

PLUTO. *Po.*, III, i, 422; 430; 433; *Ca.*, I, i, 190; *Qu.*, 131; *Chl.*, 98; 99; *Epi.*, 238; *Canaan*, 348.

J.'s allusions to Pluto are scant. He rules the lower world, where he has his palace (*e.g.*, *Theogony*, 767-769; *Works*, 152-154; *Met.*, 4. 434-445). He compelled Proserpine to be his queen (*e.g.*, *Met.*, 5. 385-508; *H.H. to Demeter*, 2. 75-87; *R.P.*, 2. 247-372). "Pluto's Court" in *Canaan* alludes to his judges; see AEACUS. With the suggestion that Love entertained the infernal deities (*Chl.*), *cf.* IXION. "Grisly Pluto" (*Epi.*) and "Pluto's casque" (*Qu.*) are indefinite; the latter may be "the dread cap of Hades," which made the wearer of it invisible; see GORGONS. Olympiodorus, in a commentary on *Gorgias* quoted in the Pausanias published without the translator's name by Priestly in London, 1824, vol. 3, p. 269, says: "And Pluto wears a helmet, on account of the darkness over which he presides. For, as a helmet conceals the head, so Pluto is the power that presides over invisible natures."

PLUTUS. *Case,* V, i, 379; *K.J.E.,* 418 and footnote; *L.R.,* 199, 200.

J. writes in *K.J.E.* that next to Irene or Peace stood Plutus "or Wealth, a little boy, bare-headed, his locks curled, and spangled with gold, of a fresh aspect, his body almost naked, saving some rich robe cast over him; in his arms a heap of gold ingots to express riches, whereof he is the god." The footnote states that this concept of Plutus as youthful was suggested by Cephisodotus in Pausanias, 9. (16. 2): "Nor was the sagacity of Cephisodotus less, who made for the Athenians Peace holding Plutus." Philostratus' *Imagines,* (2. 27. 5), are also cited; here the god is expressly said to have his sight. Contrary to this youthful concept of Plutus, J. continues, is the "blind and deformed" characterization in Aristophanes (*Plutus,* 8-14; 87-92), *Theogony,* (969-974), and Lucian (*Timon,* 26, 27). The youth of Plutus allows J. plausibly to confuse him with Cupid, especially as Philostratus, *l.c.,* specifies the god's wings. Practically all the above sources speak of Plutus as connected with gold.

Po. *Ode,* 357.
Another name for Eridanus. See CYCNUS.

PODALIRIUS. *M.L.,* V, v, 102.
See AESCULAPIUS.

POLEMOS. (POLEMIUS). *K.J.E.,* 405.
This unusual personification of war has precedent at least in Pindar's *Fragments,* 78. 1.

POLLUX. *Po.,* Apol. Dia., 508; *Se.,* IV, v, 106; *Ca.,* II, i, 228; *N.I.,* I, i, 313; *T.V.,* 19; *N.T.,* 37; *Epi.,* 235.
See DIOSCURI.

Polyphemus. *Ob.,* 174 and footnote; *Epi.,* 236.
  See CYCLOPES, and *cf.* GALATEA.

Poppea. *Al.,* IV, i, 119.
  "Nero's Poppea," his mistress, persuaded him to matricide
and uxoricide so that she might become his queen after he
had ordered her husband to govern Lusitania (Suetonius'
Nero, 35; and Seneca's *Octavia, passim*).

Portunus. *N.T.,* 33-38; *F.I.,* 77-81. See also PALAE-
MON.
  Portunus, or Palaemon, is introduced only as a sea-god
whose function is to guard the ports (Apollodorus, 3. 4. 3;
Met., 4. 519-542; *Fasti,* 6. 493-502; 546, 547; Servius on
Aen., 5. 241; Hyginus' *L.F.,* 2; Pausanias, 1. 42. 6; 1. 44. 7,
8; and others). Only Servius and Ovid's *Fasti* mention the
care that Portunus has over harbours—an honour that came
to him after his mother Ino had leaped, with him in her arms,
into the sea to escape the insane rage of his father. (Semele,
inspired by jealous Juno, had asked Jove to appear to her as
he appeared in his majestic splendour to Juno, but the vision
was too dazzling for her eyes. Bacchus, her unborn child,
was rescued by Jove, who sewed him into his thigh until time
for his normal delivery. Jove then gave him to Ino, Semele's
sister, to be cared for, and this incited Juno against Ino's
husband, Athamas. The story is related commonly, as *e.g.,*
Met., 3. 259-315.)

Priapus. *C.R.,* I, i, 230; *Po.,* III, i, 425; see WOODEN
GOD.
  C.R. associates Priapus with Venus, and *Po.* with Bacchus;
perhaps J. knew Pausanias, 9. 35. 1, who says in part: "The
Lampsaceni venerate him beyond all other divinities, and
assert that he is the son of Bacchus and Venus." Lucian
(*Gods,* 23) at least implies the same parentage, and
emphasizes the sensual nature of the god, as does *Fasti,* 1.

415-438. J. intimates that Priapus was also honoured as the deity of agricultural productiveness (see WOODEN GOD).

PROMETHEUS. *Po.*, V, i, 472; *Ca.*, III, i, 242; *Be.*, 24; *M.V.*, 238; 240-242; *Epi.*, 214; *Und.*, 369.

The concept of Prometheus as the producer of men and the assertion that men, "without Promethean stuffings reach'd from heaven," are like hollow statues reflect Pausanias, 10. 4. 4; Lucian's *Prometheus on Caucasus*, 11-13; *Gods*, 1; *Met.*, 1. 76-88; 363, 364; Juvenal's *Satires*, 14. 35; Scholium on Horace's *Odes*, 1. 3, 29, where the god is said to have stolen fire from heaven *"ad suas e terra fictas statuas animandas"*; and others. *Und.*, indicating that Prometheus, the son of Japetus (*Works*, 47-52; *Theogony*, 542; 559; *Met.*, 1. 82), stole the fire from Jove's chariot, recalls Servius on *Eclogues*, 6. 42, where Prometheus is said to have held his torch to the wheel of the sun's chariot for fire. Other sources generally do not mention the exact source of the flame. *Ca.*, containing the threat to fetch new fire "out of the head of Jove," a vaunter's daring boast, has no classical authority. In implying the aid of Athene (*Und.*), J. has in mind that she assisted Prometheus (Lucian's *Prometheus on Caucasus*, 13; Servius, *l.c.*). The scene of the punishment of Prometheus in Aeschylus' *Prometheus Bound*, 1-35, as also in Lucian, *l.c.*, is Caucasus (*Ca.*) where, as he lies chained, Jove's "own gaunt eagle" flies at him.

There seems to be no precedent for stating that Prometheus lost the fire or for speaking of the friendship of Prometheus and Nature. Prometheus' words, "I woman with her ills did fly," presumably refer to the creation of Pandora, *q.v.* See TITAN.

PROSERPINE. *B.F.*, II, i, 396; *Qu.*, 126 footnote; *Chl.*, 98; 99; *Epi.*, 238; *Und.*, 403.

Proserpine, the daughter of Jove and Ceres, *q.v.*, is the "Sicilian maid" ravished by Pluto, who made her his queen (see PLUTO). The *Qu.* footnote is quoted quite incidentally from Lucan, 6. 739, 740.

PROTEUS. *Volp.*, III, vi, 246; *Be.*, 25 and footnote; *N.T.*, 27; 33-38; *F.I.*, 77-81; *L.T.*, 88; *M.P.*, 358.

Proteus, a sea-deity, is characterized by J. in *Be.* as "the gray prophet of the sea," for which description the footnote quotes *Geor.* 4. (388,389); "gray," however, does not agree with Vergil's *"caeruleus Proteus,"* which Fairclough translates "sea-green," but which may be "dark blue" or "azure." J. uses "the blue Proteus" in *Volp.* That there was a suggestion of gray associated with Proteus is clear, though, from Vergil's description of his eyes, *"lumine glauco,"* which Fairclough translates "grey-green," but which might be called simply "grey." When Volpone vaunts that he would contend with Proteus for the love of Celia, one thinks of the struggle between Agamemnon and Proteus (*Od.*, 4. 435-461) and between Aristaeus and Proteus (*Geor.*, 4. 437-445). In both of the classic struggles, moreover, Proteus, in trying to escape, assumes the appearance of various objects, and thus J.'s "father of disguise" (*N.T.*) becomes clear. "Proteus' herds" (*N.T.*, 36; *F.I.*, 80) reflect the seals which Proteus has in his keeping (*Od.*, 4. 404-453; *Geor.*, 4. 394-436).

PSYCHE. *Hue,* 89.

Venus here is concerned lest Cupid has found "a second Psyche, and lives here disguised." Apuleius (*Met.*, 4. 28-6. 24) tells of the romance of Cupid and Psyche.

PYLADES. *E.M.O.*, IV, iv, 140; *Epic.*, IV, ii, 448.
    See ORESTES.

PYRACMON. *Und.*, 372.
    See CYCLOPES.

PYRENE. *Ode.*, 354.
    See CYCNUS.

PYTHON. *Po.*, III, i, 418; *Henry's Ba.*, 154.
  See APOLLO.

REMUS. *Ca.*, II, i, 232; *K.J.E.*, 421 footnote; 426 and footnote (Romulus).

Amulius, having seized Alba from his brother, the rightful
ruler, took pains to murder his brother's sons and to make
Rhea, their sister, a Vestal; consequently Amulius believed
that his brother would have no issue. Rhea, however, being
mysteriously violated, bore twin boys, whose father, she said,
was Mars. These boys, it was ordered, were to be drowned,
but the Tiber, receding after a flood, left them alive on the
banks where they were nourished by a she-wolf until a
shepherd of the king found them. He and his wife secretly
raised them to brave and sturdy manhood.

One day some robbers, in revenge upon the twins for having stolen their plunder, attacked them, and took Remus
prisoner. Brought before Amulius and accused of usurping
the land which Amulius had given to his deposed brother
Numitor, Remus was sent to Numitor for sentence. Meanwhile the shepherd who had raised the twins took Romulus
into his confidence, and Romulus and certain trusted friends
quietly made their way to Numitor, who had already sur-
mised the real identity of Remus, his captive. Subsequently
the twins killed Amulius, and restored the kingdom to
Numitor, whom the nation recognized.

Romulus and Remus, having decided to establish a great
city on the spot where they had been abandoned in their in-
fancy, could not agree upon which one should name it—
there being no evidence of their priority of birth. Each un-
dertook an augury. There came to Remus six vultures, but to
Romulus twelve. The former claimed his right to name the
city because he had received the first augury; the latter, because he had received more vultures. During their quarrel,
Romulus or one of his party killed Remus. There is also

a slightly different conclusion: Remus dared to jump over the walls of the city which Romulus was building, and the latter killed him as a kind of warning to all other intruders.

This story, which Livy, 1. 3-7, and Ovid (*Fasti*, 3. 11-78) relate, J. had in mind when he wrote the *Ca.* Chorus:

> Great father Mars, and greater Jove,
>> By whose high auspice, Rome hath stood
>> So long; and first was built in blood
> Of your great nephew, that then strove
> Not with his brother, but your rites:
>> Be present to her now, as then,
>> And let not proud and factious men
> Against your wills oppose their mights.

RHADAMANTHUS. *Po.*, III, i, 413, 414; *Se.*, I, i, 23, 24; *Ca.*, IV, iv, 365; *Epi.*, 239; *Canaan*, 348, 349.

See AEACUS. An examination of the contest accompanying "sweet Radamant" (*Ca.*) makes clear that it is of no classic significance.

RHEA. *Hue,* 93 footnote.

Rhea is "the mother of all the gods" (*Theogony,* 468). For her love of Atys, see ATYS. Rhea is also identified with Cybele, *q.v.*

ROMULUS. *Ca.*, V, iv, 319, 320; *K.J.E.*, 421 footnote; 426 and footnotes.

See REMUS for *K.J.E.* The *Ca.* citation substantially translates Cicero's *Against Catiline*, 3. 1. For Romulus' dedicating "March the first month" to his father Mars, see MARS.

RUMOUR. *Epic.*, V, i, 478; *J. and A.*, 477; *T.V.*, 6; *For.*, 255; *Und.*, 422.

Ovid (*Met.*, 12. 39-63) and Vergil (*Aen.*, 4. 173-195)— see FAME—offer the concept of Fame which probably is all that J. had for Rumour. He distinguishes, however, between them (*T.V.*) without specifying differences. "Bold rumour" (*J. and A.*) seems without exact precedent.

SABELLA. *Po.*, III, i, 415.

Gifford, who comments that J. is following Horace in using Sabella as a substantive, cites *Epodes;* the correct source is *Satires,* (1. 9. 29, 30). Of course this is not mythological.

SALIAN RITES. *Au.*, 423 and footnote.
See MARS.

SAPPHO. *Und.*, 374.
See PHAON.

SARON. *N.T.*, 33-38; *F.I.*, 77-81.

Apparently the only source from which J. could have acquired his information about Saron, who drowned while pursuing a hind and was buried in Artemis' grove, is Pausanias, 2. 30. 7, 8.

SATURN.

Saturn, the father of Jupiter, *q.v.*, (*Ob.*, 170 footnote; *F.I.*, 64) at the request of Earth, Saturn's mother, used a sickle to emasculate his father Uranus (Heaven) because the latter had confined some of his children in the Earth or in Tartarus (*Theogony*, 147-182; Apollodorus, 1. 1. 4). This J. humorously suggests at *T.V.*, 4. In his turn, however, Saturn made it a practice to eat his own children as soon as they were born (*L.F.*, 195), lest one of them should dethrone him—as he had learned from Earth and Heaven that one would; Here saved Zeus from this fate by wrapping a stone for Saturn to swallow, and Zeus later forced Saturn to disgorge his brothers and sisters (*Theogony*, 453-502; Apollodorus, 1. 1. 5-1. 2. 1; Hyginus' *L.F.*, 139; Servius on *Aen.*, 3. 104; *Fasti*, 4. 197-206; Pausanias, 8. 36. 3; 9. 2. 7; 9. 41. 6; 10. 24. 6; and others; see also JUPITER for

Ob., 170 footnote). Saturn's reign won the designation, "golden age," *q.v.,* as J. thinks of it at *Henry's Ba.,* 160; *T.V.,* 14; *Epi.,* 224; *For.,* 250. To *K.J.E.,* 421, J. appends a footnote giving Vergil's "Eclog. v" as his source for *"Redeunt Saturnia Regna"*; the correct citation, however, is *Eclogues,* 4. 6.

At *T.V.,* 4, Saturn is said to be "Time itself, and his name CHRONUS"; this Roman viewpoint is well put by Cicero in *De N.D.,* 2. 25. 64. The elaborate relationship based upon the concerns of Saturn (time), Venus (love), and Diana (chastity), which follows in *T.V.,* 13-19, is a pretty invention worked out by J.; *cf.* DIANA. J. also identifies Saturn with Chronus at *Ba.,* 75, where in his footnote he writes: "Saturn: who indeed, with the ancients, was no other than time, and so his name alludes, *Kronos. Plut. in Quaest.* To which confer the Greek adage, ἄγει δὲ πρὸς φῶς τὴν ἀλήθειαν χρόνος." See Plutarch's *Moralia,* ("Roman Questions," 12). In the same footnote "Truth is feigned to be the daughter of Saturn" (also at *For.,* 264), and in the *Ba.,* 76 footnote, J. writes of Truth: "Hippocrat. in a certain epistle to Philopoem. describeth her, *Mulierem, quae non mala videatur, sed audacior aspectu et concitatior.* To which Caesare Ripa, in his *Iconolog.,* alludeth in these words, *Faccia, ne bella, ne dispiacevole, &c."* See Hippocrates, *l.c.* The *Iconologia* has not been accessible.

"Aged Saturn" (*Epi.,* 224) is clarified by the explanation of Cicero, *l.c.*: *"Saturnus autem est appellatus quod saturaretur annis."* His perfect eyes and ears and his justice (*T.V.,* 18) seem to reflect his rule during the golden age (see above). Chiromantic and astronomical passages are *Al.,* I, i, 39; *S.S.,* III, ii, 281; and *G.M.,* 373. The *E.M.I.,* V, i, 145, allusion seems, possibly intentionally, to confuse Saturn with Jupiter. See also SATURNALIA.

SATURNALIA. *Ca.,* III, iii, 259; *P.R.,* 300; *T.V.,* 4, 5.

Saturnalia was the annual occasion when the slaves were permitted to exchange places with their masters, and to speak and act with absolute immunity (*e.g.,* Macrobius' *Saturnaliorum,* 1. 10; Pliny's *Epistles,* 8. 7; Lucian's *Saturn.,* 2; 3). Hence Saturn is "lord of Misrule" during these "days of feast and liberty," "where men might do, and talk all that they list" (*T.V.*).

SATURNIUS. *C.R.,* I, i, 218.

Saturnius designates a son of Saturn, particularly Jupiter, Neptune, or Pluto. For *C.R.,* see CUPID.

SATYRS.

Silenus, the satyrs' leader, is characterized by his love of drink and by his tankard (*Ob.,* 168 and footnote); to support this, J. cites Euripides' *Cyclops,* (139-176), and quotes Vergil's *Eclogues,* 6. (17). Silenus, too, was Bacchus' tutor, and the satyrs were the god's "playfellows" (*Ob.,* 167 and footnotes); see BACCHUS. For the speech of the two satyrs, Chromis and Mnasil, to their companions, "You saw Silenus, late, I fear," J. quotes *Eclogues,* 6. (13-15). Over each company of satyrs is a Silene, in whom "was nothing of this petulance and lightness, but . . . all gravity and profound knowledge of most secret mysteries" (*Ob.,* 168-178 and footnotes). For his authority, J. mentions Athenaeus, 5 and 6; actually he used 5. 197 E-201 E. This Silenus in *Ob.,* it seems, should not be confused with the notorious Silenus mentioned above. Supporting his contention that the Silenes were worthy and grave and learned, J. instances Vergil, who in writing on "the beginnings, and hidden nature of things" allowed Silenus to present the account (*Eclogues,* 6. 18-86); and J. adds that the same attitude toward the Silene is noted in Plato (*Symposium,* 215 A-C), Synesius (*Letters,* 154), Herodotus (7. 26; 8. 138), Strabo (10. 3.

7), Philostratus (*Imagines*, 2. 17. 5 probably), and Tertullian (no satisfactory passage located).

The desire of the satyrs to woo the ladies (*Ob.*, 169 and footnote) causes J. to recall Horace's *"Risores et Dicaces"* (*Ars Poetica*, 225) and "the Greek poets, *Nonnus, &c.,* style them φιλοκέρτομους." This latter epithet, meaning "laughter-loving," is not given in the standard sources upon Silenus, but suggests a very curious possibility: It seems that J. has confused the Greek for Silenus with that for Selene, for Nonnus applies φιλοκέρτομος to the moon at *Dionysiaca,* 4. 215. The footnote continues in Latin that the satyrs' dance was σικίννις, and that from this they were called σικίννισται. J. adds that this name is derived from the name of the inventor of the dance, Sicino (see Athenaeus, 1. 37), or from the movement of the dance *"qui est concitatissimus."*

In a footnote to *Ob.*, 170, J. relates that the Centaurs are sometimes confused with the satyrs: "Either of them are διφυὲς, but after a diverse manner. And Galen observes out of Hippocrates, *Comment.* iii in vi. *Epidemicor.* that both the Athenians and Ionians called the Satyrs φῆρας." *Cf.* the remainder of this footnote under CENTAURS, and see Galen's *De Morbis Vulgaribus,* 14, where only the Ionians are mentioned. Other footnotes on 170 justify the use of "grandsire" there and at 175, as an appellative of Silenus, Julius Pollux, 4. 19 (or perhaps 4. 142 is a closer specification) being cited in proof of his age, as also is Julian's *Caesares,* 309 D, where Bacchus calls Silenus παππίδιον ("little father").

The satyrs, according to 171, carry hunting staves, have an excessive love of wine, and physically have "crooked legs," "cloven feet," "tawny wrists," "stubbed horns," "pricking ears," "shaggy thighs," and hairy tails (173). Their forms are "rough and rude" (175). They are inordinately given to ornamentation, to trickery, and to love-making. The sources of these attributes probably are manifold: J. cites one piece of sculpture (see BACCHUS); Callistratus describes another sculpture of a satyr in his *Descriptions,* 1. Their lewdness (also *Volp.,* II, iii, 217) is apparent in Euripides' *Cyclops,* 69-72, and in Philostratus' *Imagines* 1. 20. The latter also brings out their love of wine, their dancing, their flattering the ladies, their "prominent ears, . . . and having the tails of horses" in 1. 22. Horace (*Odes,* 2. 19. 3, 4) speaks of "the goat-footed satyrs with their pointed ears," with which *cf.* also *Po.,* III, i, 438.

The satyrs' dancing (*Satyr,* 441; *Pen.,* 462-464; *Ob.,* 168), besides being mentioned by Philostratus, *l.c.,* is found in many other places (*e.g.,* Euripides' *Cyclops,* 25, 26; etc.; *Culex,* 116, 117). Their association with Bacchus (*Ob.,* 167 and footnote; 170-172 and footnotes) has been partially discussed under BACCHUS; see also Euripides' *Cyclops,* 1. 2; 38-40; 708. The satyr's horn (*Satyr,* 444; *Ob.,* 168) may reflect the musical skill of Pan. The latter is united with the satyrs at *Pen.,* 464-468; *Ob.,* 170, as *e.g.,* at *Culex, l.c.* For the significant passage at *Ob.,* 174, alluding to the stakes used to bore through the Cyclopes' eye, see CYCLOPES. Allusions of a general nature are *C.R.,* I, i, 225; *Po.,* V, i, 480; *Satyr,* 450; *T.V.,* 9; 10; *P.A.,* 43; *Chl.,* 101; and *For.,* 245. See also CHRONOMASTIX.

SCAMANDER. *S.S.,* I, ii, 247.

For fighting Achilles, Scamander, a river near Troy, was attacked by Vulcan and burned (*Il.,* 21. 211-382; Apollodorus, 4. 7). The "blue" of the Scamander is apparently J.'s idea, the Homeric epithet being "lovely" or "deep-eddying." Nor has "Vulcan leap'd into" the Scamander in the sources.

(SCYLLA). *Epi.,* 235.

Without naming Scylla, J. writes of

> the rock
> Made of the trull that cut her father's lock.

Scylla, madly loving Minos, who was warring against her father's country, cut off the lock of her father's hair in which his strength had its source. Pausanias (1. 19. 4; 2. 34. 7) relates that Minos, horrified at Scylla's deed, had her thrown from his ship; her body later was cast by the waves upon a headland thereafter known as Scyllaeum. Ovid (*Met.*, 8. 148-151) and Vergil (*Ciris*, 487-489) say that she became a bird, the Ciris. Hyginus (*L.F.*, 198) states that she was changed *"in piscem, cirim quem vocant."* See also Aeschylus' *Libation-Bearers*, 613-621; Propertius, 3. 19. 21-24; 4. 4. 39, 40; and various scholia. There is also a possibility, it seems, that J. has confused this Scylla with the other who dwelt in a cave on a cliff, and carried off mariners (*Od.*, 12. 73-100). Whalley's suggestion that "the old poets seem to have confounded two different stories together" is scarcely necessary in view of Pausanias' story.

SEA-HORSES. *Bl.*, 7 and footnote.
See TRITONS.

SEMIRAMIS. *Epic.*, III, ii, 393.
Semiramis, daughter of a Syrian and Derceto, was abandoned by her mother in the desert, but doves marvellously fed her. She married Onnes, a general, and during a siege captured for him the citadel of Bactra. Thereupon Ninus, the king, wished to wed her, and Onnes killed himself. Shortly after bearing Ninus a son, Semiramis succeeded to the throne. One writer reports that she tricked Ninus into turning over the rule to her for five days, during which she ordered that he be executed. Another says nothing of the cause of the death. Semiramis reigned brilliantly, building cities and subduing countries. After a reign of forty-two years, she resigned the kingdom to her son, and disappeared to become one of the gods or merely an immortal dove. J. probably knew of Semiramis from Diodorus, 2. 4-20, and Hyginus' *L.F.*, 240; 243.

SERENITAS. *Be.*, 29 and footnote.

J.'s personification of Serenitas seems original, and his footnote lends confirmation to this opinion: "As this of serenity, applying to the optics reason of the rainbow, and the mythologists making her the daughter of Electra." Aristotle (*Meteorology*, 3. 2) makes a scientific explanation of the rainbow which J. seems to have personified.

SEVEN WISE MASTERS. *E.M.I.*, III, ii, 80.

The seven most distinguished men living from approximately 620-550 B.C. have been given this title. See *e.g.*, Plutarch's "Banquet of the Seven Wise Men" in *Moralia*.

SIBYL. *Epi.*, 234.

The Sibyl was a maiden-priestess of Apollo and delivered oracles at his shrines, the most famous of which probably was Cumae. For *Epi.* see AVERNUS.

SIBYLLINE BOOKS. *Ca.*, I, i, 194, 195; 199, 200; III, i, 243; IV, v, 299; V, iv, 214, 215; *Two Kings*, 471.

The Sibylline books were a collection of prophecies offered to Tarquinius Superbus by the Cumaean Sibyl (see SIBYL). J. uses them only as he found them in Sallust's *Catiline*, 47. 2, and Cicero's *Against Catiline*, 3. 4, where the prophecy of the Sibyl that three of the Cornelian family would become rulers of Rome is used. The conspirators duped Lentulus into believing himself to be the third.

SILENE. *Ob.*, 169 and footnote.

See SATYRS.

SILENUS. *Ob.*, 167-178.

See SATYRS.

SIMOIS. *Po.*, I, i, 376.

The Simois is a river mentioned several times in *Il.*, *e.g.*, 21. 305-315, where the River Scamander, *q.v.*, urges the Simois to hurry to assist it. J. uses it to illustrate the enduring fame won by Homer.

Sinon. *Se.,* IV, v, 103.

"Greek Sinon" allowed himself to be captured by the Trojans so that he might weave a story that would cause them to draw the wooden horse into their city. Then at night he opened the door of the device, and allowed the Greeks to attack. Vergil (*Aen., 2.* 57-196; 257-267) emphasizes Sinon's deception:

> *Talibus insidiis periurique arte Sinonis*
> *credita res, captique dolis lacrimisque coactis.*
>
> (195, 196.)

Siren. *Volp.,* IV, i, 268; *B.F.,* II, i, 413; *S.N.,* II, i, 203; III, i, 241; *Bl.,* 15; *N.T.,* 27; 29; 35.

The Sirens, two in number, sang charming songs to mariners who sailed near their haunt, and lured the hapless listeners to destruction. To avoid this, Odysseus covered the ears of his rowers with wax, and had himself bound to the mast as the ship passed the Sirens (*Od.,* 12. 39-54; 158-200). There seems to be no satisfactory explanation of the Sirens' tresses (*N.T.*), but with the designation "harlot of the sea," *cf.* Horace's *"improba Siren"* (*Satires,* 2. 3. 14).

Sisyphus. *Al.,* II, i, 67; *Chl.,* 99.

Sisyphus is condemned in Hades to roll unceasingly a stone toward the top of a hill without success (*Od.,* 11. 593-600). Various causes for this punishment are assigned, chief of which are Sisyphus' revealing that Jove carried off Aegina (Apollodorus, 1. 9. 3; Pausanias, 2. 5. 1; Scholiast, Ed. Dindorf, on *Il.,* 1. 180) and his impiety (Hyginus' *L.F.,* 60). Ovid also implies that Sisyphus' guilt in *"furtisque et fraude"* was the cause (*Met.,* 13. 26-33); J. writes that Sisyphus "would have made Ours common." With "ceaseless rock" (*Al.*) *cf.* *"rediturum . . . saxum"* (*Met.,* 4. 460).

Sleep. *Und.,* 306; 313.

J. implies that Sleep is not easily awakened, thereby coinciding, perhaps accidentally, with *Met.,* 11. 616-621, where

the god's eyelids are "heavy with the weight of sleep," and
he "at last shook himself free of himself." The second *Und.*
citation, which implies Sleep's guilt and fear, reflects the
characterization of Sleep in *Il.,* 14. 231-360, where he con-
spires with Here against Zeus, not without some fear, however, of the latter's ire, which he had encountered upon a
previous occasion.

SOL.
See APOLLO.

SOLON. *S.N.,* II, i, 196.
Solon is famous, among other reasons, for his relief of
debtors in his realm, he having accomplished this relief without taxing either the rich or the poor; neither group, however, was satisfied completely by his arrangements (Plutarch's "Solon," 15. 1-7; 16. 1; Aristotle's *Athenian Politics,*
9-11).

SPHINX. *Epic.,* II, iv, 379; *L.F.,* 185-193 and footnote.
The Sphinx had "the upper parts and face of a woman: the
nether parts of a lion, the wings of an eagle, to shew her
fierceness, and swiftness to evil." This description tallies
closely with that of Apollodorus, 3. 5. 8.
Her "hooked hands" and her greedy nature are described
by Seneca (*Oedipus,* 99, 100). In *L.F.* the Sphinx represents Ignorance who is the enemy of love and beauty, and
who perplexes even the simplest of matters; *cf.* Seneca, *ibid.,*
101, 102. With "monster" also *cf.* Seneca, *ibid.,* 106. She pro-
poses a riddle in *L.F.* just as she proposed her famous riddle to Oedipus, who solved it (Apollodorus, Sophocles, and
Seneca, *l.c.;* Pausanias, 9. 26. 2-4; Hyginus' *L.F.,* 67; Diodorus Siculus, 4. 64; and others). Apollodorus states that
the riddle came from the Muses to the Sphinx; hence possibly comes the assistance which Love receives from the
Muses' priests in *L.F.* J. makes Sphinx the mother of the

Follies, recalling Spenser's making Ignorance the mother of Folly (Lotspeich cites *Teares of the Muses,* 311-318).

SPRING. *V.D.,* 290-294; *Chl.,* 96-99; 102-105.

For *V.D.* see FAVONIUS. The personification of Spring in *Chl.* rests seemingly upon *Fasti,* 5. 195-214, in a very general manner and in making Chloris, *q.v.,* the "mistress of the Spring" (*Chl.,* 99). With "this perpetual spring" (*V.D.,* 293) *cf.* also *Fasti,* 5. 206: *"vere fruor semper."* Spring is not, however, properly a mythological personification.

STENTOR. *S.N.,* V, ii, 291; *Epic.,* IV, i, 418.

"Stentor of the brazen voice, whose voice is as the voice of fifty other men" (*Il.,* 5. 785, 786; Juvenal, 13. 112) is used in J. to designate "sons of noise and tumult."

STEROPES. *Und.,* 372.

See CYCLOPES.

STYX. *C.R.,* I, i, 217; *Po.,* IV, iii, 455; *Ca.,* I, i, 190; III, ii, 249; *Epi.,* 233; 237; *Canaan,* 349.

The most binding of oaths among the gods was the one which invoked the Styx (*e.g., Il.,* 2. 755; *Od.,* 5. 185, 186; *H.H. to Hermes,* 4. 513-521; Apollodorus, 1. 2. 5) as in *Po.* In addition to the character of Styx as a river, it is also termed loosely "the Stygian sound" (*Ca.*) and "the Stygian pool" (*Epi.*) with which *cf. Aen.,* 6. 135: *"Stygios . . . lacus."* At other times "Stygian" seems to indicate nothing more than "infernal." For "Stygian ferry" (*C.R.*) see MERCURY, and for allusions to Charon, see CHARON.

SUN. *Hue,* 90; *L.F.,* 187; *Ob.,* 181; *M.V.,* 233; 240; *V.D.,* 291; *G.M.,* 367; *Und.,* 369; 392.

For *Hue,* see CUPID; for *L.F., Ob.,* and *Und.,* 369, see APOLLO; for *M.V.,* see NATURE; for *V.D.,* see IRIS; for *G.M.,* see HESPERUS; and for *Und.,* 392, *cf.* NATURE because "the teeming earth," *q.v.,* seems here to be substituted for Nature.

SYLVANS and SYLVANUS. *Pen.*, 462; *Ob.*, 172-180; *P.A.*, 47; *For.*, 245; 250; *Und.*, 36.

Sylvanus is compared for his hunting ability to Pan (*P.A.* and *Und.*), recalling *Aen.*, 8. 600-602, where rites to Sylvanus *"arvorum pecorisque deo"* are mentioned, and some other passages where Pan and Sylvanus are named together (*e.g.*, Vergil's *Eclogues*, 10. 24-27). More puzzling are the Sylvans encountered in *Pen.*, *Ob.*, and *For.*, for none of the ordinary sources introduces a group of Sylvans. These perform guard duty and are dignified escorts of Oberon; at least two of them are "armed with their clubs, and drest in leaves, asleep." *For.* alludes to "many a sylvan, taken with his flames." That they are not Satyrs, however, is clear from *Pen.* where the Panisks, the Sylvans, and the Satyrs "dance their wilder rounds about"; these also "cleave the air with many a shout." The beards of the guards in *Ob.* must resemble those of "Pan's goat, that leads the herds." Ovid mentions *"monticolae silvani"* at *Met.*, 1. 193, in naming classes of rustic creatures.

SYRINX. *Satyr*, 441.

The queen is described as possessing "the dame Syrinx' grace." Syrinx was an Arcadian nymph comparable to Diana in appearance, and a devotee of Diana in hunting and chastity (*Met.*, 1. 689-698). The satyr's wish that Pan were present is appropriate because Pan wooed Syrinx, and to escape him she asked that she be given another form; she was thereupon changed into the marsh reeds from which Pan made his pipe (*ibid.*, 698-712).

TAGUS. *C.R.*, V, iii, 356.

See MIDAS.

TANTALUS. *Ca.*, IV, v, 284; *Chl.*, 98.

In *Chl.* the result of Love's visit to Hades is that "half-famished Tantalus is fallen to his fruit . . . and has a river afore him, running excellent wine." The inspiration for this notion seems in part to be Claudian's *R.P.*, 2. 336, 337: *"non aqua Tantaleis subducitur invida labris."* Claudian, however, does not mention the fruit, the source of which must be either *Od.*, 11. 582-592, or *Met.*, 4. 458, 459, for both Homer and Ovid say that Tantalus was doomed to stand in a lake with fruit trees not far away, but out of his reach. Other sources (*e.g.*, Apollodorus, 2. 1, and Hyginus' *L.F.*, 82) relate that in addition to the thirst and hunger punishment, Tantulus also suffered anguish lest a pendant rock fall upon him. J. makes no mention of Tantalus' crime except that it deserved no pity (*Ca.*). In the classics he is said either to have revealed the gods' secrets or to have stolen their ambrosia for the benefit of men.

TARQUIN. *Ca.*, II, i, 228.
See LAIS.

TARTARY (TARTARUS). *Chl.*, 99.
Tartarus is the place of torture in the lower world. J. may well have had Claudian's *R.P.* 2. 333, 334, in mind, for the allusions to Ixion, Tantalus, and Tityus in *Chl.* are also in Claudian.

TAYGETE. *K.J.E.*, 428-431.
See ELECTRA.

TEMPE. *E.M.O.*, IV, vi, 153.
Tempe is the celebrated garden in the valley between Olympus and Ossa in Thessaly (Herodotus, 7. 173; *Met.*, 1. 568-576; and others).

TEMPEST. *Chl.*, 100.
"The nymph Tempest" dances with the four winds, recalling Aeneas' sacrificing a lamb to the Tempests at *Aen.*, 5. 772, and also recalling a similar sacrifice in Horace's *Epodes*, 10. 24.

TENEDOS. *Po.,* I, i, 376.

Tenedos is an island mentioned several times by Homer. (*Il.,* 1. 38; 452; 11. 625; 13. 33).

TERROR. *Qu.,* 131.

Terror is equivalent to Fear. See GORGON.

TETHYS. *Ob.,* 171.

"The pearl that Tethys wears" seems to be alluded to only by Claudian, and then only indirectly. In *Fourth Consulship of Honorius,* 8. 592, Claudian writes *"et variis spirat Nereia baca figuris,"* and a few lines after (596, 597) he asks *"quis . . . Tethyos invasit gremium?"*

TEUCER. *Po.,* Apologetical Dialogue, 513.

Teucer's ability as an archer is attested by Apollodorus, 5. 5, and Quintus Smyrnaeus, 4. 405-422.

THALASSIUS. *Hy.,* 65.

Thalassius, or a form of the word, is the name of a Sabine deity who was invoked during marriage processions. Livy, 1. 9, and Plutarch ("Romulus," 15. 1, 2; "Roman Questions," 31) state that Thalassius was the name of one of the Romans who won a wife for himself during the rape of the Sabine women, and when his party were asked for whom they were taking the woman, they answered that they were leading her to Thalassius. Because of his popularity, others joined the group, all shouting "Thalassius," and as the marriage proved happy, the term was henceforth used in marriage processions (*e.g.,* Vergil's *Catalepton,* 12. 9; 13. 16; Catullus, 61. 130).

THEMIS. *Panegyre,* 433-436; *Tilt,* 219; *L.W.Bol.,* 137.

Themis' address to James I in *Panegyre* and the allusion to her in *Tilt* recall that she preceded Apollo as the prophet at Delphi (Aeschylus' *Eumenides,* 1-8; Euripides' *Iphigeneia,* 1259-1261; Pausanias, 10. 5. 6; Apollodorus, 1. 4. 1; *Met.,*

1. 320, 321; 372-394). No source is known for "reverend Themis." For her daughters, see HOURS.

THESEUS. *Epi.*, 232.

Theseus is renowned for his having gone to Hades (Euripides' *Hercules Furens*, 619-621; Apollonius Rhodius' *Argo.*, 1. 101-104; Diodorus, 4. 26. 1; 4. 63. 1-5; Pausanias, 1. 17. 4; 10. 29. 9; *Aen.*, 6. 392-397; Horace's *Odes*, 4. 7. 27; Hyginus' *L.F.*, 79; and others), from which place Hercules is said to have rescued him.

THESPIA. *E.M.I.*, III, i, 61; *E.M.O.*, Stage, 15; *Po.*, III, i, 408; *Hue*, 93; *Epi.*, 205; *For.*, 262; 278; *Und.*, 368; *Ode*, 354.

See MUSES.

THETIS. *E. M. O.*, IV, iv, 145; *Po.*, IV, iii, 455; *Hue*, 98 footnote.

Thetis was loved by both Jove and Poseidon, but they, hearing that her son would be greater than his father, bestowed her upon a mortal, Peleus, to whom she bore Achilles (Pindar's *Isth.*, 8. 27-48; Apollodorus, 3. 13. 5; Apollonius' *Argo.*, 4. 790-804; *Met.*, 11. 217-228; Hyginus' *L.F.*, 54; *De A.*, 2. 15). For Juno's jealousy of Thetis see JUNO; for *E.M.O.*, see ACHILLES; and for *Hue*, see VULCAN.

THISBE. *Po.*, IV, i, 446.

Thisbe of Babylonia was, according to Ovid, the "loveliest maid of all the East." Next to her home lived Pyramus, with whom she fell in love. They were forbidden to see each other, but daily they conversed through a break in the wall. At length they agreed to a nocturnal tryst. Thisbe, arriving at the spot marked by a white mulberry tree, was surprised by a lioness, and leaving her cloak, she fled. When Pyramus found the cloak and the tracks, he concluded that Thisbe had been killed, and he committed suicide. She, returning, found him dying, and blaming herself, likewise plunged the blade into her breast. To commemorate their deaths, the color of the mulberry became a dark red (*Met.*, 4. 55-166). Thus is explained J.'s reference to Thisbe's "ill fortune."

THRACE. *N.I.*, I, i, 313; IV, iii, 380; *Und.*, 427.

The "Thracian barbarism" introduced in *N.I.* is explained by a reading of Herodotus, 5. 4-8. It included polygamy, and after the death of the husband, his wives contested to determine which one he loved the most; she who won this honour was then slain over his grave by her nearest relative, and was buried with him; the other wives felt the deepest disgrace. Brides were purchased, and children were sold to traders. Tattooing was a sign of nobility, and the lack of it indicated meanness of station. The Thracians drank to excess (Horace's *Odes*, 1. 27. 1-4). Herodotus adds that labour was considered disgraceful, and idleness was virtuous. See also CENTAURS.

TIME. *L.F.*, 195; *G.A.R.*, 247; *T.V.*, 4-18; *L.W.Bol.*, 139; *For.*, 264.

Of the allusions to Time, only these seem to possess mythological value. For *L.F.*, *T.V.*, and *For.*, see SATURN. J.'s meaning at *G.A.R.* is not clear, and his reference to Time's wings being deplumed and Time himself fettered (*L.W.Bol.*) has not been satisfactorily placed; it may be Elizabethan rather than classic.

TITAN. *Ca.*, III, iii, 255.

To win to him followers among the women Catiline directs Aurelia to

> Promise them states and empires,
> And men for lovers, made of better clay
> Than ever the old potter Titan knew.

This, it seems, is an allusion to Prometheus under the title Titan. Prometheus' father, Japetus, was a Titan (*Theogony*, 134; Apollodorus, 1. 1. 3). See PROMETHEUS.

TITHONUS. *V.D.*, 295.
See AURORA.

TITYUS. *Ca.*, IV, v, 284; *Chl.*, 99.

Tityus is punished in Hades because he offered violence
to Latona. J. merely suggests that his crime deserves no pity
(*Ca.*), and says that Sisyphus, *q.v.*, when Love visited in
Hades, found "Tityus' breast (for six of the nine acres) . . .
the subtlest bowling-ground in all Tartary" (*Chl.*). Among
those who mention that Tityus lay stretched over nine acres
in the lower world are Homer (*Od.*, 11. 576-581), Vergil
(*Aen.*, 6. 595-600), Hyginus (*L.F.*, 55), Lucretius, 3. 984-
994, and Claudian (*R.P.*, 2. 338-342). Claudian is quite
probably J.'s source, for he is likely to have used it in connection with Ixion and Tantalus, *q.v.*

TRITONS. *Epic.*, IV, i, 416; *Bl.*, 6-9 and footnotes; 15.

For his description of the Tritons, "their upper parts human, save that their hairs were blue, as partaking of the sea-
colour: their desinent parts fish, mounted above their heads
. . . and their music made out of wreathed shells," J. cites
Met., 1. (333-335) and *Aen.*, 10. (209-212). Moreover,
his authority for mounting Oceanus and Niger on sea-horses
(Centaurotritones or Ichthyotauri), J. says, is in Lucian's
Rhetorician, (51. 6), and Statius' *Thebais*, (2. 45-47 probably) picturing Nilus and Neptune, respectively.

TRIVIA. *C.R.*, V, iii, 355.
See DIANA.

TROY. *E.M.I.*, IV, ii, 106; *C.R.*, IV, i, 285; *Volp.*, II, ii,
214; *S.S.*, I, ii, 247; *K.J.E.*, 429; *Hue*, 95; *Qu.*, 132 footnote; *For.*, 269; *Und.*, 407; *Canaan*, 348.

Troy, of course, is familiar as the setting of the war between the Greeks and Trojans over Helen (*e.g.*, *Il.*, 1. 128,
129, *et passim*; Apollodorus, 3. 28-5. 23). She was present at
the fall of Troy, according to *Volp.*; see HELEN. This vic-

tory was won when the Greeks enclosed many of their bravest warriors in a huge wooden horse (*Canaan*), and then seemingly sailed away. The Trojans dragged the horse into their city, and at night Sinon, *q.v.*, opened it, and allowed the Greeks to emerge and to sack and burn the town (*e.g., Od.*, 4. 271-289; 8. 492-515; 11. 523-532; *Aen.*, 2. 13-804). Venus' cheering Troy after the massacre and fire, J. says, is from *Aen.*, 1. (314-401); in this passage Vergil relates that Venus appeared to Aeneas to direct him to the Tyrian city of Dido. The *Und.* statement that Vulcan did not spare "Troy, though it were so much his Venus' care" corresponds with *Aen.*, 2. 311, where the destruction of Troy continues *"Volcano superante."* The "brave men" of the store "that Homer brought to Troy" (*For.*) are Homer's heroes (*e.g.*, Agamemnon, Achilles, Ajax, and Idomen, *q.v.*); for the inspiration behind this thought, however, Whalley quotes Horace's *Odes*, 4. 9. (25-28). For *S.S.*, see SCAMANDER; for *K.J.E.*, see ELECTRA; and for *Qu.*, see ACHILLES.

TURNUS. *Qu.*, 133 footnote.

Camilla was among those, J. says, who came to aid Turnus against Aeneas (*Aen.*, 7. 783-792; see also AENEAS).

TYDIDES. *N.I.*, I, i, 325.

Tydides signifies Diomedes, *q.v.*, the son of Tydeus.

TYNDARIDES. *For.*, 269.

See DIOSCURI.

TYPHOEUS. *Se.*, V, x, 142.

At the moment of Sejanus' ruin, Caesar's envoy cries, "Come down, Typhoeus." Typhoeus, the child of Earth and Tartarus, was an immense, infuriated monster possessing one hundred snake-heads, dragon-tongues from which issued many different sounds, and fiery eyes. He warred with, and nearly overcame, Zeus (*Theogony*, 820-868; Pindar's *Py.*,

1. 15-28; Aeschylus' *Prometheus,* 353-367; *Met.,* 5. 321-331; Hyginus' *L.F.,* 152).

ULYSSES. *C.R.,* I, i, 234; *Volp.,* II, i, 196; *N.I.,* I, i, 313; 325; *F.I.,* 65, 66; *Epi.,* 232; 236; *Und.,* 423.

Ulysses' "tedious and ten years travels" (*C.R.*) are, of course, those which followed the Trojan war; Ulysses was away from his home twenty years (*Od.,* 17. 326, 327; 23. 100-102), approximately nine of which were given to war (*Od.,* 22. 226-228). His eloquence and wisdom (*N.I.*) may reflect *Il.,* 2. 278-335, where he addresses the Achaeans during the war. "Ulysses' slights" (*N.I.*) may be the trials which the hero bore so patiently that Homer terms him "much-enduring" (*e.g., Od.,* 17. 280) and Ovid *"experientis Ulixei"* (*Met.,* 14. 159). "Sly Ulysses" (*Epi.*), Root says, is to be found in Golding's translation of *Met.,* ff. 160b, 167a, but is not literal. *Cf. e.g., "facundus"* (*Met.,* 13. 92), *"fallacis Ulixis"* (*Met.,* 13. 712), and *"aptus Ulixes"* (*Fasti,* 6. 433). Also *cf.* J.'s "the politic Ulysses" (*C.R.*). The visit of Ulysses to Hell (*Epi.*) is recounted in *Od.,* 10. 487-11. 640, and by Apollodorus, 7. 17.

The *Volp.* passage alludes to

> That idle, antique, stale, gray-headed project
> Of knowing men's minds and manners, with Ulysses.

The only explanation for this seems to be Dante's *Inferno,* 26. 96-98, where Ulysses tells the poet that he made his long travels "to explore the world, and search the ways of life." The significance attached to Ulysses' hat on these travels (*C.R.*) is not known. For *F.I.,* where J. merely uses the trick of Ulysses, who called himself Outis, see CYCLOPES; and for *Und.,* 423, see PENELOPE.

VENUS.

The birth of Venus, or Aphrodite, from the waves of the sea—as Hesiod (*Theogony,* 188-200) relates it—is apparently J.'s source for his allusions to "sea-born" Venus, "Neptune's niece," in *Bl.*, 16; *Lethe*, 274; *N.T.*, 36; *F.I.*, 80; and *L.T.*, 90, 91. Venus is Neptune's niece, for in some accounts (*e.g.*, *Aen.*, 1. 254-256; *Od.*, 8. 308) Jupiter is her father (*Po.*, IV, iii, 454, 455; *L.T.*, 91). The marriage of Venus and Vulcan (*Po.*, IV, i, 443; iii, 454; 461; *Hue*, 97; *Christmas*, 262, 263; *Und.*, 399; 406; 407; 409) and the affair of Venus with Mars (*Po.*, IV, i, 449; IV, iii, 454; *Volp.*, III, vi, 251; *Ba.*, 81, 82; *Tilt*, 215, 216; 219; *For.*, 261) are found in many versions (*e.g.*, *Od.*, 8. 266-302; *Theogony*, 933-937; *Met.*, 4. 171-189; Lucian's *Gods*, 15) ; J. mentions (*Se.*, III, i, 70; *M.V.*, 238; *For.*, 243) the net which Vulcan fashioned to capture Venus and her paramour.

For the parentage of Cupid, see CUPID, and to the citations there listed of Venus as his mother, add these wherein her relationship to Cupid is but hinted: *E.M.I.*, IV, i, 99; *S.N.*, IV, i, 253; and *L.F.*, 186. Another child of Venus is Aeneas (*Hue*, 94 and footnote), his father being the hero Anchises. To this romance of Venus with a mortal J. refers in declaring that she could "love a man" (*N.T.*, 36; *F.I.*, 80) ; the most complete source for this narrative is probably the *H.H. to Aphrodite*, 5. 45-290, but *cf. Theogony*, 1008-1010; *Il.*, 2. 819-821; 5. 311-313; *Fasti*, 4. 35-38.

The beauty of Venus, emphasized by her triumph over Juno and Minerva (*Und.*, 298), is also common material, but Gifford has shown the resemblance between J.'s reference and that of Angerianus (*Erotopaignion*, inaccessible). Her beauty is specified at *E.M.I.*, IV, i, 99; *Po.*, IV, i, 445, 446; *Volp.*, I, i, 160, 161; II, ii, 214 (see APOLLO) ; V, i, 289, 290; 294, 295; *Ca.*, II, i, 228; *S.N.*, II, i, 210; IV, i, 253 (Aphrodite's feet are particularly mentioned in *Theogony*, 194) ; *N.I.*, III, i, 358; *Be.*, 34; *Bl.*, 15; *Tilt*, 216; 219, 220; *Christmas*, 262, 263; *Und.*, 297; 302; 377, 378. No source has been discovered for J.'s allusions to Venus' cheeks, "Cupid's baths, wherein he uses to steep himself in

milk and nectar" (*C.R.*, V, ii, 329, 330) or "where he doth
steep himself in milk and roses" (*Und.*, 363) ; see also *Und.*,
298.

The most remarkable of Venus' attributes is her ceston,
mentioned at *C.R.*, I, i, 218 (see MERCURY) ; *Volp.*, V, i,
289, 290; *Hy.*, 63 and footnote (J. recalls the ceston as described in *Il.*, 14) ; *Tilt*, 214, 215; *L.T.*, 91 ; *Und.*, 298; 378;
443. Gifford correctly specifies *Il.*, 14. 214 (-223) as the
source J. had in mind. The doves and swans of Venus (*C.R.*,
IV, i, 292, 293; *Hue*, 88 and footnote (J. cites *Met.* 10 and
11) ; *Hy.*, 68; *Tilt*, 217 (see CUPID)) are found in *Met.*,
10. 708, 709; 716-720; 13. 673, 674; 14. 597; 15. 386, but
J.'s *Met.*, 11, proves inaccurate. Her chariot (*Hue*, 88; 94;
97) is also specified or implied in the above-named sources
and in numerous others (*e.g.*, Ovid's *Heroides*, 15. 91).

Another attribute which J. gives Venus is her golden fruit
(*Be.*, 31 and footnote) "the notes of loveliness, and sacred
to Venus. See *Phil*. . . ." These apples the Cupids throw at
each other, "whilst on the ground leverets picked up the
bruised apples, and left them half eaten." See Philostratus'
Imagines, 1. 6, where there are many little Cupids, some pelt-
ing each other with the apples, others attempting to catch a
hare, "an offering most pleasing to Aphrodite. . . . It possesses the gift of Aphrodite to an unusual degree. . . ." The
golden apples of Venus are found at *Met.*, 10. 647-680; Apollodorus, 3. 9. 2; and Servius on *Aen.*, 3. 113.

For Venus' leading the "Idalian brawls" (*V.D.*, 294; *T.V.*,
17; *Epi.*, 208), see IDA. The sources listed under IDA are
also sufficient examples of the union of Venus and the Graces
—a very frequent concept in classical works—which J. alludes to at *S.S.*, I, ii, 248; *Hue*, 88-90; 93; 97; *F.I.*, 78; *Epi.*,
208; *For.*, 261 (the "tribade trine") ; and *Und.*, 420. No
source for the assertion that the Graces were the nurses of
Cupid has been found although J. uses this idea at *Tilt*, 219,

220; *L.T.*, 91; *L.W.Bol.*, 137. *Cf.* HOURS. For *S.N.*, IV,
i, 253, see AMBROSIA; and for *Und.*, 407, see TROY.
J. acknowledges *Aen.*, 1. (81-401) as his source for *Hue*,
95:

> she [Venus] did cheer,
> After a tempest, long-afflicted Troy,
> Upon the Lybian shore.

Bacchus' union with Venus and the Graces (*Und.*, 420) has
many precedents (*e.g.*, *Anacreontea*, 38. 1-6; 44. 6-16). No
particular poem, however, supports Whalley's declaration
that "wine it is the milk of Venus" (*Verses Placed*, 73) is
Anacreontic. "Cytherea" (*C.R.*, II, i, 250; V, iii, 344) and
"Cypria" (*Po.*, IV, i, 447; *Ca.*, II, i, 228; *Hy.*, 62; 68) are
explained by Hesiod: "Cytherea because she reached Cythera,
and Cyprogenes because she was born in billowy Cyprus"
(*Theogony*, 198, 199); in a footnote to *Hy.*, 68, J. says of
"Cypris": "A frequent surname of Venus, not of the place,
as Cypria: but *quod parere faciat, ἡ τὸ κυεῖν παρέχουσα*,
Theoph. Phurnut. and the grammarians upon Homer, see
them." Whom J. means by "Theoph." is not made clear either
by an examination of different writers named Theophrastus
or by standard sources of epithets. "Phurnut." designates
Phurnutus (Cornutus); he thus alludes to Venus in his
Theoria under *"De Venere,"* p. 64.

Concepts of Venus as the patroness of unchaste love (*C.R.*,
I, i, 230; IV, i, 289; *Hy.*, 61; *For.*, 261 ("light Venus");
Und., 298; 302; 399 ("loose wife"); 406; and 443) are
not uncommon in the classics; *cf.* HYMEN, and *cf.* her mis-
conduct with Mars and Anchises (above in this article and
e.g., *Fasti*, 4. 133, 134). More pleasant allusions to Venus
as the prefect of marriage are found at *Hy.*, 61, 62 (for
Cypria's strewing "many a lily, many a rose" at marriages
(*cf. L.T.*, 92) J. cites Statius (*Silvae*, 1. 2. 11-23 is close),
Claudian (25. 116-119), "and others"); 67; 68 (Venus' influence upon human fertility, J. says, is confirmed by *Il.*, 8,

but he probably had in mind 5. 429; or 14. 198-221; or 14. 292-351; by Lucretius' *De Rerum Natura*, 1, and by Vergil's *Geor.*, 2, but this also seems unlikely, for the only reference to Venus (line 329) is scarcely appropriate); *Hue*, 87; 92 (for confirmation of J.'s footnote on Horace, see CUPID); 94 (J. correctly cites Pausanias, 4. (30. 5), and Plutarch's *Moralia*, (138 CD)); 97 (J.'s footnote quoting Catullus, 61. (61, 62) is correct); 101; 102; *Qu.*, 134, 135 (see BERE-NICE); *L.T.*, 91. For the antagonism between Venus and Cynthia (*C.R.*, V, iii, 340; *T.V.*, 18, 19), see DIANA.

General citations of Venus as the queen of love occur at *C.R.*, IV, i, 292, 293; V, ii, 328; *Se.*, I, ii, 30; *Ca.*, II, i, 228; III, iii, 355, 356; IV, v, 375, 376; V, iv, 391; *N.T.*, 36; *F.I.*, 80; and *Und.*, 443. Invocations to Venus are *C.R.*, IV, i, 296; 297; *Po.*, IV, i, 443; *Ca.*, II, i, 219; 222. Chiromantic and astrological allusions to her are *Al.*, I, i, 39; IV, i, 123; *G.M.*, 364; 373; 378. For *stella Veneris* (*S.S.*, III, ii, 281; *Hy.*, 61, 62 and footnote; 66; *Hue*, 88; 94; 97), see HES-PERUS, and for the court of love (*N.I.*, III, ii, 394 ff.), see CUPID.

VERTUMNUS. *Se.*, III, i, 66; *S.N.*, III, i, 221.

Vertumnus, wooing Pomona, assumed divers disguises to win audiences with her in her garden (*Met.*, 14. 641-660; Propertius, 4. 2. 21-48).

VESPER. *G.M.*, 367.

Vesper, a variant of Hesperus, is used by Catullus, 62. 1, 2.

VESTA. *Po.*, IV, i, 446; *Se.*, I, ii, 35 footnote; *Al.*, II, i, 46; *Ca.*, I, i, 202; *C.A.*, III, iii, 355, 356; *Hy.*, 66 and footnote.

Vesta, the deity of the domestic and civic hearth, particu-larly of the flame on the hearth (*e.g.*, *Fasti*, 6. 295-301; *Aen.*, 2. 296, 297; Servius on *Aen.*, *l.c.*), early devoted herself to virginity and won the honour of presiding over the family as her reward (*H.H. to Aphrodite*, 5. 21-32; *Fasti*, 6. 253,

254; 283-294) ; hence she is represented as modest and serious. At *Se.* J. recalls Justus Lipsius' *"comment. in Tacit."*
(3. 69) that Silanus was confined at the request "of his re-
ligious sister" of whom J. quotes: *"Torquata virgo vestalis,
cujus memoriam servat marmor Romae."* In *Hy.* the bride
is directed to raise her feet "above the threshold high"; in
explanation J. writes: "Servius saith, because it was sacred
to Vesta. *Plut. in Quaest. Rom.* remembers divers causes."
See Servius on *Aen.*, 2. 469, and Plutarch's *Moralia,* "Roman
questions" (29). Plautus (*Casina,* 4. 4. 1) and Catullus, 61.
162-164, also allude to this custom of brides. *Al.* refers irrev-
erently to the virgins who kept the fire before Vesta's image
constantly burning (*e.g., Fasti,* 6. 435-460).

VICTORY. *Hue,* 88; *Henry's Ba.,* 156.

Victory is usually described as winged in the classics (*e.g.,
Met.,* 8. 13: *"Victoria pennis"*; Tibullus, 2. 5. 45: *"volitat
Victoria"*), but the only presentation of her as golden seems
to be in Pausanias (*e.g.,* 5. 10. 4). She is generally sculp-
tured with a wreath or garland (*e.g.,* Pausanias, 5. 11. 1,
states that the statue of Zeus at Olympus held a garlanded
Nike (Victory) in the hand).

VIRTUE.

Of J.'s allusions to Virtue, few seem to have mythological
value. She is the goddess of manly valour and had a temple
(see HONOUR), but J. neglects this concept in favour of
that of Perseus, *q.v.,* whom he accepts as "expressing heroic
and masculine VIRTUE" (*Qu.,* 130, 131; 139-144). See also
FAME, but Virtue in that article is used as equivalent to
Perseus' character—not Virtus'. For the suggestion and instances of the notion that Virtue is opposed to Fortune, see
FORTUNE, and for the allegory of Pleasure and Virtue
(*P.R.,* 302; 303; 305-310; *Wales,* 330), see PLEASURE.
Other references to Virtue seem to be but personifications.

VOLSCIANS. *Qu.,* 133 footnote.
See AENEAS.

VULCAN.
Vulcan is the son of his mother alone ("father thou hadst
none," *Und.,* 404) ; she was Juno, according to *Theogony,*
927-932; Apollodorus, 1. 3. 5.; Lucian's *De Sacrificiis,* 6.
In Homer (*Il.,* 1. 578, 579; 20. 11; *Od.,* 8. 311, 312) Vulcan speaks of Jove as his father, as Apollodorus says. (Critics
who claim that the Homeric view merely indicates the general
fatherhood of Jove over gods and men are obviously unaware
of the *Od.* passage: "I was born misshapen. Yet for this is
none other to blame but my two parents—would they had
never begotten me!") J. indicates the Jove-Juno parentage
of Vulcan at *Po.,* IV, v, 456.

That Juno was frightened by the appearance of her son
(*Und.,* 404) and threw him from heaven is found in *Il.,*
18. 394-398 and *H.H. to Py. Apollo,* 3. 316-318, but J.'s
passage accords more closely with Lucian's *Gods,* 5, where
Jove, to justify his opposition to Vulcan's becoming his cupbearer, reminds Juno that her son's appearance prevents her
kissing him. Another version of this story is that because
Vulcan tried to assist his mother during one of her disputes
with Jove (see JUNO), the latter threw him from heaven
(*Und.,* 400) ; he landed on Lemnos where the inhabitants
nursed him, but thereafter he was lame (*Il.,* 1. 590-594;
Apollodorus, 1. 3. 5; Lucian's *Charon,* 1). Gifford has quoted
two lines from Catullus (36. 7, 8) for "thou lame Lord of
fire" (*Und.,* 399). With "polt-foot" (*M.V.,* 234; *L.W.Bol.,*
135) *cf.* Homer's "crook-foot" (*e.g., Il.,* 18. 371; 21. 331).
Vulcan's lameness is also alluded to at *E.M.O.,* Stage, 15,
and *Po.,* IV, iii, 443. For *Po.,* IV, iii, 456, 457, where Vulcan serves nectar to the gods to stop a quarrel between Jove
and Juno, see JUNO.

Vulcan was honoured as the artificer. At *Hue,* 95 and footnote, J. recalls that Vulcan made Achilles' armour in *Il.,* 18. (468-618), and Aeneas' armour in *Aen.,* 8. (439-453; 608-731). Again, at *M.V.,* 238, J. recounts that "Mulciber heretofore has made stools to stir, and statues dance, a dog of brass to bark, and . . . a woman to speak," as *Il.,* 18. 373-377; 419-423; *Od.,* 7. 91-94; and Hesiod's *Works,* 60-89; *Theogony,* 570-612, respectively relate. With Vulcan's creating Pandora (*Und.,* 409), see PANDORA. At *Hue,* 98 footnote, J., who has made Vulcan the artificer of the dance, says that when Homer "makes Thetis for her son Achilles, to visit Vulcan's house, he feigns that Vulcan had made twenty tripods or stools with golden wheels, to move of themselves miraculously, and go out and return fitly," again alluding to *Il.,* 18. (373-377).

The appearance of Vulcan "attired in a cassock girt to him, with bare arms, his hair and beard rough; his hat of blue, and ending in a cone; in his hand a hammer and tongs, as coming from the forge" (*Hue,* 96) corresponds broadly with *Il.,* 18. 410-417: his anvil and tools, "his mighty neck and shaggy breast, and put upon him a tunic," but here J. omits Homer's emphasis upon Vulcan's lameness. With the *Hue* description and with "hammer-armed Vulcan" (*L.W.Bol.,* 135), *cf.* the Homeric epithet, "the god of the two strong arms" (*e.g., Il.,* 1. 607; 18. 393; 614). Vulcan's assistants at the forge were the Cyclopes, *q.v.,* (*Po.,* IV, iii, 456; *Hue,* 96; *M.V.,* 233, 234; *L.W.Bol.,* 135). Other allusions to Vulcan's rôle as an artificer are *C.R.,* I, i, 218 (see MERCURY); *Se.,* IV, v, 102; *Hue,* 98; *For.,* 261; *Und.,* 404; 408, 409.

J. also asserts that Vulcan is "the god of fire and light. Sometimes taken for the purest beam" (*Hue,* 95 footnote). He recalls that Orpheus in the *Hymns,* (65. 6), celebrates Hephaestus "for the sun and moon," and that Euripides in *Troiades,* (343-345), makes him *"Facifer in Nuptiis.* Which present office we give him here, as being *Calor Naturae,* and *Praeses Luminis."* J. further recommends Plato's *Cratylus* (407 C), and *"Pausan. in Eliac."* (seemingly Pausanias, 5. 19. 8). For Vulcan as the fire-god, see also *Hue,* 98; *Henry's Ba.,* 151; *M.V.,* 233; and *Und.,* 399; 409.

For Vulcan's part in the birth of Pallas from Jove's head (*For.,* 261; *Und.,* 400) and for his attempt to win her love (*Und.,* 400; 404), see MINERVA. For the relationship of Vulcan with Venus and Mars (*Po.,* IV, i, 443; IV, iii, 454; 461; *Hue,* 96, 97; *Und.,* 399; 406; 407 (see TROY); and 409), and for Vulcan's net (*Se.,* III, i, 70; *M.V.,* 238; *For.,* 243), see VENUS. The fact that Vulcan, married to Venus and to Charis, *q.v.,* sought to win Pallas seems sufficient explanation for "uxorious Vulcan" (*Hue,* 95). For *S.S.,* I, ii, 247, see SCAMANDER. Other allusions to Vulcan are *Po.,* II, i, 392, and *Und.,* 400, but for the latter, see MARS.

VULTURNUS. *Be.,* 27 and footnote; 33.

Vulturnus is an early Latin name for the southeast wind, which came to be more generally known by the Greek name of Euros. In his footnote J. quotes *"Denuntiat igneus Euros"* from Vergil (*Geor.,* 1. 453). But Vulturnus was not, as J. suggests, a gentle wind: Lucretius calls it *"altitonans"* (5. 745), and Livy mentions the hot dust which it flung into the faces of the Romans at Cannae (22. 43; 46).

WOLF. *E.M.O.,* V, vii, 193.

Gifford quotes Vergil's *Eclogues,* 9. (53, 54) as evidence of the ancient belief that if a wolf saw a man before the man saw the wolf, the man would lose his power of speech.

WOODEN GOD. *Ca.,* III, i, 240.

Priapus is intended in Catiline's desire to be

> that wooden god
> That keeps our gardens, and could not fright the crows.

Wooden figures of Priapus, *q.v.*, were set up in gardens against thieves and birds (Vergil's *Geor.*, 109-115; Tibullus, I. I. 17, 18; *Met.*, 14. 640, 641).

WOOD GODS. *Ob.*, 172.

The Wood Gods and their "ratling pipes" are indefinite, for the designation can be applied to various classes of rural divinities. *Cf.* especially PANISCI.

ZEPHYRUS. *Al.*, II, i, 45; 49; *Pen.*, 461-464; *V.D.*, 290-294; *F.I.*, 77; *Chl.*, 96; 97.

See CHLORIS and FAVONIUS.

BIBLIOGRAPHY

Aeschylus (H. W. Smyth). Loeb Classical Library. 4 vols. New York, 1927.

Albricius, *De Deorum Imaginibus Libellus* (ed. T. Munckerus). Amsterdam, 1581.

Allen, Percy, *Shakespeare, Jonson, and Wilkins as Borrowers.* London.

Anacreontea in *Lyra Graeca* (J. M. Edmonds). Loeb Classical Library. 3 vols. New York, 1931.

Angerianus, *Erotopaignion.* Florence, 1512.

Anthologia Lyrica (T. Bergk; ed. E. Hiller). Leipzig, 1890.

Apollinaris, Sidonius (A. Ludwich). Leipzig, 1912.

Apollodorus, Library (J. G. Frazer). Loeb Classical Library. 2 vols. New York, 1921.

Apollonius Rhodius, Argonautica (R. C. Seaton). Loeb Classical Library. New York, 1921.

————, *Scholia* (ed. H. Keil). Leipzig, 1854.

Apuleius, *Oeuvres Complètes* (tr. *sous* M. Nisard). Paris, 1842.

Aristophanes (B. B. Rogers). Loeb Classical Library. 3 vols. New York, 1924.

Aristotle, *Constitution of Athens* (tr. E. Poste). New York, 1892.

————, *Meteorology* (E. W. Webster). Oxford, 1931.

Arnobius, *Adversus Nationes* (ed. F. Oehler). Leipzig, 1846.

Arnold, Matthew, *On the Study of Celtic Literature and on Translating Homer.* London, 1903.

Athenaeus, Deipnosophists (C. B. Gulick). Loeb Classical Library. 5 vols. published, 2 in preparation. New York, 1928.

————, (C. D. Yonge). 3 vols. London, 1854.

Bacchylides (ed. and tr. R. C. Jebb). Cambridge, 1905.

Bion. See *Greek Bucolic Poets.*

Boccaccio, *De Genealogia Deorum Gentilium.* Probable ed., 1532. Title-page missing.

Bruchmann, C. F. H., *Epitheta Deorum.* Leipzig, 1893.

Callistratus, Descriptions and *Philostratus, Imagines* (Arthur Fairbanks). Loeb Classical Library. New York, 1931.

Camden, Wm., *Britannia*. London, 1607.

Casaubon, Isaac, *De Satyrica Graecorum Poesi* (ed. T. Crenius). Leyden, 1699.

Catullus, Tibullus, and Pervigilium Veneris (F. W. Cornish). Loeb Classical Library. New York, 1925.

Chaucer, Geoffrey, The Complete Works of (F. N. Robinson). New York.

Cicero, De Natura Deorum and Academica (H. Rackham). Loeb Classical Library. New York, 1933.

————, *Orations* (C. D. Yonge). London, 1897.

————, *Speeches* (N. H. Watts). Loeb Classical Library. New York, 1931.

Claudian (M. Platnauer). Loeb Classical Library. 2 vols. New York, 1922.

Dante Alighieri, The Vision of (H. F. Cary). Everyman's Library. New York.

Dio's Roman History (ed. H. B. Foster; tr. E. Cary). Loeb Classical Library. 9 vols. New York, 1924.

Diodorus Siculus (tr. A. F. Miot). 7 vols. Paris, 1834.

————, (C. H. Oldfather). Loeb Classical Library. 2 vols. published, 8 in preparation. New York, 1933.

Diogenes Laertius (R. D. Hicks). Loeb Classical Library. 1 vol. published, 1 in preparation. New York, 1925.

Dunn, E. C., *Ben Jonson's Art*. Northampton, 1925.

Euripides (A. S. Way). Loeb Classical Library. 4 vols. New York, 1912; 1925.

Festus, Sextus Pompeius, *De Veborum Significatione*. 3 vols. London, 1826.

Galen, *Commentariei Aphorismos Hippocratis* (ed. A. Toll). Leyden, 1633.

Greek Anthology (W. R. Patton). Loeb Classical Library. 5 vols. New York, 1926.

Greek Bucolic Poets (J. M. Edmonds). Loeb Classical Library. New York, 1923.

Herodotus (A. D. Godley). Loeb Classical Library. 4 vols. New York, 1924.

The History of Herodotus (tr. George Rawlinson; ed. E. H. Blakeney). Everyman's Library. 2 vols. New York.

Hesiod, *Carmina* (ed. Thomas Gaisford). Leipzig, 1823.

Hesiod, Homeric Hymns and Homerica (H. G. Evelyn-White). Loeb Classical Library. New York, 1920.

Hippocrates, *Oeuvres Complètes* (E. Littré). 10 vols. Paris, 1861.

Homer, *Iliad* (A. T. Murray). Loeb Classical Library. 2 vols. New York, 1924.

————, *Commentarii Eustathii*. 2 vols. Leipzig, 1827.

————, *Scholia Graeca in Homeri Iliadem* (Dindorf). 6 vols. Leipzig, 1875.

————, *Odyssey* (A. T. Murray). Loeb Classical Library. 2 vols. New York, 1927.

————, *Scholia Graeca in Homeri Odysseam* (Dindorf). Oxford, 1855.

Homeric Hymns. See *Hesiod*.

Horace, Odes and Epodes (C. E. Bennett). Loeb Classical Library. New York, 1921.

————, *Satires, Epistles, and Ars Poetica* (H. R. Fairclough). Loeb Classical Library. New York, 1926.

————, *Scholia* (ed. J. Cruquius). Antwerp, 1578.

Horapollo Nilous, *Hieroglyphics* (tr. A. T. Cory). London, 1840.

Hyginus, *Astronomica* (ed. B. Bunte). Leipzig, 1875.

————, *Fabulae* (ed. B. Bunte). Leipzig.

————, (ed. M. Schmidt). Jena, 1872.

Isocrates, *Orationes* (ed. F. Blass). Leipzig, 1888.

————, (ed. and tr. G. Matthew and E. Brémond). 2 vols. Paris, 1928.

Jonson, Ben, The Works of (ed. Peter Whalley). 7 vols. London, 1756.

————, (biography by W. Gifford). London, 1860.

————, (ed. W. Gifford and F. Cunningham). 9 vols. London, 1875.

Jonson, Ben, *The Works of* (G. H. Herford and Percy Simpson). 5 vols. published, 5 in preparation. Oxford, 1925-1937.

Julian (W. C. Wright). Loeb Classical Library. 3 vols. New York, 1913-1923.

Juvenal and Persius (G. G. Ramsay). Loeb Classical Library. New York, 1920.

Juvenal, *Oeuvres Complètes* (tr. *sous* M. Nisard). Paris, 1845.

Lactantius, *Opera* (ed. Gersdorf). Leipzig, 1842.

Lactantius, Placidius, Commentary on Statius' *Thebaida* and *Achilleida* (ed. R. Jahnke). Leipzig, 1898.

————, *Opera*. Paris, 1600.

Livy, *History of Rome* (D. Spillan). London, 1857.

Lotspeich, H. G., *Classical Mythology in the Poetry of Edmund Spenser*. Princeton, 1932.

Lucan (J. D. Duff). Loeb Classical Library. New York, 1928.

Lucian of Samosata, The Works of (tr. H. W. and F. G. Fowler). 4 vols. Oxford, 1905.

————, *Oeuvres Complètes* (tr. Eugene Talbot). 2 vols. Paris, 1882.

Lucretius, *Of the Nature of Things* (tr. W. E. Leonard). Everyman's Library. New York.

Macrobius (ed. F. Eyssenhardt). Leipzig, 1893.

Marlianus, *Antiquae Romae Topographiae*. . . . 1534; 1544; 1560.

Martial's Epigrams (W. C. A. Ker). Loeb Classical Library. 2 vols. New York, 1925.

————, *Les Epigrammes* (tr. P. Richard). Paris, 1931.

Martianus Capella (ed. F. Eyssenhardt). Leipzig, 1866.

Milton, John, The Complete Poetical Works of (N. H. Dole). New York.

Moschus. See *Greek Bucolic Poets*.

Nicander, *Theriaca* (ed. O. Schneider). Leipzig, 1856.

Nonnus, *Dionysiaca* (ed. A. Koechly). Leipzig, 1857.

Olympiodorus. See *Pausanias,* London, 1824, for quotation.

Orphica (G. Herman). Leipzig, 1805.

Osgood, Charles G., *The Classical Mythology of Milton's English Poems*. New York, 1900.

Ovid's Fasti (J. G. Frazer). Loeb Classical Library. New York, 1931.

————, *Heroides and Amores* (Grant Showerman). Loeb Classical Library. New York, 1925.

————, *Metamorphoses* (F. J. Miller). Loeb Classical Library. 2 vols. New York, 1926.

————, *Tristia and Ex Ponto* (A. L. Wheeler). Loeb Classical Library. New York, 1924.

Pacuvius, *Poetarum Latii Scenicorum Fragmenta* (ed. F. H. Bothe). 5 vols. Halberstadii, 1823.

Parthenius, *Love Romances* (S. Gaselee). New York, 1916.

Pausanias, Description of Greece (W. H. S. Jones). Loeb Classical Library. 6 vols. New York, 1918.

————, (probable tr. Thomas Taylor). 3 vols. London, 1824.

Persius. See *Juvenal.*

————, *Oeuvres Complètes* (tr. *sous* M. Nisard). Paris, 1845.

Pherecydes, *Fragmenta Historicorum Graecorum* (ed. Mueller). Paris, 1874.

Phillipus. See *Greek Anthology.*

Philostratus, *Apollonius of Tyana* (tr. J. S. Phillimore). Oxford, 1912.

————, *Imagines.* See *Callistratus.*

Photius, *Bibliotheca* (I. Bekker). Berlin, 1824.

Phurnutus, *Theoria.* . . . Cambridge, 1670.

Pindar, The Odes of, Including the Principal Fragments (John Sandys). Loeb Classical Library. New York, 1927.

————, Scholia (ed. Eugenius Abel). Berlin, 1884.

Plato (W. R. M. Lamb; H. N. Fowler; R. G. Bury; Paul Shorey). Loeb Classical Library. 12 vols. New York, 1919.

Plautus, in *Theátre Complet des Latins* (tr. *sous* M. Nisard). Paris, 1844.

Pline le Jeune, *Lettres* (tr. C. Sicard). 2 vols. Paris, 1931.

Plinius Secundus, *Naturalis Historiae* (various ed.). 5 vols. Leipzig, 1860-1878.

Plutarch, *Lives* (tr. John Dryden). Boston.

————, (B. Perrin). Loeb Classical Library. 11 vols. New York, 1928.

Plutarch, *Morals* (translations ed. by Wm. Goodwin). 5 vols. Boston, 1883.

————, *Moralia* (F. C. Babbitt). Loeb Classical Library. Vols. I-V and X published, others in preparation. New York, 1928.

Proclus, Commentary. See Hesiod (ed. Gaisford).

Propertius (H. B. Butler). Loeb Classical Library. New York, 1912.

Puteanus, *Comus*. Paris, 1608; 1613.

————, Oxford, 1634.

Ripa, Cesare, *Iconologia*.

Root, R. K., *Classical Mythology in Shakespeare*. New York, 1903.

Roscher, W. H., *Ausführliches Lexikon der Griechischen und Römischen Mythologie*. Leipzig, 1893.

Rufus Festus Aviens, *Carmina* (A. Holder). 1887.

Rufus, Quintus Curtius, *De Rebus Gestis* (ed. F. Schneider). 3 vols. London, 1825.

Sallust (J. C. Rolfe). Loeb Classical Library. New York, 1921.

Seneca's Tragedies (F. J. Miller). Loeb Classical Library. 2 vols. New York, 1917.

Servius, *Commentarii in Vergilii Carmina* (ed. G. Thilo and H. Hagen). 2 vols. Leipzig, 1881.

Silius, Cajius (Italicus), *Punica*. 2 vols. London, 1792.

Smyrnaeus, Quintus (A. S. Way). Loeb Classical Library. New York, 1913.

Solinus; Plinianae *Exercitationes* in C. Julii Solini *Polyhistor*. 1689.

Sophocles (F. Storr). Loeb Classical Library. 2 vols. New York, 1912.

————, (A. S. Way). 2 vols. London, 1909.

Statius (J. H. Mozley). Loeb Classical Library. 2 vols. New York, 1928.

————, *Opera*. 4 vols. London, 1824.

Strabo, Geography (H. L. Jones). Loeb Classical Library. 8 vols. New York, 1927-1932.

Suetonius (J. C. Rolfe). Loeb Classical Library. 2 vols. New York, 1914.

Synesius of Cyrene, Letters of (tr. Augustine Fitzgerald). London, 1926.

Tacitus, *Opera* (ed. Justus Lipsius). 2 vols. Paris, 1599.

Theocritus. See *Greek Bucolic Poets*.

Theophrastus, *Characters* (ed. I. Casaubon). Cambridge, 1670.

————, (J. M. Edmonds). Loeb Classical Library. New York, 1929.

Tibullus. See *Catullus*.

Tzetzes, Commentary on *Lycophron*. Oxford, 1647.

Valerius Flaccus, *Oeuvres Complètes* (tr. *sous* M. Nisard). Paris, 1843.

Valerius Maximus, *Oeuvres Complètes* (tr. *sous* M. Nisard). Paris, 1843.

Varro, *De Lingua Latina Libri* (ed. L. Spengel). Berlin, 1885.

Virgil (H. R. Fairclough). Loeb Classical Library. 2 vols. New York, 1925.

Xenophon, Memorabilia and Oeconomicus (E. C. Marchant). Loeb Classical Library. New York, 1923.

Zenobius, *Centuria* (ed. Andrea Schottus). Antwerp, 1612.

INDEX

Only the Introduction has been indexed in full. Works referred to in it and also in the Sources are listed under the names of the authors.